op cloth
1999 pbk $1.6⁵/⁹⁵

)st)0ᵈ

SWINBURNE

SWINBURNE
The Poet in his World

Donald Thomas

Weidenfeld and Nicolson
London

ISBN 0 297 77605 3

Set, printed and bound in Great Britain by
Cox & Wyman Ltd
London, Fakenham and Reading

Contents

Illustrations

Preface

IT is a truism of Swinburne's life and writing that he was a child of the Victorian age. William Empson, looking back on his poetry from the perspective of 1930, found even in the Venus and Tannhäuser romance of 'Laus Veneris' the unmistakable décor of the 1860s. In Swinburne's poem, 'it is lighting-up time; the indoor Victorian-furnished Venusberg becomes hotter, stuffier and more enclosed, more irritating to sick headache and nervous exhaustion, and the gas-jet will have to be popping from now on'.

In terms of chronology, Swinburne's life is almost a model of one type of Victorian experience. Tennyson, Browning, even Dickens, were launched upon their careers before Victoria came to the throne. Swinburne, born in the year of her accession, experienced Eton at the time of its transformation into an Arnoldian public school and Balliol during a period of new intellectual vigour which Jowett's Mastership was later to characterize. Yet Oxford also introduced him to Rossetti, Morris and the Pre-Raphaelite painters of the Union Society murals. In part as their companion, he outraged bourgeois susceptibilities in the raffish and Bohemian society of London in the 1860s. This was the decade of his discovery and adulation of the Marquis de Sade.

More obviously than Rossetti or the Pre-Raphaelites, he was the figurehead of rebellion and modernity in literature. His verse proclaimed a revolution in poetry and morals, as much as in the political affairs of Europe. Yet even in this moral and spiritual rebellion he was a child of his time, more conformist in this respect than he would have cared to admit. The bottle and the brothel, not least the literary brothel of pornography, had already been adopted by thousands of less rebellious contemporaries, at a time when Henry Mayhew and others put the number of London prostitutes at anything up to eighty thousand. Even his portrayal of lamp-lit lesbian embraces and erotic cruelty had been anticipated; Gautier's *Mademoiselle de Maupin*, published before Swinburne was born, and the poetry of Baudelaire were hardly to be improved upon in the former genre.

As for the use of means of discipline as a sexual stimulus, this was so widespread in the London brothel trade that the term 'le vice anglais' was coined to describe it.

On the whole, alcoholism is less fertile as a vice of literary interest than the sado-masochistic tastes which Swinburne gratified in the brothels of the 1860s. Yet it was brandy which promised to kill him thirty years before his time, not the Sadean capers of his favourite girls at their elegantly furnished premises in St John's Wood. And if there was a figure of Victorian homily more cherished than the dying drunkard, it was surely the reclaimed drunkard. The advent of a lawyer, friend and man of letters, in the person of Theodore Watts-Dunton, might have seemed a homiletic exaggeration. Yet the manner in which Watts-Dunton gained the confidence of the ailing poet and then carried him off to thirty years of useful sobriety at No. 2, The Pines, Putney, could hardly belong to any other period.

At Putney, as the national self-congratulation of two royal jubilees united all classes in a sense of imperial achievement, the rebellious poet turned to the praise of the queen whom he had once so vigorously lampooned. He denounced the Irish Nationalists and the Liberal supporters of home rule. During the Boer War, England could scarcely have asked for a more jingoistic bard. There was even talk of making him Poet Laureate. The old erotic enthusiasms still ran in his mind, but the currents flowed deep and hidden, no longer chuckling in the sight of the world.

With the publication of his most private letters, fifty years after his death, it seemed that time and the changing tastes of the later twentieth century had played a cruel trick upon him. Swinburne, who aspired to be a great poet with a sardonically rebellious sex-life in addition, seemed merely a sexual curiosity who had written a mass of tedious verse. But for the fact that he had once been the greatest name in contemporary English poetry, even his secret compulsions would perhaps have rated no more attention than those of thousands of other sexual eccentrics.

The truth is that the details of Swinburne's private life remained buried in his letters and similar documents. Yet the nature of his obsessions was clear from his published work. It was of course possible, for those who so wished, to ignore some of the less agreeable implications. He had been a vehement atheist since his days at Balliol, yet his expression of this in public was oblique. After his death, his surviving sister and his closest cousin were able to take

comfort in the belief that their beloved Algernon 'was in communion with the Church of England all his life'. They also believed that
he had never been drunk and was too well bred to speak to a woman
whose virtue was in question. Yet, as with his unbelief, the character
of Swinburne's other enthusiasms has always been on public display
in his poetry. To many readers Sappho, Hermaphroditus and
Dolores, 'Our Lady of Pain', spoke for themselves.

*   *   *

Swinburne chose his own place in the history of English literature,
more specifically than Dickens or Tennyson had done. He was
selfconsciously the leader of a new movement and a new generation
in the 1860s. An older Pre-Raphaelite like Rossetti, or a younger
one like William Morris, might have done the same, but Rossetti
published no book of poems until 1870, and Morris had
hardly fulfilled his early literary promise. Apart from this, the
Pre-Raphaelite concern was increasingly with visual art.

During the decade, Swinburne was spoken of as a possible 'successor' to Tennyson and the Brownings. Tennyson had begun to
write within a few years of the death of Keats and in much the same
tradition. Yet as Poet Laureate he had become more bland and
platitudinous, while even Browning was in the last decade of his
greatest work. This was the point at which Swinburne raised the
banner of *l'art pour l'art*, later and more loudly proclaimed as 'Art
for Art's sake'. He defended the poetry of George Meredith as well
as his own in these terms, allowing that some verse might deal in
moral preaching – as Tennyson's had done in the recent past – but it
was 'all the worse and all the weaker for that'.

As T. S. Eliot remarked, the problem with Swinburne's own
poetry is to choose from its greater quantity those pieces on which
his claim to excellence may safely depend. On reading *Atalanta in
Calydon* and *Poems and Ballads*, for instance, the enthusiasm of his
young contemporaries can be easily understood. As leader of that
new generation, he was qualified both by vigour of style and colour
of subject to shake the throne of Tennyson. He may lack the obvious
energy of his much admired near-contemporary Gerard Manley
Hopkins, but surely equalled him with the less convulsive dramatic
tempo of *Atalanta*.

In some respects, Swinburne was a leader of the *fin de siècle* born
too soon. He detested the social drama of Zola, Ibsen and Shaw, yet

as a poet of the perverse and the decadent, as a novelist of wit and sophistication in *Love's Cross-Currents*, he would hardly have been out of place in the age of Wilde, Beardsley and the mature Meredith. Indeed, there is much in common between a novelist like Ronald Firbank, who was too late for the *fin de siècle*, and Swinburne, who preceded it. In fiction, they share a style of wit, an interest in lesbian amusements, even a sardonic appreciation of sado-masochism, as in Firbank's *Valmouth* ('"The mistress, I presume, is with the scourge," the butler announced, peering impassably around').

Many of Swinburne's modern affinities appeared too late for Edmund Gosse and others to observe them. Gosse, both in his essay of 1912 and in his biography of Swinburne five years later, was apologetic over the eagerness of young men in the 1860s to accept Swinburne as a figure of modernity. Though his later verse had obscured this achievement, he had more in common with the poetry of the twentieth century than Gosse could suspect. Swinburne's affinity, in this respect, was not with the intellectual modernity of T. S. Eliot or Ezra Pound but with the traditional technical virtuosity of a poet like W. H. Auden. Many of the truest echoes of *Atalanta* or *Poems and Ballads* ring not in the 1880s or 1920s but in the 1930s and 1940s.

As a literary figure, Swinburne was the visible and striking symbol of the new order, conspicuous in his appearance and behaviour. The rebellion which his poetry represented spread to other spheres of writing. He perpetrated a number of hoaxes designed to make fools of the solemn bourgeois readership of certain periodicals. In public disputes, he relished the exchange of insults with the delight of one who could effortlessly outgun his opponents, even to the point of precipitating a libel action against one of his publishers. His excitement in such matters was evident to his friends. After a public quarrel with Emerson over the morality of *Poems and Ballads*, Swinburne denounced the great sage as a senile ape chattering on its perch and living on its own excrement. As soon as the insult had been delivered, Swinburne was seen 'chuckling and twitching and snapping his fingers' with the sheer pleasure of battle.

In the last sixty years, Swinburne has been well served by a number of biographies, strongly contrasted in type and purpose. Edmund Gosse's *The Life of Algernon Charles Swinburne* (1917) remains pre-eminent as the work of a man who knew Swinburne for forty years and knew the society in which he lived. Harold Nicolson, in *Swinburne* (1926), combines literary analysis and polished generalities on the secret truths of Swinburne's life, which Gosse had not introduced. Nicolson's stated refusal to write his biography in terms of drink and sado-masochism was probably the means of informing most people that these were major problems in Swinburne's life. Georges Lafourcade's *La Jeunesse de Swinburne* (1928) is a two-volume study of the poet's life and works until the age of thirty and the reception of *Poems and Ballads*; for wealth of detail and analysis it is unlikely to be improved upon. Lafourcade's *Swinburne: A Literary Biography* (1932) is a more general account of the entire life. Among recent studies, the late Philip Henderson's *Swinburne: The Portrait of a Poet* (1974) is the most worthy successor to these earlier volumes. As with all Swinburne studies of the past twenty years, it enjoys the advantage of having as a source Cecil Y. Lang's edition of *The Swinburne Letters* (1959–62). This collection, bringing together the previous volumes of letters as well as many unpublished manuscripts, remains the most distinguished monument to Swinburne scholarship since the poet's death. The work of any writer on Swinburne has been immensely facilitated by its appearance.

The purpose of the present book is to depict Swinburne in relation to the society in which he lived. To that extent, it is not primarily a new essay in psychological analysis nor a linguistic dismemberment of his poetry, though his poetry and personality determine the perspective. With the scope of eighty thousand words, however, I have chosen to portray Swinburne and the world through which he passed, rather than Swinburne under analysis by that world.

I have simplified two points of nomenclature. Edward Burne-Jones acquired his hyphen in 1894 but in the interests of typographical consistency I have given it to him *ab initio*. Theodore Watts-Dunton was Theodore Watts until 1896, when he added his mother's maiden name to his own, provoking Whistler's heartless salutation, 'Dear Theodore, What's Dunton?' Here, too, I have given him his hyphenated form after the initial reference.

In discussing Baudelaire and Swinburne I have made verse translations of the former, on the principle that the general form of poetry should take preference over interpreters' English.

Among a number of acknowledgements I must first record my gratitude to Mr Vincent Quinn, Fellow Librarian of Balliol, for his help on material in the college library relating to Swinburne and Jowett. I am grateful, too, to the Keeper of Western Manuscripts, the Bodleian Library, for making available other papers relevant to Swinburne's undergraduate career. I am indebted to the British Library for the use of printed and manuscript material, and particularly to Mr T. A. J. Burnett of the Department of Manuscripts and to Dr D.W.G.Clements of the Department of Printed Books, who made my work so much easier in this respect. To the Librarian and staff of the London Library I must record my thanks for their assistance and, particularly, for access to the unpublished autobiography of John Addington Symonds. Among other assistance, I am grateful for the facilities offered by the University of London Library, and the library of the University of Wales Institute of Science and Technology. The study of literature and society is, appropriately, a speciality of the latter institution. Finally, my principal debt is to my wife's patience and encouragement during the months of writing the book.

Chapter 1

Blue Blood

IN 1855 the painter William Bell Scott noticed a young man on a long-tailed pony riding hard across the Northumberland moors from Capheaton to Wallington. Scott was struck by the manner in which the rider's appearance combined the look and figure of a boy with 'a certain mature expression on his handsome high-bred face'. During the mid-Victorian summers which followed, the same young man was to be seen walking or riding on the moors and bathing in the cold northern seas which lay twenty miles or more to the east. He rode with his 'bright, coarse yellow hair flowing on his shoulders, and flashing out round his head', and with a bundle of books strapped to his saddle, 'like those of a schoolboy'.[1]

As a rule, his destination was Wallington Hall, an eighteenth-century country seat in well-kept parkland, where Lady Pauline Trevelyan was friend and hostess to William Bell Scott and to men more famous than he. John Ruskin, John Everett Millais and Effie, who was in turn the wife of both, were among her guests, as was Dante Gabriel Rossetti. Capheaton Hall, from which the youthful rider had set out, was no less than Wallington a symbol of long-established family wealth that had acquired a new lease of prosperity in an industrial age. Its owners had rebuilt it in the seventeenth century in a style of simple classicism which has endured to the present day. The vision of this young man flying at full gallop across the Victorian skyline, caught between the patrician calm of Capheaton and the heady stimulation of Wallington, might well have served as an emblem for the fame or notoriety soon attached to the name of Algernon Charles Swinburne.

Reviewing his family's turbulent history from the mid-point of his own life, Swinburne remarked, 'I think you will allow that when this race chose at last to produce a poet, it would have been at least remarkable if he had been content to write nothing but hymns and idylls for clergymen and young ladies to read out in chapels and drawing-rooms.'[2] Exaggeration and self-advertisement were among his more prominent traits, yet the history of the Swinburnes was hardly calculated to inspire those lyrics of simple piety and moral example of which Mrs Felicia Hemans had been the popular exponent. It was unthinkable to him that the descendant of men who had stood for centuries in the path of Border wars and Stuart rebellions, dark crimes and secret murders, should be content with the subjects of the drawing-room and the parlour.

From the obscurity of medieval history, the Swinburnes emerged in the twelfth century, during the reign of Henry II, as lords of Chollerton. The estate was in the valley of the North Tyne, some thirty miles from the river's mouth. They were also lords of Swinburne Castle, a few miles away, which they retained until 1695 when it had already fallen into ruins. Their enduring fortune was founded by Sir Adam de Swinburne who acquired the Capheaton lands in 1274. He and his kinsmen held them during the long struggle between Edward I and the Scots, which brought invading armies and raiding parties over the borders of Northumbria. Equally important, the family survived the greater convulsion of civil war four centuries later and eventually emerged on the winning side. Though John Swinburne of Capheaton, head of the family, was stabbed to death in an obscure local feud in 1643, his successors were rewarded beyond their expectations in 1660. Charles II, at his restoration, conferred a baronetcy on the dead man's son.

Sir John celebrated this triumph by employing a fashionable architect, Robert Trollop, to build him a substantial house, Capheaton Hall, a foursquare design with an air of solid wealth and good sense, lightened somewhat by the neo-classical ornamentation of the new age. It remains, in Nikolaus Pevsner's description, 'One of the most interesting houses of its date and character in England ... provincial and endearing Baroque.'[3] It owes a good deal of its charm to the improvements which followed. A new north front was built by William Newton in the eighteenth century, while the gardens with their formal lake and avenue of tall trees were laid out by another famous Northumbrian, Capability Brown. From Capheaton the family faced the world with a self-assured affluence which was evident even in the young visitor to Wallington in 1855. Scott was struck by the absence of humdrum cares and preoccupations in the life of this new acquaintance. 'He was a creature above all the ills of life or difficulties of art, emancipated from ordinary annoyances.'[4] It was later to seem that, precisely by preserving him in this vacuous tranquility, the fates had mocked his genius.

As though to belittle his family fortunes at a time when inherited wealth, by a poet of revolution above all, was hardly respectable, Swinburne claimed grandly that his predecessors had 'given their blood like water and their lands like dust for the Stuarts'.[5] He himself was to expend equal quantities of ink on this most romantic of lost causes in British history. The allegiance of the Swinburnes to the exiled kings had, he insisted, led to the confiscation of half their estates. A less picturesque truth is that they had lost some territory in 1735 in a legal dispute with Swinburne's own Oxford college, Balliol, which claimed part of the family's land at Stamfordham. Yet both parties were to be richer than they knew from their respective shares. As the enthusiasm for industrial development seized the nation at the end of the eighteenth century, the lands were found to be rich in coal, enabling the owners of Capheaton to enter the Victorian period with a new lease of prosperity.

As for Swinburne's recent ancestors, there were few with whom he could be expected to have much intellectual sympathy. The only literary figure was that of his great-great-uncle, Henry Swinburne, who had made some reputation as a writer of travel books designed for those who could afford to make the Grand Tour only in their imaginations. He was best known for *Travels through Spain* (1779) and *Travels in the Two Sicilies* (1783–5). During the war with France he was sent to Paris in 1796 as commissioner for the exchange of prisoners of war, a role in which he distinguished himself by failing to secure the exchange of anyone at all. Hannah More met him in 1783 and thought him 'a little genteel man', the type of glancing description applied a century later to those who saw his great-great-nephew on his best behaviour.[6]

Yet there was one member of the family who was, in every respect, Swinburne's idol: his grandfather, Sir John Swinburne. Sir John was born in France in 1762, where the family passed a number of years after the failure of the Jacobite rising of 1745. He lived to be ninety-eight, dying in 1860 when his grandson had already left Oxford and embarked on a literary career. Sir John combined reformist political views with intellectual rationalism and an active appreciation of the arts. In Swinburne's view, 'He was (of course on the ultra-Liberal side) one of the most extreme politicians as well as one of the hardest riders and the best art-patrons of his time. ... It was said that the two maddest things in the north country were his horse and himself.'[7]

Despite the Catholic faith in which he was brought up, Sir John

Swinburne was the friend and sympathizer of Mirabeau and John Wilkes, belonging, as his grandson described him, to the age of Voltaire. He became Member of Parliament for Launceston and, again according to the younger Swinburne, led a spirited attack on the Prince Regent in 1812 when John and Leigh Hunt were sent to prison for reminding the readers of the *Examiner* that His Royal Highness was not, as the *Morning Post* proclaimed him, 'an Adonis in loveliness', but 'a corpulent man of fifty'.[8] Sir John was also the friend of a number of artists, including Turner and Mulready. 'I wish to God he had discovered Blake,' said Swinburne wistfully.[9]

Sir John did not believe in taking his political radicalism to extremes. He lived to see the first emergence of socialists in France, whom he recognized by the light of Voltairean rationalism as 'enemies of liberty'. His grandson, though prepared to move further towards absolute revolution and wishing to see, at various times, the Pope, Napoleon III and the Austrian emperor hanged as criminals, found his own aristocratic lineage and privileges entirely in accord with his political ambitions. As Victor Hugo told him in 1869, he and Byron and Shelley were prime examples of *noblesse oblige* in terms of revolutionary leadership.[10]

His own father, the second son of the radical Sir John, was born in 1797 and entered the Royal Naval College in 1810. For one determined upon a naval career, he had timed his appearance in the world badly. By 1810 the war was almost exclusively a matter of land campaigns, since the last attempt by the French fleet to escape the Biscay blockade had been frustrated at the Basque Roads in the previous year. By the time that the young man 'passed for lieutenant' the Royal Navy had too many career officers competing for too few active commissions in its reduced peace-time role. It took him a quarter of a century to reach the rank of captain in 1835. After that, he worked his way up the seniority lists, stepping into dead men's shoes and emerging as rear-admiral on the half-pay list in 1857. He progressed to vice-admiral in 1863 and admiral four years later, after fifty-seven years of duty and patience.

It was not a life of active service. Apart from punitive bombardments and the policing of the slavers' routes, there was little enough of that. But he was, as Edmund Gosse described him, 'devoted to mechanics', which had a direct relevance to the great naval issue of the day.[11] It certainly put him on the side of Lord Cochrane, Earl of Dundonald, and those who believed that the Royal Navy must develop modern gunnery, and steampower for more uses than manoeuvring a ship when the wind happened not to be favourable. Among their chief opponents was Lord Minto, First Lord of the Admiralty, who thought it inconceivable in 1843 that anyone should be so rash as to 'steam the *Vanguard* or the *Queen* at the rate of ten miles an hour'.[12]

The years of peace gave the future Admiral Swinburne leisure to be a family man. In 1836, the year after his captaincy, he married the daughter of the third Earl of Ashburnham, Lady Jane Henrietta, who was then twenty-five years old. Their eldest child, Algernon Charles Swinburne, was born on 5 April 1837 at 7 Chester Street, Grosvenor Place, London, while his parents were making a visit to the capital. This first child was to be followed by four sisters, Alice, Edith, Charlotte and Isabel, and by one brother, Edward, the youngest of all the children.

If the Swinburne lineage reads like the object of Dickens' satire on family pride in the opening chapter of *Martin Chuzzlewit*, that of the poet's mother is even more a self-parody of ancient pride. The family home of the Ashburnhams in the Victorian period was Ashburnham Place, Battle, but their residence in Sussex went back beyond the Norman Conquest. Indeed, it was Bertram de Eshburnham who as sheriff of Sussex had led the defence of Dover Castle against William the Conqueror and had been beheaded in consequence. Like the Swinburnes, the Ashburnhams had supported the royalist cause in the Civil War and John Ashburnham had arranged the safe conduct of Charles I from Oxford to the Scottish army at Newark in 1646. Though the Ashburnham estates were confiscated by the victorious Cromwellians, the property was recovered at the Restoration, with the additional consolation of a baronetcy in 1689 and an earldom in 1730. There was even a Northumbrian connection, since Swinburne's Ashburnham grandfather, the third earl, married a sister of the Duke of Northumberland. Swinburne, as Gosse remarks, might be a republican but he was no democrat in such matters.[13] Not only did he prize having a duke as his great-uncle, he informed Emilie Venturi that he had even managed to trace a relationship to an earlier Duke of Northumberland, by a marriage in his father's family.[14]

With a sure instinct for choosing a home which combined the best of Victorian fashion with the most promising return for the financial outlay involved, Swinburne's parents settled at East Dene, Bonchurch, on the south-eastern coast of the Isle of Wight, in 1836. The island was one of the 'discoveries' of high society in the early

Victorian period, described in its guide book for 1840 as 'a place to which Fashion has "set her seal", and which, in consequence, becomes the annual resort of thousands'.[15] Its mild climate, picturesque woods and lawns sloping to the sea had drawn visitors to it for half a century. William Gilpin, connoisseur of romantic scenery, and Ann Radcliffe, *doyenne* of the Gothick novel, had described its beauties. More to the point, the founding of the Royal Yacht Club in the month of Waterloo and the annual regatta which followed brought the wealthy and the titled in considerable numbers. The little towns of Cowes and Ryde grew and prospered as the Royal Thames Yacht Club and the Royal Victoria followed the example of their predecessor. The foundation stone of the Royal Victoria's club house was even laid by Prince Albert himself in 1846. By 1850, the Royal Victoria Arcade at Ryde or the fine new villas of men like the Marquess of Donegall or Earl de Grey at Cowes showed how wise Captain and Lady Jane Swinburne had been in their choice of a home. Nor was there anything fast or raffish about the tone of the fashionables who frequented these new resorts. Just beyond Cowes there rose the Italianate towers of Osborne, a palace by the sea designed largely by the Prince Consort himself, where he and the queen were to listen to the summer nightingales, and where they could walk alone through the grounds 'without being followed and mobbed', as she explained to Lord Melbourne.[16]

In choosing East Dene and Bonchurch, the Swinburnes had gone to a remoter and quieter coast. In 1850, their home was described in Bonchurch as 'The principal villa ... enjoying a most exquisite position near the church, and remarkable for the *interior* of the house being finished and furnished in the true antique style of the Elizabethan period, at great expense'.[17] From the outside the house was an early Victorian vision of Tudor imitation combined with creeper, conservatories and wide, smooth lawns running down to a prospect of what Edmund Gosse called 'limitless ocean'.[18] Landslips at the cliff's edge had produced strange 'amphitheatres of rock' as Ann Radcliffe termed them, in a world of green vegetation stretching above them 'with wildest pomp. . . . The look-down on the shores and seas is indeed tremendous.'[19] If, as Prince Albert thought, Osborne with its balmy climate and blue seas on the northern coast resembled the bay of Naples, Bonchurch was distinctly more Grecian or Aegean. Such comparisons were less absurd in an age when experience of exotic climates was, for most men and women, confined to reading about them and when, for instance, a poem of tropical enchantment like Tennyson's *Lotus-Eaters* was inspired by a visit to Torquay.[20]

Until he went to Eton at the age of twelve, Swinburne's life was divided almost entirely between East Dene and Capheaton, much of it spent in the company of his grandfather, Sir John Swinburne, as well as in that of his parents. Sir John was part of the immediate family, either staying at East Dene or entertaining its inmates at Capheaton.

* * *

In their care for their eldest child, the Swinburne parents evinced a tone of anxious indulgence, utterly unlike anything in their son's later sado-masochistic fantasies. The three of them called one another by affectionate nicknames, coined in Swinburne's child-hood, to which they remained faithful, even in their letters, unto death. His father was 'Pino', his mother 'Mimmie', and Swinburne himself 'Hadji', perhaps an echo from James Morier's Persian romance *The Adventures of Hajji Baba of Ispahan* (1824). Lady Jane Swinburne always wrote to 'My dearest Hadji', until he was fifty-two years old, when he became 'Darling Hadji'.[21]

The events of Swinburne's childhood were subsequently over-shadowed by the scenes of youth and upbringing in his two novels *Love's Cross-Currents* and *Lesbia Brandon*. There is every indica-tion that he identified himself with the child victim of innumerable floggings in each book. There is no evidence whatever to identify Captain Harewood, the sadistic father in *Love's Cross-Currents*, nor Denham, in *Lesbia Brandon*, with Captain Swinburne. As Swinburne admitted of Reginald Harewood in the earlier story, 'nothing can possibly be more different than *his parents* from mine'.[22] He wrote this to William Michael Rossetti, who had met his father and found him a 'kindly, conversible man'.[23]

The future Admiral Swinburne subsidized his son's literary career and his publications, showing pride in Algernon's achievements and even taking his part in disputes with authority. Both parents were inevitably upset when their protégé's name appeared as author of celebrations of lesbian love or erotic cruelty. As Swinburne's father admitted to Ruskin, these poems had caused pain and sorrow. But far worse than that, they had checked 'the longing desire to be pleased', which both he and his wife felt towards his son's writing.[24] At the first opportunity that pleasure burst out with an engulfing affection. Lady Jane Swinburne, for instance, wrote to him in 1870 about their delight at his English version of Hugo's 'Children of the Poor'. She had hastened 'to tell you how lovely Pino & I both think your "Children of the Poor". Pino says "Tell him with my love that the oftener I read it (& that is very often) the more I admire and like it". It really is wonderful.'[25] The tone of such exchanges is far more informative than the birch-ridden fantasies of Swinburne's later life.

Whatever the truth of his relations with his parents, Swinburne remained obsessed by childhood memories. In the poetry of his mature years he returns frequently and lovingly to landscapes of childhood, Northumbria and particularly the visions of East Dene, where,

> In a coign of the cliff between lowland and highland,
>   At the sea-down's edge between windward and lee,
> Walled round with rocks as an inland island,
>   The ghost of a garden fronts the sea.[26]

The sea, 'the great sweet mother' of his poem 'The Triumph of Time', obsessed the rhythms and the imagery of his verse. One of his earliest and happiest memories was of being 'held up naked in my father's arms and brandished between his hands, then shot like a stone from a sling through the air, shouting and laughing with delight, head foremost into the coming wave'.[27] As a child he swam and floated by the hour beyond the lawns and foreshore of East Dene, lapped in the blue waters and the languid summer tides, as though in the Aegean of his Hellenic dream-world. Hypnotic movement, waves sliding timelessly over the drowned past, echoed through his poetry for the rest of his life.

> We shall hear, as one in a trance that hears,
> The sound of time, the rhyme of years;
> Wrecked hope and passionate pain will grow
>   As tender things of a spring-tide sea.
>
> Sea-fruit that swings in the waves that hiss,
>   Drowned gold and purple and royal rings.
> And all time past. . . .[28]

At this level, Swinburne's early childhood mirrors the cliché of a Victorian idyll of smooth lawns and summer waves, the close attachment of his parents and the sunlit security of coloured bricks on the nursery floor, or the paints on the schoolroom table where the governess read stories to the brothers and sisters from *The Penny Reward*.[29] Old Sir John Swinburne renounced Catholicism on his return from France, but the family had taken up the Anglo-Catholicism of the Oxford Movement, which seemed less plebeian than the scrubbed and selfconscious earnestness of the Church of England's evangelical wing. Under this moral aegis, the education of the children was careful but not priggish. Lady Jane Swinburne was a woman of considerable education and culture, well taught in French and Italian, from whom Algernon caught an early enthusiasm for European literature.

Swinburne was brought up on the Bible and retained a daunting ability to quote aptly from it for the rest of his life. Despite his loss of religious belief at Balliol as an undergraduate, he was selected to assist Benjamin Jowett in the production of a *Children's Bible* in 1872. In the secular curriculum of East Dene there was no unsupervised novel-reading, though the children were read to, and in this respect, as Swinburne remarked, Dickens became 'a household god'.[30] Best of all, the child was given unrestricted use of Bowdler's *Shakespeare*. Unlikely though it might seem, the expurgator of Shakespeare thus earned a place among Swinburne's literary heroes, in company with the Marquis de Sade. For, as Swinburne remarked, Bowdler had done Shakespeare an incalculable service when he 'made it possible to put him into the hands of intelligent and imaginative children'.[31] As the eldest child, he was also 'privileged to have a book at meal-times ... at tea-time especially'.[32]

*   *   *

The first intrusion into this childhood world was made by Mary Gordon, Swinburne's cousin, who was three years his junior and who remains one of the most mysterious figures in the story of his life. To her we owe the early descriptions of Swinburne as a child, riding a Shetland pony led by the family servant York, and of Swinburne and his sister Edith walking briskly across the downland – he with 'that springy, dancing step which he never entirely lost' – leaving the smaller children to catch up as best they could.[33]

Lady Jane Swinburne's sister had married Sir Henry Gordon, whose house, The Orchard, at Niton, was about five miles from East Dene. It was inevitable that the young cousins should see much of one another, though the bizarre relationship which developed between Swinburne and Mary Gordon was one which their contemporaries could not have predicted nor, perhaps, understood. As a safeguard against mutual sexual demands, they described their relationship as one of brother and sister. Under this guise, in childhood and in adult life, they indulged their enthusiasm for the birch and for girls who played the part of boys. Much of this, at least, took the form of literary fantasy. It formed a strong bond between them in their twenties, before Mary's marriage, and during her widowhood when they were in their fifties. The central fantasy seems to have been of the type of school which Swinburne created in his imagination, and in which Mary played the part of a 'minor' or younger boy.[34]

Their shared interests became the erotic themes of Swinburne's fiction. *Lesbia Brandon*, on which he worked from 1864 until 1878, also presents incestuous desire between half-brother and half-sister, a close parallel to the attachment to Mary Gordon. The novel deals openly with flagellation and obliquely with unrequited lesbian love of one of two half-sisters for the other. Lesbianism, sadism and incest combined to ensure the novel's suppression. It appeared at length in 1952. Mary nostalgically recalled Swinburne reading her the manuscript during the autumn of 1864, though she gives little hint of the book's obsessions.[35] Yet she remembered, in this connection, a letter from him at about this time, in which he described how he had taken a room in a schoolhouse and 'overheard a flogging going on in the schoolroom', an anecdote whose manner she found 'amusing'.[36]

In the story of Swinburne's childhood, it is Mary Gordon who is primarily responsible for the image of Captain Swinburne as 'a stern disciplinarian'.[37] It is at least possible that this belief was either the result of her own preoccupations or of fantasies invented for her benefit by 'Cousin Hadji', as he was later to invent them for the world at large.

At the end of 1848, when Swinburne was eleven, he and Mary were thrown together in different circumstances. He was sent to lodge with the Reverend Foster Fenwick, vicar of Brooke, close to the Gordons' other house on the Isle of Wight at Northcourt. The time had come for him to learn the rudiments of Latin and Greek in preparation for his departure for Eton. He and Mary were frequent companions, 'playing at horses', as she called it, but also acting 'people' as well.[38] Swinburne's taste for dressing up in amateur theatricals was part of the domestic fashion of his age and class. He adapted *Dombey and Son*, 'himself taking the part of Mrs Skewton in her Bath chair'. The part of Carker was to be given to 'whoever could show the best set of teeth'. Mary Gordon put on 'a tremendous grin', and won the competition.[39] In their shared secret fantasies, too, drama and suggestion were more evocative than any physical act. In erotic daydreams, above all, it was the function of art to improve upon life.

*   *   *

If Swinburne's adult reminiscences were to be believed, the years at Eton shaped his obsessions and enthusiasms for the rest of his life. Eton provided intellectual nourishment, the visions of Hellenic grandeur and Elizabethan excitement; it offered the exhilaration of sado-masochistic stimulus; and it established a dominion in personal loyalty which even a republican and atheist acknowledged with alacrity. In short, the marine idyll of his childhood was at an end, and the world opened before him.

Captain and Lady Jane Swinburne might have thought their slightly built and nervous son ill adapted for survival in a Victorian public school. Dr Arnold's reforms at Rugby in the 1830s had not become universal. A Royal Commission on Public Schools reported on this in 1864, too late to help Swinburne. Meanwhile, physical cruelty, moral inertia and homosexuality were the snares awaiting new arrivals, the first two condemned openly and the third hinted at knowingly. The problems were not new. In 1785, for instance, the poet William Cowper had issued a warning to parents in *Tirocinium: or, A Review of Schools*.

> Would you your son should be a sot or dunce,
> Lascivious, headstrong, or all these at once,
> That in good time, the stripling's finish'd taste
> For loose expense and fashionable waste,
> Should prove your ruin and his own at last; –
> Train him in public with a mob of boys,
> Childish in mischief only and in noise,
> Else of a mannish growth, and five in ten
> In infidelity and lewdness men.

The poem adds that a pupil will find how 'taverns teach the knowledge of the heart', and seek in 'some street-pacing harlot his first love'. The power of education and authority is self-corrupting.

> The management of tyros of eighteen
> Is difficult, their punishment obscene.[40]

Fifty years later, the father of Lord Suffield, the son being a contemporary of Swinburne and a friend of the Prince of Wales, was torn between submitting the boy to the horrors of Eton or imprisoning him within the narrow confines of private tuition. 'I dread the waste of time and vices at Eton; I dread the selfishness, the illiberality and, in a tenfold ratio, the vices of a private system of tuition.'[41]

In the first half of the nineteenth century Eton, like most public schools, relied upon comparatively few masters teaching a great many boys and keeping order by means of physical authority. Keate and seven masters in the upper school at Eton were in charge of 515 boys. Discipline was maintained with the aid of captains in the school. The Reverend C. A. Wilkinson recalled nostalgically in the *Guardian* on 30 June 1875 how he had once, as a senior boy at Eton, 'superintended a noted general whipping of upwards of a hundred boys'. Ten years later he wrote his schoolboy reminiscences at book length, revelling in comic and grotesque accounts of Eton floggings, deriding the 'old ladies' who opposed the system.

At no point in such accounts is there any hint of the type of sexual trauma which Freud was later to describe in his essay 'A Child is being Beaten'. The system was taken as a proof of manhood and courage on the part of its victims, an important element in Swinburne's own attachment to it. Wilkinson, for instance, dismisses with casual contempt those Eton contemporaries who were not severely beaten. 'The little mamma's darlings,' as he calls them, 'got little more than a tickling which would scarcely warm them up on a cold morning.' They 'hardly could say that what boys called the "college arms" were stamped upon them'.[42]

Wilkinson naturally considered that the public school system of punishment 'can do no real harm to anyone'.[43] He presumably overlooked such cases as that of a boy named Stewart at Harrow in 1853 who suffered such injury from thirty-one blows of the cane that he was permanently disfigured. He also ignored the protests of such men as Henry Salt, who had been boy and master at Eton, one of the so-called 'holders-down' during these punishments, and who emerged finally as 'a socialist, a vegetarian, and a free-thinker'.[44] Salt resigned from Eton in 1884. 'It's the vegetarianism, I fear,' said Dr Warre, the headmaster, pityingly. Salt remarked that it was the socialism. Warre threw up his hands and cried: 'Socialism! Then blow us up, blow us up! There's nothing left for it but that.'[45]

It was Salt who added an unwelcome gloss to the beloved

Victorian motto of 'Spare the rod and spoil the child' by pointing out that it came not from the Bible but from Samuel Butler's *Hudibras*, that the child in question was Cupid, and that the advice came from a lady who was advising the man in question to submit to a flogging as a stimulant to sexual intercourse.[46]

For all that, the exercise of physical punishment by authority was less awesome than some of the other ordeals awaiting the new arrival at Eton. As Wilkinson remarked, the system of small boys acting as fags for their elders, despite the bullying it involved, 'did more good than harm'. Yet even he might have had qualms over a more lethal form of amusement – tossing in a blanket in the Long Chamber. He witnessed the incident in which the young Rowland Williams hit the ceiling and came down scalped, or rather with 'the scalp hanging down over the neck and back suspended only by a small piece of skin'.[47] Yet such experiences could hardly dull 'the excitement of a good spin up to the ceiling', and Wilkinson adds, 'Bold little fellows liked it.'[48]

There was some reason to suppose that the delicate young Swinburne might be toughened physically by life at Eton. It was less certain that he would acquire much refinement. Even in the nineteenth century, cockfighting and badger-baiting survived at the school among the nation's future leaders. The irrepressible Wilkinson also looked back affectionately on the practice of cornering rats in the dormitories and bludgeoning them to death. 'It really was glorious fun – try it, some of you young fellows.'[49]

Within Eton, as well as in the adult world, there existed a raffish and well-heeled society which could afford to dispense with the selfconscious refinement of the mid-Victorian period. Sir Alexander Duff Gordon proudly showed off the letter which had been written to him from the school by his ten-year-old son on 4 December 1861. 'One fellow took a shot at the ball and caught Freeth such a toe on the ass which made him rub it I can tell you so we all hollowed out how is your ass Freeth which made him fearfully baity.'[50]

All these things only touched the surface of the brutality and viciousness at which moralists hinted in the Victorian public-school system. Benjamin Jowett, writing to his young second cousin, Sidney Irwin, who was about to go to Wellington in 1860, remarked circumspectly, 'Boys about your own age or a little older are sometimes very vicious and indecent both in word and also sometimes in action.'[51] He himself had endured the verbal persecution of being

'Miss Jowett' at St Paul's School, as Stanley, the biographer of Dr Arnold, had been 'Nancy' at Rugby. But there remain the memoirs of the poet and critic John Addington Symonds, which are still unpublished, and which give an appalling picture of the mid-Victorian public school from his own memories of Harrow. Direct quotation from this manuscript is not permitted, but it is sufficient to say that every good-looking younger boy was named as a girl and became either the 'bitch' of a particular older boy or the sexual property of his elders at large.[52]

Symonds, who was a self-confessed homosexual as an adult, was not shocked by adolescent affection as such, but by the nude *tableaux* which it was impossible not to see, and by the violence of what can only be described as homosexual rape, the victim finally beaten and spat upon by his assailants. He gives the names and houses of those involved in this. The *Harrow School Register* further identifies their adult roles in Victorian society. The victims included one wealthy coal-owner and one amateur rackets-player; among the rapists, for want of another term, were a hero of the Maori War, a judge, a magistrate and one of Her Majesty's Inspectors of Schools.[53] If Swinburne later sympathized with Sade's belief in the corruption of all authority, that sympathy may have been strengthened by the sight of men sentencing their social inferiors for crimes less brutal than they or their peers had committed in their youth.

Nor were these activities confined to the boys. It was widely held by his friends that William Johnson, alias William Cory, was 'the most original, perhaps the oddest of Eton masters, and by common consent the greatest teacher that Eton has produced'.[54] Johnson, who was known to the world for his translation of Callimachus' famous epitaph on Heraclitus, was dismissed for an indiscreet note to a boy at the school. Yet this could hardly equal the bizarre situation at Harrow, where the headmaster himself, Dr Vaughan, was having affairs with the boys entrusted to him. Some of his love-letters reached the hands of the parents, who confronted him with the choice of resignation or prosecution. He resigned and was promptly offered the choice of the bishoprics of Worcester or Rochester by a grateful government. The parents intervened to prevent him from accepting either. He was allowed to become vicar of Market Harborough and later president of University College, Cardiff. No official impediment was put in the way of his career, though, according to Wilberforce, the Bishop of Oxford, both the prime minister and the Archbishop of Canterbury had been informed of Vaughan's activities at Harrow.[55]

*   *   *

Such were the adolescent jungle and predators which waited Swinburne at the age of twelve, and of which Oscar Browning – both boy and master at Eton – wrote, 'I will say nothing about the moral and social aspects of the place because the less said about them the better.'[56] Yet even here the ancient name of his family and the double prestige of parental lineage assured him a more favoured position. Etonians had traditionally been divided into Collegers, who lived in the main buildings of the school, and the more fortunate Oppidans, who lived in the houses of their tutors. Oscar Browning recalled the winter misery of life as an early Victorian Colleger, the icy wind through broken windows, the iron basin and cold water, which left the hands still 'begrimed with dirt and seamed with bleeding cracks'.[57]

In place of this, Swinburne and the other members of his house lived with his tutor, James Leigh Joynes, who was twenty-five years old, had been a boy at Eton, President of Pop and Captain of the School, went to Cambridge as Scholar and then Fellow of King's, and had just returned to Eton as a master. The atmosphere of the house, presided over by Joynes and his wife, was much more that of a family than was the bear-garden ferocity of the Collegers' lives. Swinburne remembered the couple with affection and wrote of Mrs Joynes as having been 'infinitely kind to me, at an age when I most needed kindness'.[58]

Captain and Lady Jane Swinburne brought their son to Joynes's house on 24 April 1849. Lady Jane remained at Windsor until Algernon had settled in, returning when he was unwell to sit by his sick-bed and read Shakespeare to him. It was on this occasion that she had to leave her maid to continue the reading for a few minutes. Swinburne, noticing the more careless style of delivery, made a spirited recovery, seized his glass of water and threw it impatiently in the poor woman's face.[59]

Upon his arrival, Swinburne was left to the care of his cousin, Lord Redesdale, who had already been at Eton for three years. Redesdale later recalled the sight of this 'fragile little figure', standing between his parents and hugging his leather-bound copy of Bowdler's *Shakespeare*:

He was strangely tiny. His limbs were small and delicate; and his sloping shoulders looked far too weak to carry his great head, the size of which was exaggerated by the touzled mass of red hair standing almost at right angles to it. Hero-worshippers talk of his hair as having been a 'golden aureole'. At that time there was nothing golden about it. Red, violent aggressive red it was, unmistakable unpoetical carrots.[60]

If Swinburne survived the vicissitudes of public-school life, it was by choosing the role of oddity and recluse rather than by winning popularity. He appeared to Redesdale 'an inspired elfin – something belonging to another sphere'.[61] Lord St Aldwyn, another Eton contemporary, put the matter less obliquely, describing him as 'a horrid little boy, with a big red head and a pasty complexion, who looked as though a course of physical exercise would have done him good'.[62] This last reaction lends some support to Osbert Sitwell's recollection of meeting an octogenarian Etonian, who remarked to him:

I remember well when I went to Eton. The head boy called us together and pointing to a little fellow with curly red hair, said, 'Kick him if you are near enough, and if you are not near enough throw a stone at him.' . . . I have often wondered what became of him – his name was Swinburne.[63]

Though his cousin Redesdale loyally insisted that 'None dreamt of interfering with him . . . he was absolutely courageous. He did not know what fear meant', Swinburne's courage was needed for enduring persecution rather than preventing it.[64] One morning he returned to the house in despair and begged Joynes to excuse him from going into college to face 'those dreadful boys'. 'Oh, sir, they wear tail-coats! Sir, they are men!' Whereupon Joynes read him a psalm, by way of consolation, and sent him back.[65]

In two contrasting respects, it was Joynes who was Swinburne's closest acquaintance. He encouraged the boy's reading of Elizabethan drama and, in Swinburne's fantasies at least, he carried out beatings in circumstances of Firbankian decadence. In the first case, he lent his pupil an edition of *Dodsley's Old Plays*, though with an embargo on John Ford's *'Tis Pity She's a Whore*. Swinburne's time was spent in the library in Weston's Yard, where Redesdale remembered him, 'sitting perched up Turk-or-tailor wise in one of the windows looking out on the yard, with some huge old-world tome, almost as big as himself, upon his lap, the afternoon sun setting on fire the great mop of red hair'.[66] Such reading was undertaken entirely for his own pleasure, since the literature taught at Eton was that of Greece and Rome. Yet by the age of thirteen he had acquired an impressive knowledge of such dramatists as Marlowe, Webster, Ford and Massinger, who were little studied at the time. His enthusiasm spread to English literature as a whole and, within a year or two, Redesdale also described him as 'devouring the great classics of France and Italy'.[67]

His memory was prodigious and his enthusiasm for what he had read seemed hard to contain. Years later, his contemporaries recalled him moving through Windsor Forest with his 'peculiar dancing step', which Mary Gordon had noticed long before, proclaiming the beauties of the Elizabethans, or of France and Italy.[68] A less exalted memory was of Mrs Joynes or her assistant bringing round the 'night-dose' for those boys suffering from winter colds, and finding a wild-eyed figure ranting upright on his bed. Fearing delirium, she was relieved to be told that it was 'only little Swinburne reciting as usual'.[69]

Yet Joynes was to hold a more extraordinary place in the mythology of Swinburne's childhood than any other figure of authority. In 1863 Swinburne assured Richard Monckton Milnes, the future Lord Houghton, that his tutor was not content to birch him repeatedly in the customary way. He would prepare the flogging-room with burnt scent, or choose a fragrant spot out of doors, or even beat Swinburne when his face had been saturated in eau-de-Cologne. The aim was to increase the pain, in Swinburne's view, but he confessed that for him it increased the pleasure.[70]

The account is less useful as the record of an actual event than as a glimpse into the world of comic and melodramatic fantasies to which Swinburne owed much of his intellectual allegiance. Joynes was not empowered to punish the boys in his care, merely to put them in the 'list' for the headmaster. Swinburne, as a diligent pupil, was one of the least likely to incur punishment, anyhow. The notion of master and pupil sauntering through Windsor Forest, seeking a leafy grove for their purpose, seems intentionally ridiculous. The ridicule is still more evident if one considers the appearance and character of James Leigh Joynes. A. C. Benson, who described him quite independently of Swinburne, recalled him as small, sturdy and bow-legged. This, combined with a large head, gave him 'a somewhat gnome-like aspect'. He had 'a large aquiline nose, stiff, wiry, upstanding hair, grizzled and cut short, and a short "Newgate fringe"'. He sported a tall hat and 'high, crumpled, cheek-scraping

Gladstone collars, the danger of which seemed to be that a sudden movement might cause the collar point to pierce the eyeball'. Joynes was, in appearance at least, the complete comic schoolmaster. 'He ran rather than walked, his big feet twinkling along, and rounded corners at a great pace with a suggestion of a caper.'[71] From such unpromising material, Swinburne devised a figure who apparently combined the most outrageous traits of Des Esseintes, the Baron Charlus, and Wackford Squeers.

Worse still, for the Swinburne legend, Joynes had been 'modest, kindly, and universally popular . . . he set his face firmly and courageously against all bullying and oppression . . . he seldom or never set a punishment. . . . He was very kind and fatherly in manner.'[72] Who better, in short, to do duty as the butt of a joke between two flagellophiles, to appear as the Sadean genius burning incense in the flogging-room, or beating boys who were steeped in the perfumes of the boudoir? Whatever the explanation, it is hard to read Swinburne's description as anything but another of what Cecil Y. Lang aptly calls Algernonic hoaxes. That Swinburne was birched at some time in his Eton career seems likely, that he saw others birched is very probable. It would have taken no more than that to stimulate his enthusiasm. That it happened in the way he described requires considerable credulity to accept.

The fate which awaited the Joynes family was more bizarre than anything which Swinburne devised. The tutor's son, himself a master at the school, wore long curls down his back and was sacked after he had been arrested as a revolutionary agitator. The tutor's daughter, Kate, married H. L. Salt, the socialist and vegetarian rebel. She was more entirely a lesbian than any of Swinburne's Sapphic heroines, and her only consummations of love were with her own sex.[73] From his photograph as Lower Master of Eton, James Joynes stares at the world with the air of one for whom life holds no more surprises.

Under his guidance, however, Swinburne became a good and even a moderately distinguished pupil. He took easily to *Poetae Graeci*, the Eton anthology, and to Latin poetry. 'Very well; Very well; Very creditable,' wrote Joynes on his exercises, and Swinburne was twice 'sent up for good', so that the headmaster's approval might be given to his achievement.[74] In 1852 he won the Prince Consort's Prize for Modern Languages, an area of study which had led him to *Notre-Dame de Paris* and stimulated his enduring enthusiasm for Victor Hugo.

Within a short time of his arrival at Eton, according to his sister Isabel, Swinburne had begun his first original work, a play strongly influenced by the bloodthirsty Jacobean dramas he was then reading. This was *The Unhappy Revenge*, into which, as he later claimed, he had 'tried to pack twice as many rapes and about three times as many murders' as were contained in Cyril Tourneur's *Revenger's Tragedy* (1607), upon which it was modelled.[75] On 4 June 1851 a poetic occasion of a very different sort was provided by the queen's visit to Eton, and Swinburne responded with 'The Triumph of Gloriana', which echoed both the Elizabethans and the pastorals of Pope.

> What Muse shall boldly raise a humble lay
> To celebrate the glories of this day?
> When glittering myriads flock, a countless crowd
> Confus'd with hearts upraised and voices loud.

The poem also glanced approvingly at such figures as Wellington and Chatham, with a self-satisfied reference to Eton and a snub to Harrow.

Every account of Swinburne at this time describes him as a solitary boy, who spent his leisure in the literary dream-world of Greece and Rome, of France, Italy, and the Elizabethans, as well as in the pages of Dickens, whose *Bleak House* he bought and read with enormous delight as its parts were published.[76] He kept apart from the well-heeled 'scamps' upon whom the Reverend C. A. Wilkinson bestowed his fatuous adulation, the victims of the birch and the heroes of the playing-fields whose devotion to sport enabled at least one of them to escape from Russian hands in the Crimea by a display of sprinting, leaping and hurdling which left his captors stupefied.[77].

The Eton to which Swinburne remained devoted was very much a paradise of his own fantasies. It was the pastoral academe for which he wrote his 'Eton: an Ode'.

> Still the reaches of the river, still the light on field and hill,
> Still the memories held aloft as lamps for hope's young fire to fill,
> Shine, and while the light of England lives, shall shine for England still.

And alongside this, though not for publication, the elderly poet was composing a rather different poem, 'Eton: another Ode', in which the vision is not that of pastoral nostalgia but a nursery nightmare.

'Tell me, Swinburne, does shame within burn as hot (Swish! Swish!) as your
                                                         stripes my lad,
Burn outside, have I tamed your pride? I'm glad to see how it hurts you –
                                                              glad –
Swish! I wish it may cure you. Swish! Get up.' By Jove, what a dose I've had.

The first of these, which might almost have come from the pen of
Sir Henry Newbolt, commemorated Eton's 450th anniversary. The
second, setting aside its subject matter, has a modernity which
Swinburne's later poetry rarely achieved and in its tone bears a
remarkable similarity to the verse autobiography of Sir John
Betjeman.

The double attachment to childhood fantasies was in no way
affected by the manner in which Swinburne was removed from
Eton. It was said that he had had disagreements with his housemaster 'of a rebellious kind' during the summer of 1853, when
Swinburne was in his seventeenth year. He was certainly impulsive,
excitable and visibly nervous throughout his life. His parents
became worried about his habitual mannerisms, such as drawing
down his shoulders stiffly and giving 'quick vibrating jerks' with his
hands, or suddenly kicking his legs and twisting his feet in excitement while sitting down. A specialist was consulted who pronounced that these involuntary spasms were not the warnings of
some impending fit but merely the sign of 'an excess of electric
vitality'.[78]

For all that, Swinburne had grown more difficult to control – let
alone repress – and was even known among the other boys at
Joynes's house as 'Mad Swinburne'. Joynes, however kindly in other
respects, showed little relish for harbouring this growing oddity.
There were those who later found Swinburne an hysteric and others
who thought him epileptic. Whatever the cause of his misgivings,
Joynes communicated with Captain and Lady Jane Swinburne, and
Algernon left Eton at the end of the summer.

He bore no grudge, only an enduring and hazy affection. In 'The
Triumph of Gloriana', he had compared his childhood world to the
primordial beauty of ancient Greece. To the Aegean fantasies of
East Dene he had added Eton, which he described in the poem as
Athens, reincarnate for him in 'the grey towers, Windsor, the
Forest, the Brocas, the Thames, Cuckoo Weir'.[79] As for Joynes, he
later remembered Swinburne only for his red hair. Swinburne had
sent him his poetry when it was published but Joynes would respond
only with a cold silence. Of course, Swinburne could not be

expected to guess that the dark-haired girl whom he knew only as his housemaster's daughter was an active lesbian. On the other hand, a devout old high Tory, with the traditions of Eton behind him but seeing the catastrophe of his child's marriage, could hardly be expected to respond with enthusiasm to Swinburne's relish for Sappho and the intrigues of bisexualism.

Chapter 2

Oxford

S WINBURNE'S adolescence had by no means been confined to the routine of Eton and the leisure of East Dene or Capheaton. His introduction to the wider Victorian world had included two visits to the most eminent poets of his day. The first of these occurred in the summer of 1849 when the family was on holiday in the Lake District. In September he and his parents visited Rydal Mount, where the boy was presented to the elderly Poet Laureate, Wordsworth. 'He was so very nice to Algernon, especially at the last,' wrote Elizabeth Sewell, who witnessed the encounter, 'that I could have cried, as Algernon did when we went away.' Some three years later, it was Samuel Rogers, an even more ancient poet, who was presented with the young Swinburne. Wordsworth had merely communicated with a certain smugness that 'He did not think Algernon would forget him.' Rogers did better. At the close of the formal interview, 'he solemnly laid his hand on Algernon's head, and said, "I prophesy that you will be a poet too"'.[1]

As it happened, Swinburne's ambitions were drawn in a quite different direction during the two years between his leaving Eton and going up to Balliol. It was late in 1853 that he informed his parents of a primary ambition – to become a cavalry officer.

It was less absurd than it sounded. His cousin, Lord Redesdale, remarked, 'He was no horseman and had no opportunity at home for riding. But in the matter of horses he was absolutely without terror. He, unskilled though he was, would ride anything as fearless as a Centaur.' Cavalry training might cure him of falling off horses and the slightness of his build would perhaps equip him for a commission in a regiment of light dragoons. In normal circumstances, the cavalry might still have seemed an odd choice. But the months following Swinburne's departure from Eton were anything but normal.

On 2 July, Russia had invaded the Turkish Danubian provinces. This was followed by the sinking of the Turkish fleet in November and the encroachment of Russian power upon Britain's sea-routes to India. The first few months of Swinburne's freedom from Eton saw the demand of the English press and public for action against Russia grow with irresistible strength. The Peace Movement, sponsored by the Quakers and supported by men like Cobden and Bright, was swept aside. War was not declared until March 1854 yet in the new year the troop transports whose eventual destination was the Crimea were already anchored off Portsmouth, in Spithead, and even in the Swinburnian Aegean of East Dene. The vast enthusiasm of cheering crowds, who packed the streets as the regiments marched off to war, became a cliché of contemporary journalism. Sergeant-Major Timothy Gowing, of the Royal Fusiliers, described the roaring encouragement in the Portsmouth streets. 'Stick to them, my boys! ... Give it to them, if you get a chance! ... We'll not forget you!'[2]

Against such a background, Swinburne's enthusiasm for the life of a cavalry officer was the type of ambition shared with thousands of his young contemporaries. It was the one clear chance of proving his manhood and his daring beyond any question. When the news of the glory and the folly of the light cavalry charge at Balaclava on 25 October 1854 reached England, he was lost in admiration for the lancers and hussars who had taken part in it. The courage of the Light Brigade 'eclipsed all other visions', as he put it. To be prepared for such a chance was the 'one dream of my life'.[3]

It remains difficult to imagine the intensity of enthusiasm for the war, on the part of the most unlikely men and women, as the news of its major battles reached England in the late autumn of 1854. While Swinburne thrilled to the news of Balaclava, Charles Kingsley wrote to Thomas Hughes, 'I have nothing to sing about those glorious fellows, except "God save the Queen and them".'[4] Two months earlier Kingsley had written, 'This war would have made me half mad, if I had let it. It seemed so dreadful to hear of those Alma heights being taken and not be there; but God knows best, and I suppose I am not fit for such brave work.'[5]

In the wake of Balaclava, Swinburne's parents decided that their son was unsuited to such work too. His size and apparent frailty determined them in the matter. 'My father resolutely stamped out my ambition for a soldier's work.'[6] In other respects, it is easy enough to imagine Swinburne in the mess of a cavalry regiment. His madcap horsemanship, if he had survived it, would have added colour to his reputation. His tendency to drink too much or to indulge in visits to brothels would be no disqualification in the mess.

Even flagellation houses in the mid-Victorian period had their quota of cavalry officers.[7] Above all, he had the money to buy his way to command of a cavalry regiment. The prospect of Lieutenant-Colonel A. C. Swinburne of the 10th Prince of Wales's Hussars, regarded as a character in the mess and known for verses – serious or comic – which he wrote as a sideline, is not as outlandish as it might appear. Ironically, when verses signed 'A.C.S.' appeared in *Fraser's Magazine* in 1848 and '49, they later proved to be not the work of Swinburne's infant genius – as Edward Thomas thought – but the mature productions of Sir Anthony Cunningham Sterling, KCB, Major in the Highland Brigade.[8]

With his military ambitions frustrated, Swinburne sought some way to prove his manhood and courage. Despite the Freudian incorporation of school punishments into the canon of sexual traumas, birchings at Eton were seen far more as proof of bravery. It is almost as though Swinburne, having remained one of C. A. Wilkinson's 'mamma's darlings' at that time, now sought to make amends. By Christmas 1854, he had decided that 'it was all very well to fancy or dream of "deadly danger" and forlorn hopes and cavalry charges, when I had never run any greater risk than a football "rooge".'[9] His parents had taken three days to think over his request to join the army and had turned it down. It was in the wake of this that he walked by the sea near East Dene and decided, on the spur of the moment, to put his courage to a decisive test. After sousing himself in the winter sea to steady his nerves, he set about climbing the face of Culver Cliff.

Forming the eastern headland of the Isle of Wight, Culver presented 'a great face of chalk picturesquely striated with bands of flint'. At the first attempt to scale it, he came to an overhanging ledge and had to make his way down again. Choosing another route, he returned to the task at once and 'felt like setting my teeth and swearing I would not come down alive again – if I did return to the foot of the cliff again it should be in a fragmentary condition'. He edged his way upward to the higher surface of the cliff face and then stopped at 'a sudden sound as of loud music, reminding me instantly of "the anthem" from the Eton Chapel organ'. From a hollow in the cliff below the place to which he clung, high and sheer above the cold sea, a swarm of gulls rose about him in 'a heaving cloud'. He thought of the gruesome possibility that they might attack him, their beaks thrusting for his eyes, while he could not use either hand to defend himself. But the danger passed. He had almost reached the top of the cliff face when the chalk on which he was standing crumbled beneath him, and he was left dangling 'by my hands from a ledge on the cliff which just gave room for the fingers to cling and hold on'. In his own account, he saved his life by swinging his feet gingerly sideways to another ledge, and finding sufficient purchase to pull himself up the last stretch of the cliff. At the top he lay immobilized by exhaustion and, as he began to lose consciousness, he thought 'what a sell (and what an inevitable one) it would be if I were to roll back over the edge after all'.[10]

The choice of Culver Cliff as the challenge to his manhood was less arbitrary than it seemed. The great age of Victorian mountaineering was at hand, its most distinguished pioneer being Swinburne's near-contemporary Edward Whymper, whose first successful ascent of the Matterhorn took place in 1865. To underline the hazards, Lord Francis Douglas, brother of the Marquess of Queensberry, and three companions, died on the ascent.

After the scramble on Culver Cliff, Swinburne returned to East Dene and informed his mother that he had put his courage to the test. 'Nobody ever thought you were a coward, my boy,' she told him. Swinburne's reaction was 'that was all very well: but how could I tell till I tried?'[11]

With manhood vindicated, despite the vanished prospect of a career in the cavalry, Swinburne was prepared for Oxford. He was tutored for a while by the Reverend John Wilkinson, perpetual curate of Cambo, Sir John Swinburne's parish in Northumberland. It was during this visit that William Bell Scott saw him for the first time, riding over the moors with a bundle of books strapped to his saddle. Then there was a visit to Cologne and Wiesbaden, accompanied by his uncle, in August. This provoked only a few dutiful letters to Lady Jane, embodying the commonplace observations of a young tourist. It was at the beginning of 1856 that he was sent up to Oxford, matriculating at Balliol on 24 January.

* * *

Superficially, mid-Victorian Oxford still preserved much of its romantic charm, retaining the image of the medieval city described by Gerard Manley Hopkins, who missed Swinburne at Balliol by only three years.

Towery city and branchy between towers;
Cuckoo-echoing, bell-swarmed, lark-charmed, rook-racked, river-
                                                        rounded. . . .[12]

At the extreme of romanticism, the physical charm of the pre-industrial city led Matthew Arnold into a wistful elegy of an Oxford which had ceased to exist anywhere, save in his own mind. 'Beautiful city – so venerable, so lovely, so unravaged by the fierce intellectual life of our century, so serene ... steeped in sentiment she lies, spreading her gardens to the moonlight, and whispering from her towers the last enchantments of the Middle Age. ...'[13] Those who passed their lives there found the enchantment skin-deep and the ravaging rather more apparent. The religious upheavals, first of the Anglo-Catholic tractarianism of the Oxford Movement and then of the more liberal theology of Jowett and his colleagues, had set man against man and college against college. Mrs Humphrey Ward recalled this Oxford of her youth 'still within sight and hearing of the great fighting fires of an earlier generation ... Balliol versus Christ Church – Jowett versus Pusey and Liddon – while Lincoln despised both, and the new scientific forces watched and waited'.[14] The battle raged after Swinburne had left Oxford. True, religious controversy did not lead the Tractarians to hiss and snowball the Vice-Chancellor as he left the Sheldonian Theatre, as they had once done; C. P. Golightly, the moving Protestant spirit behind the Martyrs' Memorial, no longer feared to walk the streets of Oxford at night lest he 'might fall into a Tractarian ambush'. Yet in 1863, seven years after Swinburne's arrival and two years before Arnold's elegy, Benjamin Jowett himself was indicted for heresy in the Vice-Chancellor's court, on a motion of Dr Pusey.[15]

As if this were not enough, Oxford in Swinburne's last year was to be the scene of the great debate of religion and Darwinism, staged at the meeting of the British Association for the Advancement of Science between T. H. Huxley and Bishop Wilberforce. But more important than these intellectual conflicts – at least in the story of Swinburne's life – Oxford was also discovered by the Pre-Raphaelites.

Swinburne's Oxford was a reformed university and Balliol had been one of the leaders of that reformation by throwing open scholarships to public competition and electing Fellows who were not candidates for holy orders. In 1854 the 'Old Master', Dr Jenkyns, had died after thirty-five years in office. There was a contested election between Robert Scott and Benjamin Jowett, who was to become one of the great and lasting influences on Swinburne's life. Jowett was undeniably the more distinguished of the two men, but his religious orthodoxy was suspect. So it remained. When Kate Vaughan, sharing the general suspicion of him, heard that Frank, elder brother of Bertrand Russell, was going up to Balliol in 1883, she wrote: 'Oh, my dear boy, beware of Jowett; he will turn you out a polished infidel.'[16]

To Jowett's dismay, and to his greater humiliation, he lost the election to Scott. That he was appointed Professor of Greek in the following year, by the intervention of Lord Palmerston, was poor consolation. As Harold Nicolson puts it, Jowett withdrew from college life and sulked like a Victorian Achilles in his tent.[17] John Addington Symonds, who went up just after Swinburne, recalled going to see Jowett with a letter of introduction from his father. The hopeful young man went to see the great scholar on a winter afternoon. He found him in his darkened, panelled room, dozing in front of the fire. Jowett roused himself, read the letter, then said, 'I do not think I know your father.' There was a long and awkward pause, broken at last by Jowett, who said, 'Goodbye, Mr Symonds,' and went back to sleep.[18]

Jowett remains one of the most extraordinary and undervalued characters of the entire Victorian period, almost the only figure of moral or intellectual authority who contrived to exercise an intelligent influence over Swinburne's life. Born in 1817, the son of an improvident furrier, his early years suggested the eighteenth century rather than his own. Poverty broke up the family home. The eleven-year-old Jowett was sent to fend for himself in lodgings in City Road, and to attend St Paul's School as a day-boy. With ferocious determination, he made the best of this and won a scholarship to Balliol in 1835. He was so obviously poor that another undergraduate sent him an anonymous gift of money to pay for extra tuition. With this assistance, Jowett won the Hertford and was elected a Fellow of the college while still an undergraduate.

His appearance was as odd as his antecedents. He was slightly built, curly haired, somewhat effeminate in appearance, and with a voice which remained squeaky and almost unbroken. Though he was the friend of Florence Nightingale, Tennyson and Browning, he distrusted sentiment and emotional attachments, remaining a bachelor. His style was marked, as E. F. Benson recalled, by 'an arid incisiveness ... fatuousness withered in his presence'.[19] His wry farewell to the future Margot Asquith was a superb Victorian epigram: 'My dear child, you must believe in God in spite of what the clergy tell you.'[20] His withering treatment of bores and philistines was precisely of the kind to appeal to Swinburne's vindictive streak. After displaying an obvious distaste for one group of visitors at Balliol, Jowett's coldness provoked one of them to say encouragingly, 'Oh, you mustn't think too hardly of us, Master,' whereupon, Jowett's still, small voice replied, 'We don't think about you at all.'[21]

Jowett was in many respects Swinburne's exterior conscience in the years to come, drawing him away from childish imitation of sado-masochism to more worthwhile writing. Indeed, there was to come a time when Swinburne was on such good behaviour in Jowett's presence that he even became nervous over Jowett's seeing him with disreputable friends. Yet Jowett was no mere conformist. He was prosecuted for his interpretation of the Bible, even though the case was dropped. He was no prude. When an undergraduate production of Aristophanes was put on, the tutor in charge ordered the cutting of references to boys as sexual partners. Jowett summoned the unfortunate tutor and addressed him. 'I hear you have been making cuts in the Greek play ... Aristophanes wrote it. Who are you?'[22]

As a tutor, Jowett's relationship with Swinburne was less easy. He told John Addington Symonds that he found Swinburne a very singular young man whose essays were all language and no thought. Jowett received these essays, read to him at evening tutorials, with hardly more than a few words of comment. Then he would fall silent, staring at the fire and leaving the essayist in a state of increasing unease. After one of these long silences, he announced, 'When I say nothing, people generally fancy I am thinking about something. Generally I am thinking about nothing. Good night.'[23]

Swinburne took badly to the tutorial system, but Jowett's breakfast parties were even worse. The breakfast party was an institution of Victorian Oxford, flawlessly ridiculed by the future Cardinal Newman in the tenth chapter of his novel *Loss and Gain* (1848). Conversation flagged until, as Newman remarked, the cultural feast degenerated into the routine of the pig-trough. Swinburne disliked Jowett's breakfast parties, others found them paralysing. Jowett made no effort to converse with the nervous young men whom he had invited, merely sipping tea and staring vacantly ahead of him. The sense of embarrassment deepened until, as Symonds recalled, there was complete silence broken only by the sound of toast being crunched desperately by rows of youthful jaws.[24]

For all this, Jowett saved Swinburne from destruction at least twice. The second time was many years ahead but the first was at Balliol. Quite simply, he indoctrinated his pupils with the gospel of work. In all the accounts of Swinburne's life much more is made of morbid dissipation than of the great amount of work which he produced and which, whatever its quality, distracted him from less laudable pursuits. He was not a particularly distinguished classical scholar on arriving at Balliol. He got a second in Honours Moderations and did not survive until Schools. Yet the habits of work which he learnt there remained with him. As Cecil Lang remarks, with the possible exception of Milton, Swinburne was to become the most learned of England's major poets.

By the time that Jowett became Master in 1870, salvation by work had become a central dogma. 'You are a fool!' he told Walter Morrison, 'You must be sick of idling. It is too late for you to do much. But the class matters nothing. What does matter is the sense of power which comes from steady working.'[25] The preaching of this gospel by Jowett, as tutor and Master, produced a stream of distinguished apostles, among them Archbishops Tait, Temple, and Lang, Cardinal Manning, Arnold Toynbee, T. H. Green, Hopkins, Lord Curzon, Asquith and Sir Edward Grey.

Even within the college, Swinburne's life was by no means bounded by his relations with Jowett or other tutors. In the autumn of 1856 he was one of the six founding members of the Old Mortality, a society named in honour of the delicate state of health in which its first members felt themselves to be. Its proceedings were a good deal more riotous than its minute-book, 'The Old Mortality Register', would suggest, if taken at its face value. The opening leaves constitute 'A History of the institution of Old Mortality', describing how 'a company of scholars of the University of Oxford was assembled for purposes of sober & intellectual pastime in the rooms of one John Nichol of Balliol College'.[26] The members met in one another's rooms to listen to papers or readings by the chairman for that evening, following this with discussion and refreshment.

The oldest member, John Nichol, was a Scot of radical and even revolutionary views, who had already been a student at Glasgow University and was twenty-one when he came up to Balliol. He was the moving spirit of Old Mortality and a friend who had a decisive influence on Swinburne's thoughts and writings at this time. Nichol was to return to Glasgow as Professor of English, the champion of Byron, Tennyson and the moderns, who had been dismayed when Jowett told him that Thomas Moore was a greater poet than Browning.[27]

Apart from Swinburne, the other members included Algernon

Grenfell, G. R. Luke, who was drowned in the Isis six years later, A. V. Dicey, who became one of the great scholars of jurisprudence, and George Birkbeck Hill, literary scholar and editor of Boswell. The meetings of the Old Mortality were not as strictly regulated as might be supposed. On 24 October 1857, for instance, Swinburne read an essay on *Wuthering Heights*, which somehow became 'a warm debate as to whether naked statues and pictures were desirable or not'.[28] Swinburne's contributions consisted principally of readings. On 19 February 1857 he declaimed 'The Defence of Guenevere' by an unknown young poet of Exeter College, William Morris, whom Swinburne fiercely announced as superior to Tennyson.[29] On the whole, the reception of such pieces was urbane and non-committal. On 23 May 1858, the only comment on Swinburne's enthusiasm for the plays of Marlowe and Webster was that, 'The night being sultry, no discussion of any length ensued but the essay and the ices were found equally though variously good in the eyes of the Society.'[30]

Though it was suggested that John Nichol introduced Swinburne to drink, it was probably in moderation, since evidence of what Gosse called Swinburne's 'scandalous' drunkenness was not to be found before 1862. On the other hand Swinburne's extreme excitability was shown by the manner in which he followed Nichol's revolutionary enthusiasm. Above his mantelpiece, Swinburne placed a portrait of Orsini, who with his supporters had tried to assassinate Napoleon III in January 1858 by throwing three bombs at the imperial carriage outside the Paris Opera. Orsini was a champion of Italian freedom, a cause to which Swinburne, like Nichol, was now attached. The other portrait in his room was of Mazzini. Yet it was before the picture of Orsini, who had died on the scaffold, that Swinburne would 'dance solemn and solitary gavottes, raising his hands from time to time "with gestures of adoring supplication"'.[31] To the Old Mortality as a whole, and to Swinburne most of all, the name of Napoleon III was an abomination. Swinburne would give a sharp scream whenever the name was mentioned. Professor T. E. Holland recalled the slight, golden-aureoled figure of the poet 'dancing round the table, screaming abuse, and, I think, advocating the assassination of the Emperor'.[32] It was a similar glimpse which Jowett had had when he described how the vision had 'danced about like a mad thing whenever the name of Napoleon was mentioned'.[33] In Swinburne's poetry, the advocacy of revolutionary violence was unqualified.

When the devil's riddle is mastered
And the galley-bench creaks with a Pope,
We shall see Buonaparte the bastard
Kick heels with his throat in a rope.[34]

Not surprisingly, anti-clericalism in Swinburne's case was a mere
stepping-stone to atheism. T. H. Green noticed him once at a
meeting of the Old Mortality where Green himself was reading a
paper on the development of Christian dogma. He glanced up from
his script, 'and nearly burst out laughing at the sight of Swinburne,
whose face wore an expression compounded of unutterable ennui
and naif astonishment that men whom he respected could take an
interest in such a subject'.[35]

His own enthusiasm overflowed the bounds of Old Mortality and
led to some spirited contributions to Union debates during the
presidency of Diccy. Skipping nimbly to the dispatch-box, treading
deftly on the toes of the principal speakers, he delivered a vehement
denunciation of Napoleon III and, when the Prince of Wales came
into residence at Oxford, an eloquent defence of tyrannicide

Yet the enduring relationship which derived from Old Mortality
was that of Swinburne and Nichol, the one shrill and immature, the
other older and experienced in a harder background than Swinburne had ever known. Nichol was Swinburne's host in Scotland
during the summer vacation of 1857, visiting East Dene the following Christmas. It was on the latter occasion that the two young men
went over to Farringford and called on Tennyson, who asked them
to dinner. Tennyson read *Maud* to them and thought Swinburne 'a
very modest and intelligent young fellow ... he did not press upon
me any verses of his own'.[36] Swinburne's attitude towards Tennyson
and his poetry was to remain ambivalent. Yet he and Nichol had
both championed him at this point. Nichol had written indignantly
about a motion at the Oxford Union: 'That the widespread influence of the writings of Alfred Tennyson is the main cause of the
present debased state of English poetry.'[37] Swinburne too defended
Tennyson from criticism on his visits to Radley, where the Warden
was a family friend. (In what might seem an oddly regressive step,
Swinburne was 'honorary member of the prefects' common room'.)
His break with the school came during a meeting of the Debating
Society when the speakers began to criticize *Maud*. 'You're a lot of
Philistines,' he announced shrilly and then, as it was described,
bounced out of the room.[38] His parents had evidently hoped that a
continuing association with a high-church school would support the

religious teaching of his childhood. As it was, the Warden of Radley deplored what he saw as Swinburne's 'theories of free-thinking in religion', and banished him from the school for fear that he might 'inoculate the boys with sinister tenets'.[39]

It was in the autumn of 1857 that Swinburne was caught up in one of the odder developments of mid-Victorian Oxford, which finally decided the direction of his literary ambition. Between 1848 and 1850, under the fatherly eye of John Ruskin and under the more immediate leadership of Dante Gabriel Rossetti, John Everett Millais and Holman Hunt, the Pre-Raphaelite Brotherhood had evolved and had given expression to its views in four numbers of the *Germ*. It was the beginning of a new phase in the development of Victorian art and literature, a rebellion against the dead formalism of its predecessor. The movement, with Ruskin's support for its freshness and vitality, soon achieved respectability, being somewhat less revolutionary than its members might have supposed at first.

Success also brought separation of the members of the PRB for reasons both personal and aesthetic, thereby opening the restricted society to new members and to a more liberal interpretation of its beliefs. In 1853, two young men matriculated at Exeter College, Oxford: Edward Burne-Jones and William Morris. Both were reading for holy orders. Morris, like Swinburne, possessed an impressive head of curls – dark in his case – and was known as 'Topsy', after the character in *Uncle Tom's Cabin*. More to the point, Morris was rich enough to become a patron of the arts. His own interests were in poetry and, like Burne-Jones, in visual art.

These two were to form a new and welcome tributary to the older stream of Pre-Raphaelite art. So far as Swinburne was concerned, they were also instrumental in directing the interest of the PRB towards Oxford. Dante Gabriel Rossetti had come up to Oxford for the day in the summer of 1857 to visit the new university museum being built in Parks Road to the design of Benjamin Woodward. He also visited another of Woodward's buildings, the recently completed debating-chamber of the Oxford Union, a study in red-bricked Venetian revival.[40]

Rossetti was struck by the semicircular bays of the ceiling and their obvious suitability for mural decoration. He put the suggestion to Woodward, who agreed, and a slightly bewildered Union committee consented to let the artists do the work in exchange for their keep and their materials. It was, in every respect, an almost idyllic Pre-Raphaelite arrangement. In place of the more famous and established names of the movement, Rossetti chose a group of young friends who had yet to make their reputations. One of them, Val Prinsep, protested that he couldn't paint or draw. 'That makes no difference,' said Rossetti, and then referred to William Morris as 'one of my friends who is going to join us who has never painted anything, but you'll see he'll do a stunning thing. Now, you come to Oxford and see what you have to do, and don't be afraid.'[41]

Rossetti and his seven friends, who included Burne-Jones as well as Morris, descended upon Oxford in August and set to work with a cavalier disregard of the necessity for preparing the walls to receive the paint. Perhaps the rapid deterioration of the work hardly seemed to matter, since the whole enterprise had much more the atmosphere of what the twentieth century was to call a 'happening' than the selfconscious creation of an enduring masterpiece. Rossetti first took lodgings in the High Street, later in George Street, and the work which had begun in the long vacation was still proceeding when Michaelmas term began in October and Swinburne returned to Oxford.

His introduction to the Pre-Raphaelites came on 1 November in the rooms of Birkbeck Hill at Pembroke. Hill was the one founder member of Old Mortality who was not a Balliol undergraduate, a fact on which his scout congratulated him because of the appalling reputation of Balliol food and accommodation: 'In Pembroke, sir, we *lives*; at Balliol they *exists*.'[42] The meeting with Morris, Burne-Jones and Rossetti was an immediate success. One of Swinburne's contemporaries described him at this time as 'like some figure in a Pre-Raphaelite canvas, where he would not have been out of place'.[43] Yet the appeal was mutual and profound, leading Burne-Jones to pronounce: 'We have hitherto been three and now there are four of us.'[44] The exuberant frivolity and the contrasting intensity of an 'improvised Bohemia' opened Swinburne's eyes to a world unlike any he had yet experienced. The Old Mortality was a society of clever and agreeable young men, dedicated to the agility of the mind rather than to the visions of art. Swinburne took at once to the exuberance of Rossetti, the amiability of Burne-Jones and the literary example of William Morris.

Swinburne was easily incorporated into the company of artists now busily covering the Union ceiling with scenes from Malory's *Morte d'Arthur*. Burne-Jones had chosen 'The Death of Merlin', Morris 'Sir Tristram and Lady Iseult', and Rossetti 'Sir Lancelot's Vision of the Holy Grail'. It was the last of these which inspired Max

Beerbohm's portrayal of Jowett staring at the ceiling in mild disapproval, inquiring: 'And what were they going to *do* with the Grail
when they found it, Mr Rossetti?'[45]

The scenes of activity in the Union debating-chamber were a
perfect match for Swinburne's own nervous excitability with the
reports of 'laughter, and songs, and jokes, and the volleys of soda-
water corks; for this innutrient fluid was furnished to them without
stint at the Society's expense, and the bill from the Star Hotel close
by amazed the treasurer'.[46] Expense in the eyes of the artists themselves was no object, as Rossetti indicated when on upsetting a pot
of costly lapis lazuli into another of real ultramarine, he met the
nervous protests of his patrons by saying casually, 'Oh, that's
nothing, we often do that.'[47]

Rossetti had at once seized on the Pre-Raphaelite possibilities of
Swinburne's appearance by inviting him to act as a model. Yet
before the mural could be carried out Rossetti was called away from
Oxford by the illness of his mistress, Lizzie Siddal, leaving Swinburne
to improve his acquaintance with Morris and Burne-Jones.
Of the two, it was Burne-Jones who became his firm friend, addressing him as 'Little Carrots' and allowing Swinburne to call him 'Ned'
in return. It was a world away from Oxford life where close friends
still followed the social custom of addressing one another as 'My
dear Swinburne', or 'My dear Nichol'. For the time being, however,
it was William Morris who had the greater influence over the new
recruit to the Pre-Raphaelite cause. Rossetti had yet to publish a
book of poetry but William Morris's *Defence of Guenevere* was to be
issued in a few months more and he was the most obvious poet of the
movement. Before the agreeable Bohemia of the Union artists
disintegrated, Val Prinsep recalled, Rossetti would recline on the
sofa in the evening and invite Morris to 'read us one of your grinds',
which Morris would do, jiggling his watch-chain nervously and
reciting in a sing-song voice, while Burne-Jones worked at a pen-
and-ink drawing:

> Gold on her head and gold on her feet,
> And gold where the hems of her kirtle meet,
> And a golden girdle round my sweet;
>   *Ah! qu'elle est belle La Marguerite.*[48]

For Swinburne's benefit, Morris read 'The Haystack in the Floods'.
Swinburne later told S. C. Cockerell that the 'poignancy and splendour of the ending caused him an anguish which was more than his

nerves were able to bear'.[49] It is easy to see the appeal to Swinburne of the strong drama of the poem, the condemned girl whose escape is frustrated and who sees her lover killed before her eyes; the colour and imagery of the neo-medieval picture, reflecting in words the style of the Union decoration, and the headlong rhythm of the short lines. For the time being, at least, it was William Morris who was the living example of a modern poet.

*   *   *

Apart from the society in which he moved, Swinburne had also found at Oxford those sources of literary inspiration which were to dominate his writing for the rest of his life. This was obviously true in the more academic sense, in respect of his study and lifelong admiration of Aeschylus and Sappho. His enthusiasm for English drama of the sixteenth and seventeenth centuries had grown to include those writers of Jacobean pastiche whose verse dramas were an accompaniment to the Romantic Revival in the 1820s. These included C. J. Wells, *Joseph and his Brethren* (1824), and Thomas Lovell Beddoes, *Death's Jest-Book*, begun in 1825 but not published until 1850. Apart from these, and the more obvious enthusiasm for *Maud*, Browning and the Brontës, he had also discovered the riches of French literature in the library of the Taylorian Institute. Indeed, he was to win the 1858 Taylorian Scholarship.

It was French literature which offered him the material of one of his dominant themes: lesbianism and bisexualism in more general terms. He certainly read *Fragoletta* by Henri de Latouche, whose central character appears to be a girl but is in fact hermaphrodite. In this role, Fragoletta attracts the love of a young army officer, while actually having an affair with his sister as a male character. Fragoletta poses as her own twin brother for this purpose and in this guise is challenged to a duel by the young officer, who kills her without ever discovering that she is his mistress.

In terms of bisexualism, Swinburne's wide reading of Balzac, whose novels were regarded with grave suspicion by English moralists, opened him to the influence of *La Fille aux yeux d'or*.[50] Henri de Marsay, the hero of the melodrama, is presented as having an affair with Paquita Valdès who, at the moment of orgasm, calls out another girl's name and reveals her lesbian past. Returning to avenge himself upon her, de Marsay finds Paquita bloodily and fatally stabbed by the Marquise de Réal, the slighted lesbian lover,

who then proves to be de Marsay's half-sister, both being illegitimate children of Lord Dudley.

The culmination of this obsession with lesbianism in European
literature of the period was, of course, Théophile Gautier's
Mademoiselle de Maupin, which though it had appeared in 1835
seemed effortlessly to achieve a perfection for which later authors
laboured in vain. It remains the great erotic *tour de force* of its
century and perhaps of all modern European literature. Swinburne
acknowledged it as such.

> This is the golden book of spirit and sense,
> The holy writ of beauty; he that wrought
> Made it with dreams and faultless words and thought.[51]

The skill of the novel, which influenced Swinburne from his
acquaintance with it as an undergraduate, is in a lyrical and almost
caressing attachment to the discussion of feminine beauty; the effect
of black worn on a white skin and the appeal of a woman in
mourning; the settings for making love; the use of playful violence
by a lover and the woman's pleasure in it; the ultimate dream of
possessing a harem of beautiful women of all types and races. It is in
the second half of the novel, with the discovery that Théodore's
page-boy is in fact a girl dressed as a boy and that Théodore is a
young woman – Mademoiselle de Maupin – that the lesbian theme
becomes explicit. In a production of *As You Like It*, the part of
Rosalind is, according to Shakespearean tradition taken by a youth
– in this case by Madelaine de Maupin masquerading as a boy in
order to act as a girl. Her appearance in feminine form reveals to her
mistress, Rosette, the truth about the supposed 'Théodore'.
Madelaine's final encounter with her male lover, D'Albert, is
followed by her disappearance to another room. Next day,
Rosette's bed is found 'tossed and in disarray, bearing the imprint of
two bodies'. The only indication of the identity of Rosette's lover is
a pair of pearls found among the sheets, recognized as those which
Madelaine de Maupin, alias Théodore, wore in her hair while playing the part of Rosalind. Gautier's manner is polished, oblique in its
description, evocative and suggestive in a supremely erotic style.

> Here is that height of all love's eminence
> Where man may breathe but for a breathing-space
> And feel his soul burn as an altar-fire
> To the unknown God of unachieved desire.[52]

Like so many of his literary contemporaries, Swinburne's knowledge of lesbianism came from imaginative writings, not from any recognition of it in girls like Kate Joynes whose path crossed his. He had not, of course, read Baudelaire at this point but the poetic treatment of the theme in the condemned section of *Fleurs du mal* was a direct parallel to his own later obsession with the subject.

As to his own writing, Swinburne claimed that before going up to Balliol he had burnt 'every scrap of MS he had in the world'.[53] In the style of Oxford prize poems he wrote 'The Temple of Janus' in 1857, during his first acquaintance with the Pre-Raphaelites, and failed to win the Newdigate with it in 1858. In 1860 he entered for another prize at Oxford, whose poetic subject was 'The Discovery of the North-West Passage'. In 1845, Sir John Franklin's expedition had set out to find the North-West Passage and had disappeared a few months later. After a number of attempts, first to rescue and then to recover the remains of the expedition, those remains were found in 1859. It was a subject as poignant in its way as Captain Scott's fate was to be over half a century later. Swinburne entered for the competition and, once again, failed to win it, though his entry was awarded second place. Certainly the poem was to show a force and vigour of description beyond anything else he had so far written, as well as uniting the courage of Franklin and his doomed companions with that shown by the Elizabethan explorers or the Nelsonian heroes of nineteenth-century sea-fights. In his entry, which Swinburne entitled 'The Death of Sir John Franklin', it is the Arctic scenery which appears as the implacable agent of disaster, starkly and compactly described.

> For the laborious time went hard with these
> Among the thousand colours and gaunt shapes
> Of the strong ice cloven with breach of seas,
> Where the waste sullen shadow of steep capes
> Narrows across the cloudy-coloured brine,
> And by strong jets the anger'd foam escapes,
> And a sad touch of sun scores the sea-line
> Right at the middle motion of the noon,
> And then fades sharply back, and the cliffs shine
> Fierce with keen snows against a kindled moon,
> In the hard purple of the bitter sky.[54]

By the end of 1857, the Old Mortality had given birth to *Undergraduate Papers*, a magazine giving Swinburne his first means of publication. His only poem in the short-lived paper was 'Queen

Yseult', a single canto of a poem in the style of Pre-Raphaelite medievalism. Its debt to William Morris was embarrassingly evident, though the embarrassment might have been as much Morris's as Swinburne's. Like a parody, its verses show the worst of the Pre-Raphaelite style and little of the best.

> In the noble days were shown
> Deeds of good knights many one,
> Many worthy wars were done.
>
> It was time of scath and scorn
> When at breaking of the morn
> Tristram the good knight was born.
>
> He was fair and well to see
> As his mother's child might be:
> Many happy wars had he. . . .[55]

Swinburne also produced a good deal of prose for the magazine, attacking Matthew Arnold, then Professor of Poetry at Oxford, and, of course, Napoleon III. Yet his most interesting piece was a review of *The Monomaniac's Tragedy, and other poems* by Ernest Wheldrake. Beyond question, Wheldrake's subjects seem the most extraordinary in all Victorian poetry. In Wheldrake, Swinburne found the hero who, in order to write a poem about murder, burgled his brother's house and strangled the infant child in order to taste 'the red kiss'.

> Oh! ah! oh!
> Ha! ha! it burns me.

Wheldrake also describes his sinister amusement on the death of his mistress and depicts himself subsequently, in one of the poems, tearing up her lace underwear into tooth-shaped fragments and gloating over her skirts. Introducing Wheldrake to his readers, Swinburne remarks sadly: 'Nothing is so tenacious of life as a bad poet. The opossum, we are credibly informed, survives for hours after its brains are blown out with a pistol. The author of "The Monomaniac's Tragedy" lives, writes, and finds a publisher.'[56]

There was, of course, one minor disappointment for those who hurried out to buy the poems of this mid-Victorian lunatic who savoured the joys of murder in the last thrilling spasms of his child victim or tore at his mistress's small-clothes with his teeth. Ernest Wheldrake, including the long quotations from his poetry, had been invented by Swinburne for the purpose of the article. Among the earnest and strident contributions to *Undergraduate Papers*, the Wheldrake hoax stands out as the magazine's supreme achievement.

His own poetry was a more serious matter, in Swinburne's view, as Birkbeck Hill reported. He was invited to Swinburne's rooms on 3 March 1857 to hear the latest poems read 'with such an earnestness, so truly feeling everything he had written'. Hill wrote to Annie Scott, his future wife, 'I wish you knew the little fellow; he is the most enthusiastic fellow I ever met, and one of the cleverest.'[57]

Arguably, it was Swinburne's supreme poetic talent and his desire to be 'clever' which were in conflict. Wheldrake was not his only literary hoax. He had also written two acts of a pseudo-Elizabethan play and endeavoured to pass it off on the academic world as the genuine article. 'The first edition of this rare play was printed in quarto, 1609; the second in 1622. I have noticed their variations in the footnotes.'[58] It has been suggested that Swinburne saw himself as a second Chatterton, but his enthusiasm for these hoaxes can be more easily explained. Duping his intellectual victims and then witnessing their subsequent annoyance was a rare pleasure, and one which he was to indulge frequently in the future. Pastiche continued to take up much of his time at Oxford with the writing of three acts of *Laugh and Lie Down*, a Jacobean piece whose title was taken from Cyril Tourneur. The comedy involves sufficient sexual ambiguities to make it worthy of its source. Imperia, a courtesan, is loved by the Duke of Milan, among others. She herself is in love with Frank, alias Francesca, who appears as both page-boy and girl, and who is beaten regularly throughout the action. The fact that his twin, Frederick, also appears as both boy and girl adds to the general confusion. It may be that the unfinished comedy shows something of Swinburne's sexual ambiguity in late adolescence. It certainly reflects the same theme in *Mademoiselle de Maupin* with the dressing-up of a girl as a page-boy, or the story of a girl masquerading as a boy, in order to dress up as a girl in *As You Like It* and thus confront the woman she loves.

It may simply have been that Swinburne was intent on devising the most sexually outrageous plot. The shrill delight of putting his elders and betters to the blush was one which he tasted, for instance, with Burne-Jones in the newly painted debating-chamber of the Union. He and Burne-Jones were engaged in a loud argument with two friends on the nature of heaven, which Swinburne suggested was only conceivable as a sexual paradise, 'a rose-garden full of stunners'. As respectable members of the university came to look at the new pictures, the debate on religion as sexual bliss continued, and 'Atrocities of an appalling nature were uttered.' The respectable Oxonians stood and looked dumbly at the group of friends, heard the language of the discussion, and 'literally fled from the room'. The result was immensely gratifying. 'Conceive our mutual ecstasy of delight,' wrote Swinburne.[59]

Even the Old Mortality had lost its sobriety, so far as Swinburne was concerned. His last performance there was a reading of comic features from *Household Words* by George Augustus Sala. It was uproariously successful and received with 'shouts of laughter'.[60] Sala was well known subsequently as the *Daily Telegraph* correspondent during the American Civil War and as the author of popular travel books. Yet he had a closer association with Swinburne than appeared on the surface. He was privately much interested in fetishistic aspects of female underwear and in the use of the birch in girls' schools. He was credited with having started an entirely bogus correspondence on the latter subject in the *Englishwoman's Domestic Magazine* which ran for almost a year in 1870 and was reissued as a special supplement. He was also the presumed author of *The Mysteries of Verbena House: or, Miss Bellasis birched for thieving.*[61] His pseudonym was 'Etoniensis' and the title of the novel is taken from the brothel in St John's Wood which Swinburne was later to frequent. Indeed, Swinburne himself was to share the same pseudonym for some of his pieces.

At Balliol, it was evident that Swinburne was about to embark upon the course of rebellion which had ended his Eton career. Jowett remained sympathetic, though showing a certain impatience with essays which were little more than 'a torrent of words, read very rapidly and shrilly'. After a long silence, he would merely say, 'Mr Swinburne, I do not see that you have been pursuing any particular line of thought.'[62] By 1859 Swinburne was bored with Oxford. The Pre-Raphaelites had gone, and so had Nichol. He chose to make an issue over compulsory chapel by refusing to attend. After a number of warnings, all ignored, he was gated. The members of Old Mortality, returning from an outing to Edgehill, went to his room to cheer him up and were entertained by a tirade of hysterical abuse against the system which oppressed him. Lord Bryce recalled that 'The amazing richness of his vocabulary had never, I think, struck us so much before.'[63]

Jowett intervened as a friend. He suggested to Admiral

Swinburne that Algernon should go down for a while and study privately, far away from the distractions of Oxford. The place chosen was the vicarage of Navestock in Essex, whose incumbent was William Stubbs, future Bishop of Oxford and author of the famous *Constitutional History of England* (1874–8) and Stubbs's *Select Charters* (1870).

The winter of 1859–60 at Navestock was uneventful and unconstructive. Swinburne had finished another play, *Rosamond*, taking as his subject the ill-fated mistress of Henry II and her destruction by the jealous Queen Eleanor. Stubbs expressed a polite interest and Swinburne proceeded to read the play to him. When the reading was over, Stubbs suggested that, for all its merits, he thought 'the tone of the amatory passages somewhat objectionable'. Swinburne's dwelling on the colour and texture of female flesh, the queen's perverse joy in tormenting and humiliating the beautiful young woman, had made the future bishop uneasy.

Swinburne said nothing, but fixed Stubbs with a long, silent stare. As Stubbs grew increasingly uncomfortable, the young poet let out a shrill scream, heard throughout the house, and ran up to his room. Mrs Stubbs, following nervously a little while later, could get no reply to her knock. There was only the sound of tearing and rending, and 'a strange glare through the key-hole'. Noises of one kind and another continued all night.

By next morning Stubbs was ready to humour his unpredictable guest, and he apologized for his criticism of the play. 'I lighted a fire in the empty grate, and I burned every page of my manuscript,' Swinburne announced, to the horror of his hosts. Then he added brightly, 'But it does not matter. I sat up all night and wrote it right through again from memory.'[64]

In April, he returned to Oxford, the period at Navestock having been intended to enable him to take his degree examinations in history and law. But he was never to sit the papers. Having moved into Nichol's former lodgings in Broad Street, free from the direct supervision of the college, his behaviour became uncontrollable. Late hours, drunkenness and violent conduct were alleged. Jowett had done his best to avoid having Swinburne sent down, 'Balliol thereby making itself as ridiculous as University had made itself about Shelley'.[65] Yet Jowett had also remarked significantly, 'if a poet came here, we could never hold him'.[66]

As it happened, Swinburne's academic future was determined in distinctly unpoetical terms by his landlady. 'I've had me fill of them tiresome Balliol gentlemen,' she announced.[67] It was merely a question of whether Swinburne should wait to be sent down or should leave of his own accord. He abandoned any thought of a degree and took his departure for East Dene. His friendship with Jowett, one of the most important of his life, survived the quarrel with the college. Edmund Gosse recalled: 'He used to say, very firmly, that the Master of Balliol was officially a stranger to him, but Mr Jowett an honoured and lifelong friend.'[68] As for the university in general, it was beyond forgiveness. When in 1907 the Chancellor, Lord Curzon, wrote to offer him an honorary degree, Swinburne with studied politeness told him to keep it.

Chapter 3

The Protégé

BY the time of his departure from Oxford, it was at least doubtful whether anyone took Swinburne seriously, including himself. Hoax and burlesque played quite as prominent a part in his writing as lyric fervour. His bogus Elizabethan or Jacobean drama, his inspired creation of the lunatic poet Ernest Wheldrake, his association with the painters of the Union who tempered artistic dedication with genial slapstick, all suggested a weary effort to lighten the burden and boredom of life. Faced with no sufficient challenge to his intellectual power, and no family or financial demands, the perpetration of literary jokes was at least some antidote to the tedium.

It was also an antidote to revolutionary fervour. In fact there was little enough for Swinburne to rebel against in his own life. To imitate Orsini's attempt to assassinate Napoleon III by refusing to set foot in Balliol chapel and being gated in consequence seemed absurd. This, like the other gestures of defiance against academic authority, was surely the performance of a youth acting the part of a revolutionary in a cause which did not directly concern him. He faced no danger and no hardship and, to that extent, his ridiculous patronage of Orsini, who had gone to the scaffold with matchless courage, seemed in questionable taste.

As for the deeds of military valour which had once occupied his imagination, how wise it seemed his parents had been to frustrate such ambitions. Shortly before leaving Oxford, he tried a modest jump over a gate on horseback, fell out of the saddle and landed on his chin. For a week he lay plaintively in bed and was fed upon liquids.

He lacked an immediate cause rather than the moral courage to do battle. As William Bell Scott observed, Swinburne's 'nervous excitable nature could not stand strain: pain was nothing to him, yet he would not bear the slightest inconvenience a moment'.[1] Scott witnessed this on a morning when Swinburne woke up with toothache, and swore that he would not stand it another moment. The tooth must come out. In Scott's company, he went to the dentist.

The tooth in question was 'a mighty grinder'. The dentist, exerting 'his whole muscular force', applied the forceps to the tooth and actually lifted Swinburne bodily without extracting it. Scott held him down by the head, the dentist pulled again, and this time the grinder broke with a crack. 'Swinburne swore, not against the dentist, but against the tooth, and had it out piecemeal without complaining.'[2]

There is a characteristic irony in the manner in which Swinburne's fortitude, which he dreamed of in terms of military or revolutionary glory, was at length displayed, before an audience of two, in the dentist's chair.

Yet Admiral Swinburne, though he had refused to allow his son to join the cavalry, was quite prepared to subsidize his career as an author. He paid substantially for the publication of his poems and gave him an allowance of £400 a year, which was almost exactly the sum allowed by parents to young officers of hussars or lancers to meet their mess expenses.[3] By the time he had left Oxford, Swinburne had completed his two plays, *Rosamond* and *The Queen Mother,* as well as the first of the poems which were to appear in *Poems and Ballads* in 1866. He was also well furnished with introductions to the literary society of the mid-Victorian period.

During his Oxford vacations he had, as usual, spent a certain amount of time with Sir John Swinburne at Capheaton, improving his acquaintance with the Trevelyans at Wallington. Sir Walter Calverley Trevelyan, the sixth baronet, was something of a caricature of the wealthy amateur in Victorian science. He had been the friend of the great pioneer of photography W. H. Fox Talbot and he was an enthusiast for geology and the new fad for phrenology. Among other things, he was a believer in the abolition of capital punishment and in total abstinence from alcohol. With a certain consistency, he bequeathed the contents of the Wallington cellars on his death 'for scientific purposes'.[4]

His wife, Pauline, was unequivocally described by their kinsman Sir George Otto Trevelyan as 'Algernon Swinburne's good angel'.[5] She was almost forty when Swinburne began to frequent Wallington, having been born in 1816. She had been brought up to the appreciation of painters like Turner and Copley Fielding, had visited the Royal Academy exhibitions and had taken lessons in water-colour from John Varley, a founder of the Water-Colour Society. In 1833 she met her future husband at the Cambridge meeting of the British Association for the Advancement of Science and married him two years later. Her portrait by William Bell Scott shows an alert, rather Grecian beauty. Effie Ruskin thought her 'a nice little woman, very quiet and rather pretty, excessively fond of painting'.[6]

The Trevelyans were busily improving their eighteenth-century hall, among its trees and parkland, principally by turning the central courtyard into a covered saloon. The Italianate arches were adorned with murals, and painted panels were added between some of them. With the stone balustrade and upper storey, the rich colours of the carpets, the statuary and the furnishings, the total effect was almost that of a theatrical set.

Between Swinburne and Pauline Trevelyan there was a deep affection, combined with a certain nervousness on her side as to the direction his poetry and his behaviour might take. She was no prude, however, and he evidently read to her parts of his burlesque drama *La Soeur de la reine,* based on his fantasy of Queen Victoria's prostitute sister and the queen's own promiscuity with her ministers, without causing offence. He also found Pauline Trevelyan a sympathetic listener to his simple and incisive views on European politics. 'Don't you think we shall live to see the last Austrian emperor hung? Is Garibaldi the greatest man since Adam or is he not?'[7] To their mutual friend, William Bell Scott, Swinburne also announced cheerfully, 'Nevertheless I shall see the hoary hell-beast called Pius IX hanged by the neck.'[8]

Pauline Trevelyan and her husband had travelled a good deal in Italy and her sympathies were on the whole Swinburne's in this matter. Yet she treated him with a certain affectionate ridicule for the shrillness of his denunciations. Edmund Gosse described a water-colour drawing which she had done of Swinburne, 'stripped to the waist, his red hair flying out like the tail of a comet, with a blunderbuss in either hand, striding across the top of a Parisian barricade'.[9] There exists another of her caricatures in which Swinburne addresses the people on his way to the guillotine. The warmth of his revolutionary ambitions and his advanced views formed the subject of amusement which was possible between a woman of her age and a young man of such excitability and immaturity. Chief among their projected hoaxes was that of introducing Swinburne to George Sand, presumably through the medium of correspondence, and passing him off on the great female intellect of French literature as 'the typical *miss anglaise emancipeé* and holding the most ultra views'.[10]

The Trevelyans had maintained a close contact with Swinburne, even at Oxford which they had visited in order to inspect Benjamin Woodward's new museum and the celebrated murals of the Union debating-chamber. Yet it was at Wallington that Swinburne was remembered most vividly. His enthusiasm and excitability, said Scott, had 'the charm of sunshine or champagne'.[11] The shrill, declamatory voice monopolized the new saloon. George Otto Trevelyan described him reciting his poetry to the ladies of the party in its Italian splendour. 'He sat in the middle of the room, with one foot curled up on the seat of the chair beneath him, declaiming verse with a very different intonation and emphasis from that with which our set of young Cantabs read Byron and Keats.'[12]

According to Swinburne, there was never a shadow between him and Pauline Trevelyan. When her husband entered the room and found a copy of Balzac, perhaps nothing so remarkable as *La Fille aux yeux d'or,* he picked it up with a pair of tongs and deposited it in the fire. Swinburne walked out of the house in protest but went no further than Scott's home in Newcastle. There he occupied himself, 'lying before the fire with a mass of books surrounding him like the ruins of a fortification, all of which he had read, and could quote or criticize correctly and acutely many years after'.[13]

The separation from Wallington was short-lived, Swinburne forgiving Sir Walter Trevelyan's philistinism as the price of Pauline Trevelyan's affection. He spent some of his time with Scott in Newcastle, where Scott was working on a portrait in oils of the young protégé. It was the painter who observed during these visits what seemed to be the fatal flaw in Swinburne's genius. He had learning, memory, critical ability, the facility to write, and yet seemed to lack impetus or inspiration. It was, as Jowett had remarked about his essays, as though there was a flawless talent for expression with nothing of consequence which demanded utterance. He had, perhaps, the makings of a literary critic.

In a broader sense, Pauline Trevelyan grew uneasy about the lack of direction in his life, the absence of any need for Swinburne to do anything. 'It's all very well to pitch into a party,' replied Swinburne tolerantly, 'but what *is* one to do?' There were no professions which offered the least promise. 'I can't go to the Bar: much good I should do if I did. You know there is really no profession one can take up with and go on working. Item – poetry is quite work enough for any one man.' Not that writing in itself was an appealing labour. '*I* don't want to sit in rooms and write, gracious knows. Do you think a small thing in the stump-orator line would do? .... Seriously, what is there you would have one take to? It's a very good lecture, but it's not practical. Nor yet it ain't fair.'[14]

At Oxford it had been thought by his parents that Swinburne might go to the Bar and, indeed, while being tutored by Stubbs at Navestock he had undertaken the study of Blackstone's *Commentaries* and Henry Wheaton's *History of the Law of Nations*. Yet what might have been possible to an undergraduate, imprisoned in the drudgery of working up books for final examination, was quite unthinkable to one who had tasted the freedom of a life of literature on £400 a year, with Pauline Trevelyan as his good angel and the high spirits of the younger Pre-Raphaelites to keep him company.

Admiral and Lady Jane Swinburne stood back from their son's career for the most part. The duty owed by conscience towards parental susceptibilities was reserved by Swinburne for Pauline Trevelyan, as it was later to be for Jowett, and later still for that oddest figure of moral authority, Theodore Watts-Dunton. As sexual and literary scandals darkened about him, he did his best to spare Pauline knowledge of them, swearing that there was no substance to the rumours which she had heard. His task was made somewhat easier by the speed with which the fates had shortened her life. Pauline Trevelyan's health deteriorated in the early 1860s and the time came when she was in a wheelchair at Wallington. As far back as 1850 she had been operated upon for an ovarian cyst, whose recurrence brought with it a mortal sickness which was to result in her death at the age of fifty.

Despite the presence of Scott, George Otto Trevelyan and others, Swinburne's experience of Wallington seems to have been of a predominantly feminine world, in which he figured both as the *miss anglaise emancipée* and as a reincarnation of Sarah Gamp, according to Scott. It was a world from which there radiated an intensity of feminine friendship reflected in Jane Welsh Carlyle's outburst to Louisa Ashburton, an *habituée* of the Wallington gatherings. 'O my darling! My darling! I know the effect a letter from *you* has now always on *me*; it makes me long to take you in my arms and hush you to sleep, as if you were a tired wee child, and kiss off all the tears from your eyes.'[15] Such declarations were more innocent than the hungry curiosity of a post-Freudian age would believe. For Swinburne, this feminine salon offered cultural sympathy and the emotional ease of a second home. The arena of literary battle lay elsewhere. For Pauline Trevelyan, he retained a distinctly filial

regard. Some years after her death he summed up the essence of her
beauty and her courage.

> Half humorous goodness, grave-eyed mirth on wings
> Bright-balanced, blither-voiced than quiring strings;
> Most radiant patience crowned with conquering cheer;
> A spirit inviolable that smiled and sang....[16]

*   *   *

For the time being, Swinburne's encounter with the literary world of
Victorian London was postponed by his parents who went to
Mentone for the winter and took him with them. He had first been
abroad with them on a visit to Paris in the spring of 1857. This was
the occasion when the newly promoted admiral and his family were
driving in an open carriage down the Champs-Elysées, when they
passed another carriage, containing Napoleon III himself. Not
knowing quite what to do, the Swinburne parents rose in their
carriage and bowed, while the emperor raised his hat in distant
acknowledgement. Swinburne remained seated with his hat on.
When asked if he had raised it, he replied, 'Not wishing to be obliged
to cut my hand off at the wrist the moment I returned to the hotel, I –
did – *not!*'[17]

This time Swinburne was more receptive to the city as the family
travelled through France. 'I am in love with Paris,' he assured
Pauline Trevelyan, and not least among his discoveries there was
the Louvre. Predictably, the eroticism of Giorgione's *Fête
Champêtre,* the two naked girls attending the two fashionably
dressed men in their sylvan musical picnic, made an instant appeal
to him. 'What a stunner above stunners that Giorgione party with
the music in the grass and the water-drawer is – that Gabriel made
such a sonnet on.'[18] His delight came in part from the preparation
for his first sight of the picture by Rossetti's poem, written in 1849,
describing the figures of the canvas, including the naked girl who
has just drawn the flute from her mouth.

> Whither stray
> Her eyes now, from whose mouth the slim pipes creep
> And leave it pouting, while the shadowed grass
> Is cool against her naked side?[19]

That Swinburne with his sympathy for French culture should have
responded to all that its capital could offer is hardly surprising.
Mentone was a different matter: he hated it. The Hellenic

dream-world of East Dene was one thing, but the real Mediterranean seemed profoundly uninteresting. Its landscape, as he saw it, was 'blotched, mangy, grimy, parboiled country, *without* trees, water, grass, fields – *with* blank, beastly, senseless olives and orange-trees like a mad cabbage gone indigestible'.[20] As for the reality behind that feminine eroticism of Giorgione or his own poems of Grecian sexuality, it consisted of women 'with hunched bodies and crooked necks carrying tons on their heads and looking like death taken seasick. Arrrrrr. Grrrrr.'[21]

Lacking any other distraction, he turned to his own work. This included the completion of three prose stories in imitation of Boccaccio's *Decameron*, the revision of some short individual poems, and the first sustained labour of *Chastelard,* the initial verse drama on the theme of Mary Queen of Scots, to be followed in due course by *Bothwell* and *Mary Stuart.* None of these pieces reflected the least influence of his Mediterranean experience. Nor did the other work upon which he was engaged and which, despite its scandalous reputation, was more intriguing than any of the rather stolid masterpieces at which he aimed. This was the burlesque novel *La Fille du policeman.* Written in French, the book is a skilful parody of Gallic inability to cope with English titles and nouns, while also being a hilarious fantasy of a *coup d'état* staged by Prince Albert against Victoria. With ludicrous improbability, Albert with his pudding-faced solemnity is presented as the leader of popular revolt, 'le prince prolétaire', urged on by the lecherous and sadistic Bishop of London, 'Le grand évêque Whitestick'. The truth of the story is vouched for by men of probity, including the celebrated philanthropist, 'le révérend comte sir Shaftesbury'. The geography of London is grotesquely rearranged, in the manner of the worst French fiction, so that Prince Albert's secret apartment is found where the vice-ridden promenade of the Haymarket borders the Thames at Charing Cross within sight of the Tower of London. Here he plots the revolution with the Lord Mayor, Tom Boggs, who is inevitably addressed as 'Sir Boggs'. The dialogue of Albert and Victoria is an inspired blend of broken French. 'Restez, Godam!' is his contribution, while the queen deals with her troublesome courtiers. 'My lords,' she informs a pair of them, 'vous coucherez tous deux à la tour de Londres.' But the squabble is settled by 'un handshake assez cordial'.

It is while Lord Derby is hiding in the sewers and the mob is advancing on Buckingham Palace that Whitestick quickly changes sides and the rebellion collapses. Albert, who has ordered the Alsopp-Barclay breweries to be thrown open to the people in order to fuel their enthusiasm, is defeated. He is demoted to the role of a puppet, 'il fera des exhibitions d'industrie'. The scapegoats are the unfortunate Williams Harvey, 'policeman et orateur populaire', and his daughter Nelli. His sister-in-law, Babby Prawns, has already died from an aphrodisiac administered to her following her abduction by the Bishop of London, Whitestick. Nelli herself follows the same path, carried off by Whitestick among cheering crowds in a chapter entitled 'Ce qui peut se passer dans un cab-safety'. In the last chapter Whitestick enters carrying Nelli's body, and Williams Harvey falls dead. He is denounced as an atheist policeman and his possessions are forfeit to the State.[22]

The truth is that *La Fille du policeman* shows a good deal more originality than 'Dead Love' or Swinburne's other imitations of Boccaccio. Even a verse drama like *Chastelard* is apt to read like a pastiche of a romantic revival imitation of an Elizabethan original. As Dante Gabriel Rossetti put it, 'I think he is much better suited to ballad-writing and such like.'[23] For the time being, in the tedium of the Maison Laurenti at Mentone, Swinburne was meditating his sequel to *La Fille du policeman,* a drama in the style of Dumas about the twin sister of Queen Victoria brought up as a common prostitute to remove her as a rival to the throne. It was also to reveal the unbridled promiscuity which the queen shared with her sister, Kitty, and which made her presence unsafe for her ministers and even for the Poet Laureate himself.

A more immediate relief to the boredom of winter in Mentone was the prospect of a visit to Italy. He wrote to Pauline Trevelyan and William Bell Scott seeking advice on what he ought to see in Venice and, possibly, Florence. He had already made up his mind that he must pay his respects to the hair of Lucretia Borgia, preserved in a bottle of spirit in the Ambrosian Library at Milan. He was particularly anxious to see the beauty of Venice as well, 'before it gets bombarded'.[24]

Swinburne's visit to Italy in February 1861 almost coincided with the proclamation of Vittorio Emmanuele in Turin as king of a united country. In 1859, as King of Sardinia, he had promised to respond to the *grido di dolore* of Italians languishing under Bourbon and papal rule to the south and under that of the Austrians in the north. During the same year, he and his prime minister, Cavour, had persuaded Napoleon III to support their cause by driving the

Austrians from Lombardy. After the victories of Magenta and Solferino, however, Napoleon had concluded a hasty peace with Franz Josef at Villa Franca, without pushing on from Mantua to Venice. He was evidently concerned that a prolonged conflict would bring Prussia into the war on Austria's side. He had, however, supported Vittorio Emmanuele in the annexation of central Italy in 1860, though receiving the territories of Nice and Savoy as the price of his assistance. It was this last act of political extortion which confirmed for Swinburne and other supporters of Italian independence that the French emperor was the scoundrel they had long suspected. In the summer of 1860 Garibaldi had landed in Sicily with his volunteers to support the rebellion against the Bourbons, and then led the campaign in Italy as far as Naples. At the same time Cavour had invaded the Papal States from the north. By the time of Swinburne's visit, Vittorio Emmanuele was King of Italy, with the exception of Rome, which remained under papal rule until 1870, and Venice which was still in the hands of the Austrians. As a matter of fact, Swinburne need not have feared that the Venetians were about to suffer bombardment. The Italians were content to bide their time until Austria was embroiled in war with Prussia in 1866, when they annexed Venice more peacefully than anyone had dared to hope.

During the excitement of 1860, Swinburne had responded to the campaigns for Italian freedom with his poem 'A Song in Time of Revolution', which was less remarkable for its relevance to Italy than for its enthusiasm for revolution as a universal remedy.

The heart of the rulers is sick, and the high-priest covers his head:
For this is the song of the quick that is heard in the ears of the dead.

The poor and the halt and the blind are keen and mighty and fleet:
Like the noise of the blowing of wind is the sound of the noise of their
feet.[25]

From Mentone, he travelled to Milan and stood dutifully before the treasures of the Brera and the Ambrosian Library. He went on to Verona, to the Palladian splendours of Vicenza, to Padua, and then to Venice. After the tedium of Mentone and the detested Mediterranean, Italy in the fervour of independence and the radiance of art was an invigorating experience. Swinburne took to both the country and its people, having already cast them in the role of those whose triumphant rebellion was to sweep onward through European history with irresistible power.

Wilt thou judge thy people now, O king that wast found most wise?
Wilt thou lie any more, O thou whose mouth is emptied of lies?

Shall God make a pact with thee, till his hook be found in thy sides?
Wilt thou put back the time of the sea, or the place of the season of tides?[26]

It is interesting, too, that Swinburne responded particularly to the beauty of Italian women. In the light of later rumours as to his own sexual potency or ambivalence, his most overt erotic responses seem strongly heterosexual. 'As to women, I saw at Venice ... one of the three most beautiful I ever saw. The other two were at Genoa and Ventimiglia.... By her gaze I thought I might address her, but did not considering that we could not have understood each other (verbally at least); so caution and chastity, or *mauvaise honte* and sense of embarrassment prevailed.'[27]

Twenty-two years later, the memory of the three girls still preoccupied him sufficiently for him to attempt a definition of their beauty in poetry, not least the girl who had proved so fascinating yet elusive in the Venetian dusk.

> Once more a face no glance might choose but mark
> Shone pale and bright, with eyes whose deep slow beam
> Made quick the twilight....[28]

To judge from his own response, it was the sight of this goddess which made a deeper impression upon him than anything else during his winter in southern Europe. He was to have need of such images as the raw material of much of his writing in the few years which lay ahead.

*   *   *

Swinburne returned to England in the spring of 1861, now twenty-four years old. He was a published poet, though the extent of his fame was doubtful. The two verse plays, *The Queen Mother* and *Rosamond,* had been issued in a single volume at the end of 1860. They had not, of course, been accepted by a publisher as a commercial venture. Admiral Swinburne, though he thought *Rosamond* was 'far worse than useless', according to his son, promised to pay the cost of printing the book. Swinburne went to his bookseller, Pickering, and asked him to undertake the job. Later he transferred the book to the firm of Moxon, one of the most reputable publishers of the early-Victorian period. Two hundred and fifty copies were ready in

December 1860. Volumes for review and presentation were duly sent out. And that seemed to be the end of the matter. By the time the family left for Mentone, there were no reviews and no sales.

Perhaps it was not surprising. Swinburne, after all, was writing plays to be read rather than performed and the market for such literature was strictly limited, despite Wells and Beddoes. Edmund Gosse remarked that the verse of *Rosamond* was essentially Pre-Raphaelite painting in words, as in the depiction of the heroine and the women who dress her.[29]

> Maids will keep round me, girls with smooth worn hair
> When mine is hard, no silk in it to feel,
> Tall girls to dress me, laughing underbreath,
> Too low for gold to tighten at the waist.

Not that the play was without its dash of erotic violence, the theme of the beautiful heroine, mistress of the king, condemned to die by the jealousy of Queen Eleanor. Eleanor becomes the figure of sadism triumphant, gloating over the condemned Rosamond in such phrases as, 'I have not seen/A beaten beast so humble of its mouth.'

The Queen Mother was the more important of the two pieces, based on the story of the St Bartholomew's Eve massacre of Huguenots in 1572. In Swinburne's version, Catherine de Médicis, the queen mother of the title, dominates her cruel son, Charles IX, whose interest centres on his mistress Denise. The nature of their love is indicated by the girl's complaint to him.

> And once in kissing me
> You bit me here above the shoulder, yet
> The mark looks red from it.

Catherine and her women are shown by Swinburne deriving a bizarre amusement from the massacre, directing their sexual mockery at the genitals of the naked corpses.

> it made me merry
> To hear how they did mock the make of it,
> As blood were grown their game.

'Abusing the blind thing', as Swinburne describes the women, would seem to correspond to the emblem of the phallus as 'Blind Priapus', as well as to the contemporary account of the women's behaviour by J. A. de Thou in *Historia Mei Temporis*.[30]

After so much, it seemed that Swinburne was at least entitled to one outraged review condemning the obscene innuendoes of his

bloodstained dramas. It was not to be. He returned home to find
that the volume had been reviewed briefly by the *Spectator* and the
Athenaeum. Beyond that, it had been unnoticed. At least the
Spectator was moved to acknowledge the 'painful subjects' of the
plays. Of the author, it remarked, 'He has some literary talent but it
is decidedly not of a poetical kind.... We do not believe any
criticism will help to improve Mr Swinburne.'[31] The *Athenaeum* on 4
May 1861 was equally forthright. 'We should have conceived it
hardly possible to make the crimes of Catherine de' Medici dull,
howsoever they were presented. Mr Swinburne, however, has done
so.' As for *Rosamond,* the reviewer confessed, 'we were unable to
cope with a second one'.

The latter review might, at least, be dismissed as being perfunc-
tory and hardly serious in its intention. Yet the *Spectator* had
entirely missed the point. This was not the stage in his career when
Swinburne was looking for criticism, as William Stubbs had discovered at Navestock. He seemed hungry for appreciation and, better
still, adulation.

*   *   *

After the intense mutual admiration of the young, as represented by
the cleverness of Old Mortality and the poetic enthusiasms of the
Pre-Raphaelites and their friends at Oxford, the conventional literary world of the *Spectator* and the *Athenaeum* showed an aridity
beyond belief. Their reviewers, dulled by the impact of new talent in
volume after volume, month after month, were ill qualified to
appreciate the rare, delicate poetry of a new style. They were
certainly ill disposed to be impressed by clever young men. So it
seemed to the author of *The Queen Mother* and *Rosamond.* By the
spring of 1861, it was hardly surprising that he should be eager for
something even more stimulating than the judicious good taste of
Wallington.

On 4 May he returned to his London lodgings in Grafton Street,
Fitzroy Square. The day had been spent first with Burne-Jones and
then with Rossetti and Madox Brown looking over some illustrations of Blake at Alexander Gilchrist's house in Cheyne Row.
Awaiting him on his return was a note, an invitation for the following day from Richard Monckton Milnes whose town house was in
Upper Brook Street, running off Park Lane. For the next four
years, Milnes was to be the dominant influence in Swinburne's

development and, even after their estrangement, left in the poet's mind sufficient of his presence to exercise a remote control for the rest of his life. If Pauline Trevelyan were Swinburne's good angel, in the view of contemporaries, then Milnes appeared as the angel of darkness.

Like Benjamin Jowett and Pauline Trevelyan, Milnes belonged to a generation which had become young adults by the beginning of the Victorian period and self-confidently middle-aged by the time that Swinburne came to London. Milnes, who was created Baron Houghton in 1863, seems a ubiquitous figure in the social and cultural life of mid-Victorian England. A dilettante in politics and literature, a man of wit and an influential patron, he lived at his town house or his Palladian home at Fryston in Yorkshire in an aura of almost eighteenth-century sophistication and privilege. At Cambridge he had been one of the Apostles – a distant precursor of Old Mortality – along with Tennyson and Arthur Hallam. He was one of the three Apostles who made the famous journey to Oxford in 1829 to illuminate the ignorance of that place with the genius of Shelley, only to discover that their hosts thought they were talking about Shenstone.

There was something about Milnes, in middle age, which suggested a Victorian Horace Walpole. His acquaintances included Carlyle, Tennyson, Thackeray and George Sand among writers. In politics he was the friend of Gladstone, Disraeli and Louis Napoleon. He had proposed marriage to Florence Nightingale and shared with his friend Richard Burton an enthusiasm for eastern travel. In literature, he had restored Keats to his proper place among the Romantics by means of his *Life and Letters of John Keats* in 1848. He had got a civil list pension for Tennyson, after some goading by Carlyle.

'Richard Milnes,' said Carlyle, 'when are you going to get that pension for Alfred Tennyson?'

'My dear Carlyle, the thing is not so easy as you seem to suppose. What will my constituents say if I do get the pension for Tennyson? They know nothing about him or his poetry, and they will probably think he is some poor relation of my own, and that the whole affair is a job.'

'Richard Milnes, on the Day of Judgement, when the Lord asks you why you didn't get that pension for Alfred Tennyson, it will not do to lay the blame on your constituents; it is *you* that will be damned.'[32]

In the circle to which Swinburne was now invited, wit was vigorous and uninhibited and Milnes reigned supreme. The *bons mots* which enlivened his breakfast parties and dinner tables perished, yet he seems to have had a quick tongue for the plaintive and the boring. An elderly lady, bewailing the lack of respect shown by the young, remarked that when she was a girl all the young men in London were 'at my feet'. Milnes, with an expression of weary amazement, confessed that he had no idea there were so many chiropodists in the London of her youth.[33] On a later occasion his unlikely victim was the young Lord Curzon, the 'most superior person' of the Balliol rhyme and Viceroy of India in his thirties. In an after-dinner speech, Curzon was preening himself before the others in 'a suave and polished oration'. Milnes had dozed off and came to just in time to hear Curzon announce patronizingly that his success was due to his rule of life 'only to associate with his intellectual superiors'. Milnes roused himself and said loudly, 'By God! That wouldn't be difficult!'[34]

Disraeli, who based the character of Vavasour in *Tancred* on Milnes, ascribed his failure in the House of Commons to his facility for wit. Milnes had a face like 'a Herculaneum mask or a countenance cut out of an orange'. No one took him seriously and his speeches, whatever the subject, had 'the effect of some celebrated droll . . . before he had proceeded five minutes, though he might be descanting on the wrongs of Poland or the rights of Italy, there was sure to be a laugh'.[35] Disraeli was sure that Milnes longed for office, 'to sit on the Treasury Bench with folded arms and be a man of business'.[36] In that case, he had probably been ill advised to denounce the Carlton Club as a 'political scullery', and to change his politics, as the last two lines of a rhyme about him indicated.

> I was a Tory; am a Whig;
> Once Sairy Gamp, now Betsy Prig.[37]

It would have been enough for Swinburne to be drawn into this robust masculine world which the society of Milnes represented, a clear contrast to the lively, feminine good nature of Pauline Trevelyan and her friends. Yet there was more to Milnes than this. In his eastern travels he had witnessed with genial tolerance the antics of boys dressed up as dancing girls for the amusement of their Turkish admirers. Milnes describes himself as a man of 'ideal aspirations and sensual habits'.[38] Stories of his approval of the harem system and his sampling of the sexual delights of eastern women were to be borne out by his own unpublished papers. He keenly admired a troupe of dancing girls whom Flaubert had previously noted as 'very corrupt and writhing, extremely voluptuous'.[39] A thoughtful official of the British embassy in Constantinople wrote him a note, explaining where he could buy 'a Turkish damsel' for two hundred piastres, and Milnes himself recorded a girl of twelve being offered for sale to him in Egypt.[40]

In the spring and summer of 1861, Swinburne began his acquaintanceship with the friends of Monckton Milnes. Among these was the dark and intimidating presence of Richard Burton with his long moustaches and the marks of a spear-wound on his cheeks. Famous for his expedition with Speke to Lake Victoria, and still fresh from his marriage to Isabel Arundell, Burton was a figure of fascination to Swinburne. In terms of sexual behaviour, his explorations had unearthed practices which no amount of delving into historical documents on Swinburne's part would have brought to light. In 1856, Burton had published *First Footsteps in East Africa,* including an appendix on the practice of female circumcision. His nervous publisher had first insisted that it should be written in Latin, and then had become even more apprehensive over the likelihood of a prosecution for obscene libel and had torn out the appendices from the copies before issuing them. In their place, a single line of explanation was inserted: 'It has been found necessary to omit this appendix.'[41]

Within Milnes's circle it was Burton who had the most immediate effect on Swinburne, drawing him into a more rowdy and boisterous society than that which inhabited Upper Brook Street. Lord Redesdale swore that it was Burton who was responsible for Swinburne's addiction to brandy, while Swinburne himself acknowledged the genius of Burton the adventurer, 'Who rode life's lists as a god might ride', and the splendid, erotic pageantry of Burton's translations of the *Arabian Nights* and other works.

Years on years
Vanish, but he that hearkens eastward hears
Bright music from the world where shadows are....
....All that glorious orient glows
Defiant of the dusk.[42]

From Burton came the riches of the *Kama Sutra* and *The Perfumed Garden,* including that final portion whose manuscript was burnt by Lady Burton after his death and which, more specifically, dealt with such illuminating subjects as the origins of lesbianism; the tricks of sodomites; the art of pimping; the use of parts of the female body other than the vagina, and so forth. When Swinburne and Burton met on neutral territory, including the house of George Bird who was physician and friend to both, they would retire to a room apart, whence, as Gosse reported, 'the rest of the company would be tantalised to hear proceeding roars and shrieks of laughter, followed by earnest rapid talk of a quieter description'.[43]

It was Bird who was so foolish as to ask the ferocious-looking Burton with the scars of Africa upon him, 'Now, Burton, tell me; how do you feel when you have killed a man?'

'Oh, quite jolly, doctor! How do you?'[44]

Swinburne's behaviour in Bird's house at Welbeck Street was a good deal more hysterical. Isabel Burton's parents, both strict Catholics, were present on the occasion of one his more outrageous exhibitions. 'Young, sir,' said Mr Arundell in his most sanctimonious manner, 'if you talk like that, you will die like a dog!'

For a moment it seemed that Swinburne had been shocked into a realization of his errors. With clasped hands he turned to Arundell imploringly and begged, 'Oh, don't say "like a dog!"' Then adding more brightly, 'Do say, "like a cat!"'[45]

The worst of it was that Burton was a man of physical strength and energy, 'possessed at times with a kind of dionysiac frenzy', as Gosse politely called it.[46] Swinburne was no match for him in stamina. Even Monckton Milnes began to have doubts as to the wisdom of the introduction which had taken place at the breakfast table in Upper Brook Street on 5 June 1861. He remonstrated with his young protégé over his conduct with Burton. At that point, Burton was setting off for Brazil as British consul at Santos and Swinburne replied cheerily, 'As my tempter and favourite audience has gone to Santos, I may hope to be a good boy again. . . . I may have shaken the thyrsus in your face. But after this half I mean to be no end good.'[47] It was to take more than the diplomacy of Milnes to separate the tempter and his youthful prey. In 1878 *Poems and Ballads: Second Series* appeared with a dedication to 'Richard F. Burton, in redemption of an old pledge and in recognition of a friendship which I must always count among the highest honours of my life'. In the previous year Swinburne had written to John Nichol, 'I have not heard of or from Burton for two years, but I know that no length of silence or absence can imply any chance of a breach or gap in our mutual regard.'[48]

For the time being, in 1861, Swinburne's attention was drawn to stranger secrets than the sexual anecdotes of Burton's distant explorations. They were quite as bizarre, though much more relevant to his concerns. There was an apartment in the Rue Lafitte dubbed 'The clitoris of Paris' and occupied by a former officer of the 6th Dragoon Guards, who had once been a royal page at Buckingham Palace, whose father was Governor of the Ionian Islands and whose brother was a director of the Bank of England. With the Director of the Paris Opera and Napoleon III's Minister for Foreign Trade he was reputed to have staged heterosexual and lesbian orgies at his apartment, obliging one of his girls to note down the proceedings, and to have incorporated these into a book, *L'Ecole des biches*. More to the point, he was an avaricious collector of erotic books, pictures, ornaments, *objets d'art*. Many of these were smuggled to England, with the knowing assistance of Augustus Harris, manager of the Covent Garden Opera, and the unwitting help of the diplomatic service and the Foreign Office.

The name of this enterprising supplier was Frederick Hankey, and he was apt to strike a chill into those who met him. His speciality was the binding of books in human skin and he had pestered Burton to bring him back a young female skin from his African journeys. To ensure the finest texture, he later told the Goncourt brothers, it must be removed from a living subject.[49]

Burton did the only sensible thing. Unlike the horrified Goncourts, he treated Hankey as a joke. 'Poor old Hankey,' he wrote to Milnes, 'I did so want to get him a human hide. . . . And I failed.'[50] Swinburne, predictably, was fascinated by the monster, as the Goncourts termed him. Burton maintained a tolerant affection for his grotesque petitioner, dedicating the seventh volume of the *Arabian Nights* to his memory. 'My dear Fred, if there be such a thing as "continuation", you will see these lines in the far Spirit-land and you will find that your old friend has not forgotten you and Annie.'

In 1857, when the Obscene Publications Bill was presented to the House of Commons among a good deal of moral self-congratulation, one of its few opponents had been Richard Monckton Milnes. He had not, of course, declared his particular interest, which was that he was the importer of most of Hankey's more expensive wares. The library at Fryston, behind the Yorkshire Palladian façade, was a treasure-house of erotic and sadistic literature, as well as of a remarkable collection of pictures and objects.

Chief among the literary treasures, it seems, were the works of the Marquis de Sade, the most feared and the most prohibited author of the day.

Within a very short while of their meeting, Swinburne learnt of this *enfer* at Fryston. In fact, it was more appetizing in prospect than in reality. It represented in the first place the most extreme rejection of all the family and bourgeois morality of mid-Victorian England. Secondly, it promised a gratifying literary feast for any young man whose sexual predispositions were such as his. He returned, of course, to the literary life of a fledgling poet but with, as it were, one eye upon Fryston.

Chapter 4

Figures in a Landscape

THE public image of Swinburne between his arrival in London in 1860 and the literary uproar occasioned by his publication of *Poems and Ballads* in 1866 was far removed from the red-haired satyr pawing eagerly through the *enfer* of Monckton Milnes's library. He was seen often in company with Dante Gabriel Rossetti, the stouter elder figure and the excitable young poet being regarded as master and apprentice in terms of Pre-Raphaelite art. Arthur Munby, who belonged to Rossetti's generation rather than Swinburne's, saw them together at Rouget's restaurant just after the return from Mentone, describing them as 'Dante Rossetti ... & his young disciple Swinburne'.[1] Munby was a barrister, a teacher of Latin to working girls, and a poet. He had an enthusiasm for working-class women which was both sexual and philanthropic, finally marrying his own servant-girl, who continued to work as a servant elsewhere. He was also to be the witness of Swinburne's wilder outbursts, the extreme forms of his drunkenness, and the indecent displays which he then put on.

Swinburne was later at pains to separate himself in style, though not in personal sympathy, from the Pre-Raphaelites. He admitted to John Nichol that before 1861 his poetry might have shown traces of their influence, but from 1865 onward, as he assured Nichol eleven years later, 'I cannot trace in any part of my work, classical, modern, or historic, a trace of any quality that could correctly or even plausibly be labelled "Pre-Raphaelite" either for praise or blame.'[2] In 1862, at least, Munby and others had no doubt in the matter. Munby's diary for 21 March records: 'After dinner I went up to Mudie's; and at a bookstall on the way, fell in with that strange incarnation of PreRaphaelitism, young Algernon Swinburne.'[3] Munby disliked Swinburne at first, not because he found him wild or Bohemian but precisely the opposite. Three months later he was dismissing him as 'the intolerable little prig', and a year later he visited Cheyne Walk and was uneasy over the effect which Swinburne's presence was having on Rossetti. 'Rossetti has been much injured by the constant toadying of that clever little prig Algernon Swinburne, who was present, echoing all his master said.'[4]

The greatest attraction for Swinburne in London during the summer of 1861 and the following winter was Chatham Place, Blackfriars, where Rossetti lived with his wife and model Lizzie, whom he had married in 1860. Their story concerns Swinburne only in its final and familiar stages, when Rossetti had hesitantly married Lizzie Siddal after keeping her as his mistress for ten years. Her beauty, most famous in Millais's *Ophelia,* was vividly described by Georgiana Burne-Jones. 'Lizzie's slender, elegant, figure, tall for those days ... in a graceful and simple dress ... the mass of her beautiful deep-red hair as she took off her bonnet.'[5]

There was an instant attraction between Lizzie and Swinburne. With their almost identical crops of red hair and their similar impression of pent-up nervous energy, they might have been in appearance as well as in spirit the brother and sister whom Swinburne later described. Rossetti watched their high-spirited and affectionate games approvingly. Swinburne, whether reading Dickens or Elizabethan comedy to her, teasing her or admiring, was providing both the education and the fresh impetus which Lizzie had long seemed to require. She had been deteriorating in health and had been sent to Hastings and to Nice for her lungs. Dr Acland had examined her and told Ruskin that she was not seriously ill, requiring only to be kept idle. Yet this in turn imprisoned her natural exuberance.

Even the colour of their hair became a shared personal joke. Lizzie swore that when Rossetti and a party of friends went to the theatre, occupying a row with Swinburne at one end and herself at the other, the boy selling books of the play looked at Swinburne, took fright, hurried to the other side, confronted Lizzie and withdrew, muttering, 'There's another of 'em!'[6] In their vivacious mutual affection, chaperoned by the almost paternal presence of Rossetti, Swinburne might seem to be following the evident pattern of devoting his energies to a woman from whom he need fear no sexual demands. A later age might have seen in this the classic concealment of the homosexual. In Swinburne's case, this hardly seems apt. Whatever oddities were alleged against him in his relationships with women, at least it was with women that he was preoccupied.

As for Rossetti himself, his brother William Michael Rossetti recorded that Swinburne was the most welcome friend of his married life: 'there was not, I think, anyone whom Rossetti, during his wedded life saw so constantly and delightedly as Swinburne'.[7] The young poet also made the acquaintance of William Michael, who was to be a close friend throughout life, and of Christina Rossetti. To Dante Gabriel, however, Swinburne was at this time 'the most welcome of comrades'.[8] As for Swinburne and Lizzie, 'Rossetti was much entertained by their innocent intimacy, occasionally having to call them both to order, as he might a pair of charming angora cats romping too boisterously together.'[9]

Apart from the Rossettis, Swinburne's circle of acquaintances during his first years in London also included William Morris and his newly acquired wife Jane. Jane Burden, the daughter of a groom, was an Oxford discovery, seen at the Oxford Theatre one night during the work on the Union murals. The model for Rossetti's *Proserpine,* his brother described her as 'beautiful or superb. Her complexion was dark and pale, her eyes a deep penetrating grey, her massive wealth of hair gorgeously rippled, and tending to black, yet not without some deep-sunken glow.'[10] Rossetti, whose feeling for her was to grow quite as intense as Morris's, wrote of:

this sovereign face, whose love spell breathes
Even from its shadowed contour on the wall.[11]

After their marriage in 1859, Morris had used his wealth to build the Red House at Upton, on the outskirts of London, a temple to Pre-Raphaelite style, including the furnishing and interior decoration to which he now devoted himself. For Janey Morris, Swinburne developed 'an admiration approaching to worship', though it was never of the easy, intimate kind which characterized his relations with Lizzie. The Morris children remembered him 'lying on the grass in the orchard, with his red hair spread abroad', and as he lay there the two infants 'scattered rose-leaves over his laughing face'.[12]

The Red House was also the scene of considerable artistic activity, in stained glass and other media, during the period of Swinburne's visits. He kept the artists company while they worked and read his poems to them, covering up one eye with his hand, as though suffering from astigmatism. In consequence he was useful as a model for the artists' designs as he sat in the studio with them. He was well used to this, having informed Monckton Milnes in October 1861 that Rossetti had just done 'a drawing of a female model and myself embracing – I need not say in the most fervent and abandoned style'.[13] The drawing, intended for a frontispiece to *The Early*

Italian Poets, shows both figures fully clothed, indeed costumed, engrossed in a thoughtful kiss.

Apart from Rossetti and Morris, Swinburne was the near neighbour of Burne-Jones, who lived in Russell Place, Great Russell Street. Burne-Jones had become engaged to Georgiana Macdonald, the sixteen-year-old daughter of a Methodist minister at Oxford and had married her in 1859. Being close in age, Burne-Jones and Swinburne had been among the most congenial companions at Oxford. It was Burne-Jones to whom Swinburne dedicated *Poems and Ballads* in 1866. The intimacy of 'Ned' and 'Little Carrots' persisted until many years later when Swinburne was secluded at No. 2 The Pines under the tutelage of Watts-Dunton, and his former friend was not welcome.

During his residence at Grafton Street, Swinburne would descend upon Burne-Jones and Georgie 'sometimes twice or three times in a day ... bringing his poems hot from his heart and certain of a welcome and a hearing at any hour'. It was Mrs Burne-Jones who gave the fullest description of him at this time, a cameo of the exquisite Pre-Raphaelite youth:

> His appearance was very unusual and in some ways beautiful, for his hair was glorious in abundance and colour and his eyes indescribably fine. When repeating poetry he had a perfectly natural way of lifting them in a rapt, unconscious gaze, and their clear green colour softened by thick brown lashes was unforgettable. ... He was restless beyond words, scarcely standing still at all and almost dancing as he walked, while even in sitting he moved continually, seeming to keep time by a swift movement of the hands at the wrists, and sometimes of the feet also, with some inner rhythm of excitement. He was courteous and affectionate and unsuspicious, and faithful beyond most people to those he really loved. The biting wit which filled his talk so as at times to leave his hearers dumb with amazement always spared one thing, and that was an absent friend.[14]

The friendship with the Burne-Joneses remained almost as close when they forsook central London for distant Hammersmith. In the account of their son, Swinburne would hire a cab and drive down there, bearing with him a poem of portentous length. His arrival was signalled by 'shrill screams and cries' as he argued with the cabman. Swinburne had an irremovable conviction that the fare from one place in London to any other was a shilling. Philip Burne-Jones, as a child, was therefore sent down the stairs 'with some more shillings for the indignant charioteer'. When the cabman had been despatched and the irate poet remained on the pavement, Georgie

Burne-Jones would then come down 'with soothings and consola-
tions, as for a child that has seen a naughty bogie'.[15]

It was Georgie who recorded one regret about Swinburne's work
in 1860–2, not generally noticed elsewhere. The publication of
Samuel Pepys's diary had made some literary stir, and Swinburne
promised to follow it up with a spurious diary of Mrs Samuel Pepys,
to be launched on an unsuspecting public. The omissions and emen-
dations of pious editors in the original diary were precisely of the
kind to goad Swinburne to this. When Pepys describes, for instance,
being so pressed after an evening's entertainment that he was
inclined to 'take a shit in a skimmer', Victorian ingenuity hastily
altered this, making him take 'a shot at a scholar' instead.[16] However, the diary of Mrs Pepys, at least in Swinburne's hand, was never
to materialize.

So far, the first years in London had been an extension of youth,
Swinburne's character and those of many of his acquaintances
hardly altering from what they had been at Oxford, or in his own
case at Eton. By 1862 events were at hand which were to change
that and to dispel for ever the charm of youthful hope.

*   *   *

Lizzie Rossetti's health, for all Dr Acland's reassurance, had long
been in decline. Indeed, the house at Chatham Place in Blackfriars,
overlooking the open sewer of the Thames itself, can hardly have
helped her. On 2 May 1861, Rossetti had written to his mother:
'Lizzie has just been delivered of a dead child.'[17] She sat beside the
empty cradle and, when the Burne-Joneses came to visit her, she
said softly, 'Hush, Ned, you'll waken it.'[18] To calm her and to
deaden the pain of neuralgia, the early-Victorian panacea of
laudanum was prescribed. She took it, sometimes in quantities
which made it hard for her to stay awake.

On 10 February 1862, in company with Swinburne, Lizzie and
Rossetti dined at the Sablonnière Hotel in Leicester Square.
Swinburne thought that Lizzie seemed to behave normally. By eight
o'clock the dinner was over. Rossetti took his wife back to their
home by cab and then went to the Working Men's College, where he
was due to give a class at nine. He returned to Chatham Place at
about half-past eleven. Lizzie was in bed, in a deep sleep and snoring
loudly, with a two-ounce phial of laudanum empty beside her. It was
impossible to wake her. Four doctors were called, who used a

stomach-pump in an attempt to wash out the massive dose of opiate. Despite this, Lizzie died at half-past seven in the morning.

The rumours and assertions which gathered round this story included the supposition that Rossetti was not at his class but with his future mistress Fanny Cornforth. It was said that when he found Lizzie a note was pinned to her nightdress: 'My life is so miserable I wish for no more of it.' Another version gave the note as referring to Lizzie's mentally retarded brother: 'Take care of Harry.' Whatever the truth of these stories, Rossetti was distraught, insisting on a re-examination of Lizzie's body some days later to ensure that she was not merely in a trance, and at the last moment burying the unpublished manuscript of his poems in her coffin as an ultimate gesture of contrition.

At the inquest on 12 February, Swinburne and the other witnesses swore that Lizzie had seemed normal and cheerful, in no way intent on suicide. There was nothing in the medical evidence to contradict this, and the coroner's jury returned a verdict of accidental death.

For all his more obvious failings, Swinburne was the friend and support of Rossetti in the days of desperate grief which followed Lizzie's death. 'I am only too happy to have been able to keep him company and be of a little use during these weeks,' he wrote to his mother on 13 March. He also undertook to remain with his friend. 'Rossetti and I are going to live together.... In the autumn we get into a house in Chelsea – in Cheyne Walk facing the trees and river – with an old garden.'[19] They would have moved there at once, but the house had been taken for the summer, during the season of the International Exhibition then being held in London.

*   *   *

During his friendship with the Pre-Raphaelites, Swinburne was also endeavouring to find publishers for his poetry and prose who would not be merely those firms prepared to issue his writing so long as Admiral Swinburne paid the cost. In 1861 he had written an essay on C. J. Wells, *Joseph and his Brethren*. He sent it to Monckton Milnes in October, who tried without success to place it in *Fraser's Magazine*, edited by J. A. Froude. A month before Lizzie's death, Rossetti took up the question of Swinburne's poems with Theodore Martin, translator of Heine and biographer of the Prince Consort.

A young friend of mine – 23 years of age – Algernon Swinburne, son of Admiral Swinburne – is a poet not promising in the common sense only, but certainly destined to be one of the two or three leaders who are to succeed Tennyson and the Brownings. . . . At present he has his way to make, and plenty of unpublished poems and tales – all truly admirable – *à placer*: remuneration as well as fame being of importance to him. Our friend Whitley Stokes joins with me in the highest hopes of his genius. Now were I to send you some of his MSS., and you thought as we do of them, would it be possible to you, without taxing your kindness with too much trouble, to give him an introduction to *Fraser* or some other vehicle of publicity?[20]

It seems that Prince Albert's biographer felt unable to assist. Perhaps he had heard something of the readings which Swinburne was giving of *La Fille du policeman* and the ridicule heaped upon Prince Albert in the person of the 'prince prolétaire'. George Meredith was one of those privileged to hear Swinburne read it: 'the funniest rampingest satire on French novelists dealing with English themes that you can imagine. One chapter, "Ce qui peut se passer dans un Cab Safety", where Lord Whitestick, Bishop of Londres, ravishes the heroine, is quite marvellous'.[21]

Meredith, who had already published *The Ordeal of Richard Feverel* and *Evan Harrington*, was to be one of the companions of Cheyne Walk. In October 1861 he wrote to Samuel Lucas, editor of *Once a Week*, on Swinburne's behalf: 'I want to bring little Swinburne to introduce him to you this week or next. I think you'll find him valuable.'[22] A month later, perhaps following a discouraging reply from Lucas, he wrote, 'I don't see any use in your having Swinburne to dinner.'[23]

Meredith, already thirty-three, deserted by his first wife and left with a son to bring up, was intolerant of Swinburne's more extravagant behaviour, though personally attached to him. He feared also, after hearing *La Fille du policeman*, that Swinburne was merely a clever writer with a facility for verse, that his work, as Jowett had thought, was elegant and empty. Meredith conceded Swinburne's skill but added, 'I don't see any internal centre from which springs anything that he does. He will make a great name, but whether he is to distinguish himself as an Artist, I would not willingly prognosticate.'[24]

In the event it was Monckton Milnes who provided the vehicle for publication of Swinburne's individual poems and essays. In 1862 the first of his contributions appeared in the *Spectator*, edited by Richard Holt Hutton, to whom Monckton Milnes had introduced him. There were seven poems and a number of essays, including those on Hugo and Baudelaire. *Les Fleurs du mal* had, of course, been the subject of a successful prosecution for obscenity in Paris when it first appeared five years earlier. Even with the removal of its more outspoken poems, known collectively as *Les Epaves*, the book was precisely of the sort guaranteed to win Swinburne's support.

The association with Hutton and the *Spectator* continued until the following year. He made himself at home in its pages and in the number for 7 June 1862 delivered a spirited *coup de grâce* to the reviewer who had dared to denigrate Meredith's *Modern Love* for not preaching the bourgeois gospel of marriage. The time had come for the age to accommodate itself to a new and bolder species of poetry – Swinburne's included – which dealt in terms of art rather than of morality. He denounced the poetry of his predecessors, 'whose scope of sight is bounded by the nursery walls', and informed the Tennysonians that the Muses were not to be ruled by 'her who babbles with lips yet warm from their pristine pap'.

Hutton was perfectly content to give the young contributor his head in such matters. The problem between them came with two Swinburne articles reviewing a pair of the most daring new French writers, the poet Félicien Cossu and Ernest Clouet, the author of *Les Abîmes*. Even Swinburne professed himself dismayed by the obscenity of these new authors who went far beyond anything in Baudelaire. Not one poem of Cossu's is 'fit to be read aloud in the hearing of Englishwomen'. It was difficult even to quote from such pieces as the first, on the loss of virginity at fifteen, let alone such masterpieces as *Une Nuit de sodome*, where even the latrines are singing. The poet's mistress is habitually depicted vomiting, his ideal of feminine dignity is Messalina, and his abomination is England. Cossu rejoices that all the nations of the Continent are uniting to wipe England from the face of the earth. The revulsion and indignation at the breakfast tables of Hutton's readers could easily be imagined.

Ernest Clouet was, if anything, more objectionable to Swinburne as reviewer and – no doubt – to his middle-class readers. He had heaped cruel and unjustified ridicule upon Prince Albert. He wished, in metaphysical terms, to perform a Caesarean operation upon the Supreme Being. He hinted gleefully at a sexual relationship, recently discovered, between Joan of Arc and Gilles de Rais, the notorious defiler and murderer of children.

When it was set up in type, Hutton began to have second thoughts. He wrote to Swinburne, announcing that it was impossible even to review such scurrilous writing in the *Spectator*. Swinburne withdrew from the association in disappointment. The two French authors, Cossu and Clouet, were of course entirely his own invention, as were the quotations from their work. The hoax had been carefully prepared by dropping their names in his earlier articles as modern French authors now making a name for themselves. The object of the joke was to rouse outrage on the part of Mrs Grundy's more literate partisans at the unmitigated filth which threatened to engulf them from the far side of the Channel. When they had made fools of themselves, presumably the joke would have been revealed. Ironically, Swinburne's mingling of quick-eared prurience and shocked propriety was a perfect parody of some of the reactions to his own poetry in a few years more.

*   *   *

The household which assembled at 16 Cheyne Walk in the autumn of 1862 might have been the ideal Pre-Raphaelite, or perhaps Bohemian, community. Its membership was to include Swinburne, Dante Gabriel Rossetti, William Michael Rossetti and Meredith. Meredith called the house 'a strange, quaint, grand old place, with an immense garden, magnificent panelled staircases and rooms – a palace'.[25] The ground floor contained sitting-rooms and studio with a dining-room above, while the number of bedrooms meant that the *ménage* could be expanded as much as was necessary. Tudor House, as it was also known, was a sixteenth-century red-brick dwelling with gardens in which Rossetti was able to keep the pet animals of his collection, including a wombat, an armadillo and even a kangaroo. The house looked out across the foreshore of the Thames, with the raffish bustle of Cremorne Gardens a little way to the west. William Michael Rossetti recalled the area in the 1860s as 'far more picturesque than now – less of decorum and of stateliness, more of noise and movement'.[26] The visitors to Cheyne Walk included established artists like Frederic Leighton and younger men of promise like Whistler and Frederick Sandys. The arrangement promised comradeship and devotion to art.

The wombat ate the cigars. Meredith turned out to be wittier than the others and made fun of Rossetti in front of his guests. Rossetti threw a cup of tea in his face. Swinburne's nervous energy got on Rossetti's nerves, 'dancing all over the studio like a wild cat', as Rossetti described him. William Michael Rossetti found his brother's boisterous late hours an impediment to serious work.

Swinburne wrote part of a Victorian Greek tragedy, *Atalanta in Calydon*. Then things grew worse. Meredith was revolted by Rossetti's gargantuan breakfasts, bacon surrounded by a circle of eggs. Swinburne knocked Morris into a cupboard and smashed Rossetti's china. With a new acquaintance, Simeon Solomon, he romped naked about the house, sliding down the banisters and shrilly waking the echoes. Rossetti planned to accommodate his new mistress, Fanny Cornforth, whom Swinburne out of loyalty to Lizzie always referred to as 'The Bitch'. Meredith, driven to distraction by the row, swore that he 'would certainly have kicked Swinburne downstairs had he not foreseen what a clatter his horrid little bottom would have made as it bounced from step to step'.[27]

Within a few months, Meredith left. He was followed by William Michael Rossetti. Swinburne, as Dante Gabriel's admirer, remained, though his absences were long and frequent. By August 1863, less than a year after the venture had begun, Dante Gabriel Rossetti was writing: 'I see hardly any one. Swinburne is away. Meredith has evaporated for good, and my brother is seldom here.'[28] Their places had been taken by Fanny Cornforth.

'Swinburne is away.' Between 1862 and 1864 the destination of his travels and their purpose varied widely. In 1862 he went with his parents to Pau, stopping in Paris on the way where he retired to a Turkish bath and wrote his essay on Baudelaire. The next year, returning to Paris in March 1863, he met Whistler, and Fantin-Latour, and wrote his poem 'Hermaphroditus', in tribute to the famous statue in the Louvre.

> Love stands upon thy left hand and thy right,
>   Yet by no sunset and by no moonrise
>   Shall make thee man and ease a woman's sighs,
> Or make thee woman for a man's delight.
> To what strange end hath some strange god made fair
>   The double blossom of two fruitless flowers?
> Hid love in all the folds of all thy hair,
>   Fed thee on summers, watered thee with showers,
> Given all the gold that all the seasons wear
>   To thee that art a thing of barren hours?[29]

The fascination which sexual ambiguity held for Swinburne, revealed both in his poetry and in his conversation, seems beyond that of one who was consciously homosexual. He stands outside it, as he stands outside heterosexual commitment.

By his own account, it was in 1862 or soon after that Swinburne made his one proposal of marriage. His rejection was followed by a poetic complaint in 'The Triumph of Time', and by an avowed policy of despising marriage and everything to do with it from then on.

The facts remain something of a mystery. According to Edmund Gosse, the girl was Jane Faulkner, the adopted daughter of Sir John Simon, a friend of Edward Burne-Jones. She was known as 'Boo', and Swinburne addressed her in verse by this name.

> You should love me a little my own love
>   One love for a week and a day,
> For either has hardly begun love,
>   For the space of a sickle-sweep, say –
> Suppose we should settle to try love,
>   It may be as sweet as its fame.[30]

According to Gosse, when Swinburne made his proposal, 'More from nervousness, probably, than from ill-will, she broke out laughing in his face.'[31] Swinburne rushed away to Capheaton and poured out his feelings in 'The Triumph of Time'.

Objections were raised to Gosse's account when it was later discovered that Jane Faulkner would have been only ten in 1862 and that the proposal must have been made then or a fairly short time afterwards. His cousin Mary Gordon was suggested as an alternative recipient of the proposal. She, however, swore that nothing of the kind ever happened. Before dismissing the notion of Jane Faulkner as the intended bride, it is as well to remember the Victorian possibilities of booking a wife at a tender age. In 1852, E. W. Benson had wooed Minnie Sidgwick, then coming up to eleven years old. He later married her and became Archbishop of Canterbury. Oscar Browning was let into the secret of the engagement when Minnie was fourteen. No one knows beyond question the identity of Swinburne's inamorata. Age alone, in 1862, would not rule out Jane Faulkner to whom he had already addressed the lines of a love-poem, either in whimsy or in earnest.[32]

What matters rather more than the girl's identity, in this case, is the disdain for marriage in which Swinburne was able to indulge in consequence of his rejection, and the pretext which it gave for 'The Triumph of Time', that elegy for a self whose 'whole life's love goes down in a day'.

> O all fair lovers about the world,
>   There is none of you, none, that shall comfort me.
> My thoughts are as dead things wrecked and whirled
>   Round and round in a gulf of the sea;

And still through the sound and the straining stream,
Through the coil and chafe, they gleam in a dream,
The bright fine lips so cruelly curled,
And strange swift eyes where the soul sits free.[33]

A number of these absences from Cheyne Walk, to which he
despatched his share of the rent when reminded by Rossetti,
involved visits to his family. He was with them at Bournemouth
during 1863 when his sister Edith lapsed into a long and fatal illness.
He reported vaguely that his father was disposing of East Dene and
buying another house, Holmwood, near Henley-on-Thames. The
true objects of his pilgrimages lay elsewhere. After Edith
Swinburne's death, the family set off on a long continental tour.
He joined them briefly at Genoa, then made his way alone to visit
his idol, Walter Savage Landor, living as an exile in Florence.

Landor was a living monument to the age of Shelley, the
embodiment of classical heritage and revolutionary spirit, to both
of which Swinburne owed allegiance. Expelled from Rugby
and Oxford, he had left England to avoid the libel actions which he
had brought upon himself. Bearing a letter of introduction from
Monckton Milnes, Swinburne made for the house at 93 via della
Chiesa, and threw himself theatrically upon his knees before 'the
most ancient of the demi-gods'. Landor, in his ninetieth year, was
unprepared for this performance and considerably alarmed.
Swinburne withdrew, wrote a letter of apology, and received a
formal invitation. On his second visit, Landor was in his best form,
witty and acute, 'brilliant and altogether delicious'. Swinburne's
talent for hero-worship, also shown to Hugo and Mazzini, was soon
evident. 'I should like to throw up all other things on earth and de-
vote myself to playing valet to him for the rest of his days. I would
black his boots if he were *chez moi*. He has given me the shock of
adoration which one feels at thirteen towards great men.'[34]

Happily, the urge to valet for the old rebel was superseded by
other enthusiasms at Fiesole which prompted one of Swinburne's
best short lyrics and the last impetus needed to complete *Atalanta in
Calydon*. In a walled Tuscan garden, to the sound of nightingales at
noon, he wrote *Itylus*, whose musical beauty might charm the most
censorious Victorian family, unless they actually knew the basis of
the story in Ovid's *Metamorphoses*. Tereus, King of Thrace,
married Procne and later raped her sister Philomela, whose tongue
he cut out that she might not betray him. The girl wove a picture of
the outrage, and Procne avenged the deed by killing Itylus, the son

of her marriage to Tereus. The child's flesh was cooked and served to the unwitting father, whom Procne then informed about the food he had just eaten. She was changed into a swallow and her sister into a nightingale. The poem is Philomela's lament to the mother who has forgotten her terrible deed, whose gruesome climax concludes the lyric.

> O sweet stray sister, O shifting swallow
>   The heart's division divideth us.
>   Thy heart is light as a leaf of a tree;
> But mine goes forth among sea-gulfs hollow
>   To the place of the slaying of Itylus,
>   The feast of Daulis, the Thracian sea....
>
> O sister, sister, thy first-begotten!
>   The hands that cling and the feet that follow,
>   The voice of the child's blood crying yet
> *Who hath remembered me? who hath forgotten?*
>   Thou hast forgotten, O summer swallow,
>   But the world shall end when I forget [35]

Lyricism, and an almost Aeschylean sense of drama were about to be fused in the choruses of *Atalanta in Calydon*, almost blessed by the presence of Landor as the last apostle of neo-classicism. For the time being, at least, there was every reason to accept Swinburne's assurance that his borrowed Pre-Raphaelite singing-robes had fallen from him. The spring idyll of Fiesole, the ancient amphitheatre whose stones might have echoed to the *Agamemnon* or the *Antigone* two millennia before, was the perfect scenic inspiration for *Atalanta*. At a more banal level, the final meeting with Landor had been rather trying. The elderly poet was so impressed by Swinburne's admiration that he took down from the wall a Correggio painting, once the possession of Napoleon Buonaparte, and insisted on making Swinburne a present of it to commemorate the visit. Horrified at this, Swinburne protested that he could not possibly take it. The honour of the visit alone was enough to impress it in his memory. There then followed a heated argument, Landor insisting that Swinburne must take the priceless treasure, and Swinburne adamantly refusing. Finally, Landor rose, 'purple with anger', and shouted at the young poet, 'By God, sir, you shall!' There being no alternative, the picture was sent to Swinburne's hotel and subsequently brought to England. He was somewhat disconcerted to discover later on that the painting had nothing whatever to do with Correggio or Buonaparte. It was, as Edmund

Gosse remarked, 'a worthless daub, one of the strange artistic delusions of Landor's extreme old age'.[36]

Swinburne returned from his Italian visit, during which he had also visited the Uffizi with Mrs Gaskell and met Seymour Kirkup, who had actually known Blake. His energy was remarkable. He was writing *Atalanta* and a number of poems later to appear in *Poems and Ballads*, as well as chapters of a novel not published during his life but subsequently issued as *Lesbia Brandon*. The speed with which he wrote, when the mood seized him, was phenomenal. According to Frederick Sandys, the 164 lines of 'Faustine' were written in a railway carriage between Waterloo and Hampton Court as the result of a wager to see who could produce the more rhymes for the name. In 1862, before the Cheyne Walk fiasco, George Meredith invited him down to his cottage at Copsham and witnessed the same poetic facility:

> It happened that he was expected one day on a visit to me, and he being rather late I went along the road to meet him. At last he appeared waving the white sheet of what seemed to be a pamphlet. He greeted me with a triumphant shout of a stanza new to my ears. This was Fitzgerald's Omar Khayyám, and we lay on a heathery knoll beside my cottage reading a stanza alternately, indifferent to the dinner-bell until a prolonged summons reminded us of appetite. After dinner we took to the paper-covered treasure again. Suddenly Swinburne ran upstairs, and I had my anticipations. He returned with a feather-pen, blue folio-sheet, and a dwarf bottle of red ink. In an hour he had finished 13 stanzas of *Laus Veneris*.[37]

Apart from poetry and drama, Swinburne had a flair for erudition and an enthusiasm for particular authors, which led naturally to a substantial number of literary essays. On his arrival in London from Oxford he had been greatly interested in Alexander Gilchrist's life of Blake, which Gilchrist was then writing. With Rossetti and Burne-Jones, he spent an agreeable evening in Gilchrist's company on 25 November 1861. Two children and a servant in the house were ill with scarlet fever. A week later Gilchrist himself died of the infection. Swinburne appeared eager to become his 'heir' in the matter of completing the life of Blake. Rossetti mentioned the possibility to Gilchrist's widow, but the response was unpromising. Rossetti agreed that 'congruity in the views taken throughout the book is quite indispensable'.[38] Accordingly, the work was given to William Michael Rossetti. Swinburne retained his enthusiasm for the subject, however, publishing his critical essay, *William Blake*, in 1868.

Moxon's, who were Swinburne's publishers until 1866, also began to produce a series of selections from major English poets of the past with critical introductions by Victorian contemporaries. 'I am *doing* Byron,' Swinburne informed Pauline Trevelyan in 1865, 'I am to meet my partners in the serial work, Tennyson and Browning, at a publisher's feast some time this week.'[39] Even though the storm of *Poems and Ballads* had yet to break, the choice of Byron, in Swinburne's case, was almost predictable. Byron had the alternate qualities of sardonic classicism and lyric purity. Like Shelley, and like Swinburne, he was the patrician revolutionary. In his private life, he had outraged the sexual laws of marriage by his conduct with his wife, and he had fathered a child on his half-sister. That in itself was enough. Byron's posthumous enemies were precisely of the sort whom Swinburne detested. Harriet Beecher Stowe, the partisan of Lady Byron, Swinburne rebaptized as 'Mrs Bitcher Spewe', and her famous novel he retitled 'Uncle Tom's Closet'.[40] As for his poetry, *The Vision of Judgment* had been successfully prosecuted as a seditious libel on George III,[41] *Cain* was impious by mid-Victorian standards and *Don Juan* was indecent. The Nonconformist news-agent W. H. Smith found himself at the centre of a row in 1853 when a member of the public noticed a copy of *Don Juan* on his bookstall at Waterloo Station.[42]

Swinburne's shrill enthusiasm for the details of Byron's sexual eccentricities, particularly with regard to the charge of incest with Augusta Leigh, eventually wearied his closest friends. 'About the Byron business,' wrote Dante Gabriel Rossetti to his brother, 'I have heard Swinburne allude to the connexion with his sister.... Lastly, if Byron f——d his sister he f——d her and there an end – an absolute end in my opinion as far as the vital interest of his poetry goes, which is all we have to do with.'[43]

Swinburne's *Byron* appeared in 1866 and in no way ignored the vital interest of the poetry or the poet's career. Indeed, he saw in Byron's career a mirror of his own, remarking that Byron had suffered under a triple handicap: 'youth, genius, and an ancient name'.[44] In terms of the public reaction to their work, Swinburne made the parallel between himself and the great poet almost indecently blatant.

At the first chance given or taken, every obscure and obscene thing that lurks for pay or prey among the fouler shallows and thickets of literature flew against him; every hound and every hireling lavished upon him the loathsome tribute of their abuse; all nameless creatures that nibble and prowl, upon whom the serpent's curse has fallen to go upon his belly and eat dust all the days of his life, assailed him with their foulest venom and their keenest fangs. And the promise given of old to their kind was now at least fulfilled: they did bruise his heel. But the heads of such creatures are so small that it is hard to bruise them in return; it would first be necessary to discern them.[45]

With this blast of derision to the world of critics, Swinburne turned to Byron's poetry, garbing his observations in images of comparison and a sententious grandeur of style which belonged very much to the age of Macaulay and Landor. Nothing about it resembles the algebraic niggling of literary criticism at its academic worst.

Coleridge and Keats used nature mainly as a stimulant or a sedative; Wordsworth as a vegetable fit to shred into his pot and pare down like the outer leaves of a lettuce for didactic or culinary purposes. . . . Turn now to Byron or to Shelley. These two at least were not content to play with her skirts and paddle in her shallows. Their passion is perfect, a fierce and blind desire which exalts and impels their verse into the high places of emotion and expression. They feed upon nature with a holy hunger, follow her with a divine lust as of gods chasing the daughters of men.[46]

The vivacity of Swinburne's style was admirably adapted to the uses of a popular selection from Byron. Indeed, one of the most gratifying responses to the book came from Lady Jane Swinburne, who proved to be far from the prudish woman whom some of her biographers took her for. She was full of praise for her son's book, not least for the appearance of *Don Juan*, which had been treated with such moral suspicion elsewhere. 'Never before having read any of Don Juan I am surprised at the beauty of it, it seems to me incomparably finer than any of his other writings.'[47]

The appearance of *Byron*, combined with the articles on Baudelaire and other topics for the *Spectator*, and the promise of *Blake*, established Swinburne as a new and forceful literary essayist of the 1860s. Whether that was entirely to his advantage might be doubted. It absorbed a good deal of time which he might otherwise have devoted to more original forms of writing. Perhaps it seemed to matter little at the time, since the bulk of the material which was to appear as *Poems and Ballads* was ready. Earlier still, in 1865, he went some way to justifying his title to the mantle of Tennyson and the Brownings, as Rossetti described it, with the publication of *Atalanta in Calydon*.

*   *   *

Atalanta in Calydon was issued by Moxon's, the most eminent of publishers in this field. In literary terms, the poem was a perfect pattern of that Victorian dream of the ancient world, as it permeated modern education and culture. The pure and uncomplicated vision of human life in the philosophy of Plato or the dramas of Aeschylus had been, pre-eminently, the subject of academic study in the eighteenth century. To the Victorians the vision had acquired a more romantic perspective in an age of industrialization and of political problems whose solution fell little short of mechanized warfare. In mid-century the moral appeal of Greek and Latin literature was not for its immediate ethical usefulness. Its true value was in the manner in which a memory of its cadences and philosophy, buried in the mind of a schoolboy, would help to pilot him as a man through the great crises of adult life. To a later generation still, Matthew Arnold insisted that the purity of the first great literature had been elaborated but not refined; 'the instinct for beauty is served by Greek literature and art as it is served by no other literature and art'.[48]

On this surge of cultural enthusiasm Swinburne was borne to fame as the author of *Atalanta in Calydon*. The play combines the elements of Athenian drama – martial, stoic, elegiac and Arcadian – with the grandeur of the verse choruses, the polished vigour of Victorian lyricism and a poetic energy which it would be hard to match elsewhere among Swinburne's contemporaries, except perhaps with that of Gerard Manley Hopkins, whose style remains so different in other respects.

Atalanta is the story of Queen Althea and her son Meleager. At his birth, the three Fates prophesy that he will die when a brand, now burning in the fire, is consumed. Althea snatches out the brand and keeps it safe. Meleager grows to manhood and becomes a warrior-prince and adventurer. The goddess Artemis supports the Aetolians in a war against Calydon, by sending a wild boar to ravage the country and kill its inhabitants. She relents only for the sake of the virgin daughter of Iasus, Atalanta, with whom Meleager falls in love. Meleager, after the boar has been killed in a hunt, kills his uncles who try to deprive Atalanta of the spoils of the chase. Althea, learning of the death of her brothers at the hand of her son, throws the brand in the fire and Meleager's life wastes away.

The plot is improbable as any nineteenth-century opera, or indeed many dramas of the ancient world. Yet Swinburne captures the primitive freshness of Greek theatre, the Aeschylean sense of fatalism, while at the same time the ineluctable prophesies of the three sisters, the Fates, waken echoes of *Macbeth*. The poem moves with a rapidity in which verse, thought and imagery work with a brisk modernity lacking in most translations of Greek drama. Indeed, the nearest parallel to *Atalanta*, in this respect, is in some of the long set-piece poems of W. H. Auden, such as *The Age of Anxiety*, or *New Year Letter*. Even in the pace and the alliterative beat, Swinburne anticipates these in the sure-footed poetic virtuosity which they both shared.

> Maiden, and mistress of the months and stars
> Now folded in the flowerless fields of heaven,
> Goddess whom all gods love with threefold heart,
> Being treble in thy divided deity....

The opening lines of *Atalanta*, in their movement and their echoes, anticipate such poets of the twentieth century as Auden, who were to be characterized by accomplishment rather than by selfconscious innovation. At the same time they wake the memory of twenty-four centuries, and the watchman's cry.

> Θεοὺς μὲν οὐτῶ τῶνδ' ἀπαλλαγὴν πόνων
> I seek the gods' deliverance from these tasks,

which opened both the *Agamemnon* of Aeschylus and the drama of the western world. Half a century later, Gosse found it hard to describe the manner in which Swinburne had taken the imagination of young readers in the 1860s as '"the fairest first-born son of fire", who was to inaugurate a new age of lyric gold'.[49] Yet in *Atalanta*, free from the Pre-Raphaelite reverence and the feebly Sadean silliness of his worst writing, Swinburne revelled in the pagan enthusiasm of his Hellenic choruses.

> And Pan by noon and Bacchus by night
> Fleeter of foot than the fleet-foot kid,
> Follows with dancing and fills with delight
> The Maenad and the Bassarid;
> And soft as lips that laugh and hide
> The laughing leaves of the trees divide,
> And screen from seeing and leave in sight
> The god pursuing, the maiden hid.

To those who looked for a new generation of poets to eclipse the ponderous Tennyson and his kind, here was the excitement and the rush of modernity, the vigour of which the Laureate with all his admitted powers was no longer capable. Even the images of the verse seemed to run pell-mell into one another with the speed of Swinburne's narrative, as when he describes Meleager's helmet:

> .... watch,
> High up, the cloven shadow of either plume
> Divide the bright light of the brass, and make
> His helmet as a windy and wintering moon
> Seen through blown cloud and moon-like drift, when ships
> Drive, and men strive with all the sea, and oars
> Break, and the beaks dip under, drinking death.

To the educated and influential readers of 1865, brought up on the traditions of ancient literature, the poem offered the amalgamation of two great cultures. Talk of assassination and of 'the nets and knives of privy death' might have come equally from Aeschylus or Shakespeare. Above this, however, the poem caught its readers' admiration by the sureness of its technique and its memorability.

> Before the beginning of years
>   There came to the making of man
> Time, with a gift of tears
>   Grief, with a glass that ran;
> Pleasure, with pain for leaven;
>   Summer with flowers that fell;
> Remembrance fallen from heaven,
>   And madness risen from hell.

All of which, as a literary analysis of nightmare, has less in common with Tennyson, with the Victorians, even with the poetic revolution of Hopkins, than with Auden seventy years later.

> The glacier knocks in the cupboard,
>   The desert sighs in the bed,
> And the crack in the tea-cup opens
>   A lane to the land of the dead.[50]

The praise of *Atalanta* was general, and was music in Swinburne's ears after the fiasco of *The Queen Mother* and *Rosamond*. Monckton Milnes wrote of it in the *Edinburgh Review*; the *Saturday Review* announced that, for all the dignity of the Greek model, 'Mr Swinburne is wholly a modern.'[51] F. D. Maurice, one of the mainstays of Christian Socialism, pronounced the poem a compliment to the hitherto imperfect Evidences of Christianity. 'I expect at least a lay archdiaconate,' announced the atheist poet happily.[52] 'Have you read Swinburne's Atalanta?' wrote Ruskin in January 1866, 'The grandest thing ever done by a youth, though he is a demoniac youth.'[53] The young blind poet, Philip Bourke Marston, destined to become one of Swinburne's most devoted partisans, recalled that the servants used to fancy that he was 'in a religious ecstasy', as he lay in bed, alone and sightless, comforting his solitude by chanting the great choruses of Swinburne's play.[54] Even Lord Lytton, the author of *Eugene Aram* and *The Last Days of Pompeii*, conceded the work's merits. He had long despaired of 'an age which says Pope is no poet and Rossetti is a great one'. Yet he allowed Monckton Milnes to persuade him to read *Atalanta*, which he found 'promising and vigorous'.[55] From Pauline Trevelyan and William Bell Scott came the anticipated praises of the poem's grandeur and beauty. Swinburne sardonically replied to Scott that his virgin work was about to be ravished by rampant critics hungry for a maidenhead. On this occasion, at least, he need not have worried.

*   *   *

Atalanta in Calydon appeared in April 1865, dedicated to the memory of Walter Savage Landor who had died a few months after Swinburne's visit to Florence. By August, Swinburne's next volume was ready to be issued by Moxon's, for whom J. B. Payne was now willing to pay the author for the privilege of issuing his work. The book in question was *Chastelard*, a play which he had begun at Oxford and which marks his preoccupation with the story of Mary Stuart, continued in *Bothwell* (1874) and *Mary Stuart* (1881). The play was and remains a literary curiosity rather than a great poetic achievement. In a style which too often resembles mere pastiche of Elizabethan or Jacobean drama, *Chastelard* recounts the story of the wooing of the young Queen of Scotland by Chastelard and the manner in which he first compromises her and is then executed.

At its worst, the poetry strives after archaic imitation.

> Be not wroth, lady, I wot it was the queen
> Pricked each his friend out.... I wot he made good mirth.

As in Jacobean dramatic verse, Swinburne is quick to pick upon the imagery of bizarre erudition, such as the picture of drag-nets hauling from the sea

A strange-haired woman with sad singing lips...
...so that men seeing her face
And how she sighed out little Ahs of pain
And soft cries sobbing sideways from her mouth,
Fell in hot love, and having lain with her
Died soon. ...

Yet, as the *Athenaeum* remarked in its review of the book, *Chastelard* was to be valued for its 'detached beauties of expression' rather than as a drama.[56] Whether or not he still considered himself to be under the Pre-Raphaelite influence, Swinburne's greatest success in the play was in the static description of portrait and gesture, the subtle colouring of beauty in fabric or flesh, which he showed in common with Rossetti and the art of the movement.

Chastelard was a dramatic poem to be read, rather than a poetic drama for the stage. Swinburne himself gave a reading in July 1865, for his friends, over what he called 'aesthetic tea'. It was a book to be bought for reading, and reading aloud, in those families which had taken to the bland Arthurianism of Tennyson and similar poetic visions of the past. Many of the reviews of *Chastelard* gave a muted warning that the morality – or the lack of it – in Swinburne's drama and his verse generally was unacceptable for such purposes in the 1860s. Of the principal characters, the *Athenaeum* remarked: 'besides being inherently vicious, their language will offend not only those who have reverence, but those who have taste'.[57] Hutton's *Spectator*, still smarting over the japes of Félicien Cossu and Ernest Clouet, condemned Swinburne's 'forcing-house of sensual appetite'.[58] The drawing-rooms of the decade were no place for the sea-nymph's 'little Ahs of pain ... soft cries sobbing sideways from her mouth', or the 'hot love' with which mortal men ravished her and died in consequence.

*   *   *

As usual, the outbursts with which Swinburne shocked the moral susceptibilities of such contemporaries were nothing compared to his private literary indulgences. After *La Fille du policeman*, these took the form of *La Soeur de la reine*, a burlesque drama in which Queen Victoria herself was the main butt of the joke. She is shown as a woman of insatiable sexual appetite to whom Lord John Russell and 'Sir Peel' are natural prey. Surrounded by grotesques of the court, including the Duchess of Fuckingstone, Miss Sarah

Butterbottom, the Marchioness of Mausprick, and Miss Polly Poke, the queen holds court. Unknown to the world, she has a twin sister, Kitty, who has been brought up to the trade of prostitution in order to remove all threat to the succession. The two sisters share a natural sexual depravity. In one of Swinburne's versions, according to his acquaintance John Bailey, Victoria describes her first 'unfortunate lapse from virtue', and names the man responsible. He was no prince, no lord, no cabinet minister, but a common scoundrel named Wordsworth. This wretch read her a poem called *The Excursion*, a work of such smouldering sensuality that Victoria's venereal passion was unquenchably roused and she fell a victim to the bard. The old Laureate had been right when he patronizingly took his leave of the boy Swinburne in 1850: Algernon had not forgotten him.[59]

Yet even the varying versions of *La Soeur de la reine* represented a semi-respectability on Swinburne's part, a joke suited to sharing among his sympathizers. There was a yet more secret and exciting world into which they were not, as a rule permitted, to enter. A few glimpsed it in part, and fewer still in its totality. Rossetti was privileged in this respect. In the autumn of 1864, he wrote to Frederick Sandys, apropos of Swinburne and Monckton Milnes, 'At present the young poet is in panting expectation of a high mark of favour and confidence promised him by his mentor – to wit – the loan of de Sade's *Justine*, the most immoral book in the world.'[60]

Chapter 5

Orpheus in the Underworld

AS early as the autumn of 1861, Monckton Milnes had held out to his young protégé the promise of Fryston and its literary treasures. Chief among these, in Swinburne's anticipation, were 'the mystic pages of the martyred marquis de Sade'.[1] Even without reading Sade, Swinburne adopted him as hero and mentor. Indeed, when he at length read *La Nouvelle Justine*, the book itself was disappointing by comparison with what he had expected from a man of Sade's beliefs and notoriety. Sir William Hardman, meeting Swinburne during a party at Rossetti's rooms in Chatham Place, reacted with a blend of worldly wisdom and distaste to this adulation of the Marquis.

Swinburne is strongly sensual; although almost a boy, he upholds the Marquis de Sade as the acme and apostle of perfection, without (as he says) having read a word of his works. Now the Marquis de Sade was a most filthy, horrible, and disgusting rascal, a disgrace to humanity – he wrote the most abominable bawdry books that ever were written. No one is fonder of good sound bawdry than I . . . yet the Marquis completely bowls me over. I tried once to read him, but very soon stuck fast. S——y mixed with murder and hideous cruelty are the prevailing features of his writings. The assembled company evidently received Swinburne's tirades with ill-concealed disgust, but they behaved to him like a spoiled child.[2]

Hardman, a barrister and magistrate who was to become Recorder and Mayor of Kingston and editor of the *Morning Post*, was no prude. Indeed, he relished earthy humour. His friend George Meredith, portraying him as Blackburn Tuckham in *Beauchamp's Career*, described him as 'an exuberant Tory'. His distaste for Swinburne's hero-worship reveals a first-hand knowledge of Sade's fiction, more common among the Victorians than one might suppose.

Of the three versions of Sade's most famous novel, the first and most innocuous, *Les Malheurs de la vertu*, was still unpublished. It was the third and most elaborately obscene, *La Nouvelle Justine* in four volumes, which Swinburne coveted among the treasures of

Fryston, a novel to drive 'curates and curates' pupils to madness and death', as he anticipated.[3] This version had long been available in England, in the underworld of pornographic books. George Cannon had been successfully prosecuted for selling it as far back as 1830.[4] In the same year there also appeared *The Inutility of Virtue*, 'Translated from the French by Dr ———, of Magdalen College, Oxford'. This was a vague imitation of Sade, omitting his more extravagant details, and was reprinted in a new edition in 1860. In 1889, there followed *Opus Sadicum: a Philosophical Romance*, which was much closer to being a translation of *Justine*.

In whatever form, the fiction of the Marquis fell into the most unlikely hands. Henry James recalled a luncheon party at Aldworth, where one of the guests, Sabine Greville, chanced to mention the name of a relative, Laure de Sade. The sound roused Tennyson, as James describes the incident, to a prolonged denunciation of 'the scandalous, the long-ignored, the at last all but unnameable author' of the same surname. Tennyson thundered on, to the mild bewilderment of his guests, none of whom apart from James had the least idea of what he was talking about.[5]

For Swinburne's purposes, the books which Sade actually wrote were unimportant by comparison with Sade as the martyr-victim of bourgeois respectability. Before reading *Justine*, he sat down and composed a long poem in French, 'Charenton', as his tribute to the final ordeal of Sade's life, imprisonment in the asylum where he died in 1814. It was hardly appropriate to add that Sade had comfortable apartments, his library, his mistress and Madeleine Leclerc, who at fourteen became a participant in the old man's domestic 'libertinage'. Swinburne sent the poem to Monckton Milnes, who kept it.

Swinburne's first glimpse of *La Nouvelle Justine* was at Fryston, a hasty perusal of the illustrations before church on Sunday morning. Having been entrusted with the four volumes, he bore them off to the studio in Newman Street, St James's, where he had temporary lodgings before the move to Cheyne Walk. He and Rossetti and their guests agreed to close the doors and, with some trepidation, to read aloud the satanic work to one another, nerving themselves for the eternal derangement which Jules Janin had promised in 1834 to those who soiled their eyes and hearts with such literature. After a brief interval, the studio echoed to their screams, and Swinburne, as he confessed, 'quite expected to add another to the gifted author's list of victims'.[6]

But the screams were screams of laughter. Sade was not, after all, repulsive or stimulating or even shocking: he was uproariously absurd, a possibility for which Janin and his followers had made no allowance. The book was not read through systematically, but the readers evidently chose the extracts which most appealed to them. Swinburne picked chapter 16, a *grand guignol* orgy involving the families of M. de Verneuil and Mme d'Esterval, the survivors copulating with ludicrous and manic determination among the scenes of slaughter. Swinburne's audience rolled and roared with laughter. Rossetti followed with the account in chapter 6 of the schoolmaster Rodin, whose amateur enthusiasm for surgery has led to a delight in the vivisection of his victims. The culmination of his achievements is to stage surgery and sex simultaneously, cutting open his daughter Rosalie while at the same time ravishing his own sister. The ludicrously phrased horror of the watching heroine, 'Oh, monsieur ... what have you done!' is lost in Rodin's champagne celebration of his surgical achievement.

Having read Sade, Swinburne complained to Milnes of his disappointment. 'Is this all?' he inquired. Sade, for the time being, was a fallen idol, and *Justine* a mere juggler's show, no more than 'an ingenious acrobatic performance'.[7] After all the breathless anticipation, the novel seemed neither erotic nor pornographic. Indeed, it has less in common with erotica than with other 'philosophical fiction' of the eighteenth century, like Voltaire's *Candide*. As Voltaire showed that all was not for the best in this best of all possible worlds, so Sade demonstrated that virtue was not rewarded nor vice punished, quite the contrary. His reputation as a pornographer was ensured, however, by choosing a beautiful heroine as the credulous fool for whom, as it were, the banana-skin lies eternally in wait. Ravished, beaten and abused, she comes up smiling until the very end, when even heaven grows tired of her foolish virtue and strikes her dead with a thunderbolt. It is not hard to see why this novel, much of its horror couched in terms of stage melodrama, should have struck Swinburne and his companions as superbly comic.

Having become a welcome guest at Fryston, Swinburne made the most of this. In the autumn of 1861, he spent six weeks there as Milnes's guest, holding court among the other visitors and exploring the treasures of the library. Not all those to whom Milnes had introduced him were impressed by the young poet, Matthew Arnold dismissing him as 'a sort of pseudo-Shelley called Swinburne'.[8] Henry Adams, son of the United States minister at the court of St James's, recalled Swinburne at Fryston as 'a tropical bird, high-crested, long-beaked, quick-moving, with rapid utterance and screams of humour, quite unlike any English lark or nightingale'.[9] On a later occasion, after dinner, Swinburne was invited to read to Milnes's guests, who included Thackeray and his daughters, and the Archbishop of York. He chose to read 'Les Noyades', his poem which describes 'a maiden, wonderful, white', condemned to be stripped naked, tied to a soldier also condemned to death by the revolutionary tribunal in France, and thrown into the sea to drown.

> And the judge bade strip and ship them, and bind
> Bosom to bosom, to drown and die.

As Swinburne read on, Thackeray's daughters, 'who had never heard such sentiments expressed before', began to giggle. The Archbishop appeared deeply shocked at the poem, while Thackeray and Milnes seemed delighted at the situation. Swinburne stopped in annoyance, but Milnes's wife said casually, 'Well, Mr Swinburne, if you *will* read such extraordinary things, you must expect us to laugh.' Swinburne resumed, the Archbishop 'looking more and more horrified' at the chronicle of the man's eagerness and the girl's hot blushes of shame until the hero's last boast:

> And I would have given my soul for this
> To burn for ever in burning hell.

Fortunately, all comment on the moral outrage was prevented by Milnes's butler throwing open the doors 'like an avenging angel', and announcing: 'Prayers! my Lord!'[10]

The library at Fryston, towards which Swinburne's enthusiasm was directed, contained an exemplary collection of erotica among a much wider range of other treasures. Apart from the works of Sade, the most famous – or infamous – classics of the eighteenth century were well represented in the form of illustrated editions. The works of Andrea de Nerciat, Restif de la Bretonne and the determinedly pornographic writers of the age were accompanied by merely scandalous novels, to the Victorian way of thinking, like *La Religieuse* and *Les Liaisons dangereuses*, the magnificent plates of Fragonard and lesser artists abounding among them. In 1859, Milnes had succeeded in getting a handsome edition of Carracci's illustrations to Aretino's sonnets on the various postures and pleasures of sexual intercourse. It had been piloted through the British customs with the edges of the pages gummed lightly together.

Fred Hankey was busily supplying Fryston with the best that Paris and Brussels could offer. Any gaps which remained in Swinburne's acquaintance with odder sexual tastes were speedily filled by the resources of Milnes's library. After the trial of 1857 and the condemnation of *Les Fleurs du mal*, Baudelaire's publisher, Auguste Poulet-Malassis, had withdrawn to Brussels and devoted himself to supplying the market for pornography in which lesbianism featured as a major theme. Among these volumes *L'Ecole des biches* was partly the work of Hankey and was allegedly based upon the orgies which he staged for voyeurs. It circulated in manuscript for some time before its publication in 1868 and certainly in the Fryston circle. In literary terms, it was surpassed by the anonymous work *Un Eté à la campagne*, issued by Poulet-Malassis in 1867 and consisting of letters between two girls, one a young lesbian teacher in Paris, the other a former pupil in the country who emerges from exclusive attachment to her own sex and discovers the fuller pleasures of love with a male partner. Such were the gems which found their way to Fryston during Swinburne's time there and in the years which followed.

Milnes's method of transporting forbidden books and even small statues was among the more bizarre aspects of his hobby. In order to negotiate the officers of the customs, he arranged that some of the material should be sent to him at the Foreign Office, travelling in the diplomatic bag from the Paris embassy in company with Lord Palmerston's despatches. His other method was to entrust large volumes and statuary to Augustus Harris of the Covent Garden Opera. Harris had a mild physiological oddity. His back was capable of assuming so deep an inward curve when he walked that he could conceal quarto volumes and even small statuary in the bend of it. It is he who is credited with transporting a piece by the fashionable French sculptor James Pradier, depicting two girls engaged in mutual cunnilingus. Smaller volumes and pornographic photographs were brought through customs by the valet of Hankey's cousin, who simply concealed them in the pocket of his overcoat.

Chief among the forbidden literature of Fryston, revealing an interest common to both Monckton Milnes and Swinburne, were the works dealing with sexual sadism in its varying forms. They ranged from classics of the genre like Jouffreau de Lazarin's *Histoire des flagellants* or Jouy's *Galerie des femmes* to more documentary accounts in which such scandals as that of the Hoo Union were revealed, where the master had birched adolescent girls for his own satisfaction. By a supreme irony, these latter acts of sadism were warmly applauded by the same moralists who sought to stamp out the literature in which they were described. They caught the imagination of Milnes and Swinburne equally. By 1863, Swinburne was corresponding eagerly, offering Milnes his own school flagellation fiction in exchange for Milnes's account, which was evidently a reformatory sketch of the ordeal of the adolescent girls who had been birched.[11]

It was easy to react to this rather infantile obsession in melodramatic terms, depicting Milnes as the satanic evil genius and Swinburne as the eager devil's disciple. Hardman, at least, grew more disposed to laugh at them both. In 1865 he was highly amused at the predicament of the liberal Milnes, let alone the revolutionary Swinburne, over the matter of the so-called Jamaica Mutiny. The *Daily News* and the progressively minded press was filled with stories of how the British army had responded to threats of unrest by falling upon the population, hanging a number of men and flogging the women. 'I daresay the women deserved it,' remarked Hardman. He went on to quote the outraged accounts of the *Daily News*, describing how the women were 'flogged, according to Jamaica fashion, on their naked posteriors.... The person of a woman flogged is publicly and indecently exposed in shameful nakedness.' Hardman was greatly amused by the ambivalence of such men as Milnes, who felt obliged to condemn such acts politically and yet privately envied those involved in them. 'Anyhow, the whipping of women would have gratified [his] senses ... and would probably have culminated in his asking to be similarly castigated himself.'[12]

In 1876, Fryston itself, the scene of Swinburne's eager ventures into forbidden and curious literature, suffered the only fate appropriate to such an *enfer*. On a November night the great house was ravaged by a sudden and unexplained fire, in which many of the smuggled treasures were destroyed. Whether it resulted from divine wrath or spontaneous combustion is a matter for speculation.

In 1863, during the premiership of Palmerston, Milnes was raised to the peerage. Swinburne suggested that he might take the title of Baron Tattle of Scandal. Milnes chose instead to be Baron Houghton.

There was no reason why the peerage should have made any difference to the relationship between the two men. Three years later, for instance, when Arthur Munby visited Houghton at his town house in Upper Brook Street, the latter talked of Swinburne in distinctly proprietorial terms. 'He spoke of Swinburne,' Munby noted, 'said he had been S.'s only friend (true enough, but what has he done to check S.'s drink & bawdry?): that "the evangelical old Admiral", S.'s father, is at last getting proud of him: that he, Lord H., thinks S. "will beat Alfred" i.e. Tennyson.' Houghton then regaled his afternoon guests with brandy and seltzer, and his 'favourite subject' of pornography. 'Sly, sensuous, and potentially wicked,' noted Munby after studying his host's face.[13]

Houghton's irritation with Swinburne was evident not only in his warnings over the companionship of Burton but also in his reproofs over Swinburne's outrageous and ungrateful public behaviour. In December 1865, he arranged that Swinburne and he should be presented to Tennyson who was in London staying with F. T. Palgrave, compiler of the *Golden Treasury*. Swinburne was late, and seemed to Houghton to be far from sober as they made their way to Palgrave's house. Indeed, the triumphant young poet, with the acclaim of *Atalanta* and moral outrage of *Chastelard* ringing in his ears, was in one of his most intransigent moods. There was a row with Houghton on the way and Swinburne arrived in no mood to pay dutiful homage to the Laureate of England's bourgeoisie, the poet of the 'Idylls of the Prince Consort' and the 'Morte d'Albert', as he scathingly termed him. He entered the room, where the great man's admirers stood respectfully in attendance, exchanged a few words with Tennyson, turned his back on him and hurried off to the next room. For the rest of the evening, the worshippers were assailed by Swinburne's voice, shrill and exuberant, announcing the genius of William Blake.

Angered by this display, Houghton wrote a reproving note on the following day, provoking only a caustic and unrepentent reply from Swinburne, complaining that *he* had not written to accuse Houghton of being drunk, and rejecting the 'avalanche of advice'.[14]

Neither was the friendship with Burton impeded by Houghton's warnings. At Burton's instigation, Swinburne joined the Cannibal Club which met to dine and drink at Bartolini's in Leicester Square. Cannibalism was not only a professional interest of Burton's since he had encountered it during his exploration of the Gabon in 1862. It was also a shared Sadean joke. In *Aline et Valcour*, which Swinburne knew, Sade makes one of his heroes regard with dismay an ignorant traveller who would eat the flesh of mere animals when, with far less trouble, he could dine off a delicious haunch of slave-girl. A mace upon the club's dinner table represented a negro

eating a human thigh. The dishes served were given suitably can-
nibalistic titles. The club contained two eminent atheists, Charles
Bradlaugh and Thomas Bendyshe, the former of whom kept the
mildly blasphemous *Cannibal Catechism* and the latter of whom
wrote it. The lines were chanted by the members as grace before
meat.

> Preserve us from our enemies
> Thou who art lord of suns and skies
> Whose food is human flesh in pies
> > And blood in bowls!
> Of thy sweet mercy damn their eyes
> And damn their souls![15]

   In July 1865, Swinburne had assured Houghton that Burton 'had
thought to get me off my legs' in a drinking bout but had failed.[16]
The truth was that, with or without Burton's presence, it was
becoming very easy to get Swinburne off his legs, particularly since
he had turned to brandy, at Burton's instigation. Gosse, in his
biography and in the memoir which he circulated privately after
Swinburne's death, gives some indication of the problem between
the poet leaving Balliol and the publication of *Poems and Ballads*.
Hungerford Pollen and his wife recalled an evening at Rossetti's
studio when a fearful screaming began in another part of the house,
the painter announcing that it was Swinburne 'in an awful state', and
begging Pollen to help him. It was, as Pollen discovered, 'the drink –
as usual'. Soon after Swinburne made the acquaintance of Milnes,
there was an incident at Upper Brook Street, when Swinburne
disappeared before dinner and was found in the dining-room,
having drunk the dessert wine, dancing round the table like a mad
thing in front of an audience of servants.[17]
   By 1863 Swinburne was no longer confining his drinking bouts to
the presence of friends or acquaintances. While at Cheyne Walk, he
would return incapably drunk, having spent the evening in places
which he could not remember when he revived. Rossetti was woken
at three o'clock one morning by Swinburne's return, supported in
the arms of a policeman and followed by a procession of street
urchins. Until the moment when he passed out, Swinburne would
remain 'screaming drunk' in the literal sense. On this occasion,
Rossetti reported extreme difficulty with him, 'screaming and
splashing about', before he could be put to bed.[18]
   All this might have been dismissed as the picturesque conduct of a
young poet, or 'toper', as Max Beerbohm chose to call him. Yet as

Gosse remarks, Swinburne also began to suffer from fits, at least as early as 1863. Doctors who were consulted about this were unable to agree as to the cause and nature of the fits. Gosse, who witnessed them, described them as 'epileptiform'. Swinburne's collapse 'took the shape of a convulsive fit, in which, generally after a period of very great cerebral excitement, he would suddenly fall unconscious. These fits were excessively distressing to witness, and produced a shock of alarm, all the more acute because of the deathlike appearance of the patient.'[19]

How far drink had precipitated such fits was never determined. So far as intoxication was concerned, it seemed to take very little to get Swinburne drunk, though in practice he was not content to confine himself to small quantities. According to Gosse, if Swinburne saw a bottle within reach, while he was dining with friends, he would pounce upon it, 'like a mongoose on a snake', filling a tumbler from it and drinking eagerly, his lips trembling and his eyelids opening and closing violently.[20]

Perhaps it was not surprising that the new Lord Houghton, despite his proprietorial interest in Swinburne's poetry, felt little enthusiasm for a continued relationship at close quarters. Indeed, it would have been hard to sustain a great literary friendship on the basis of the silly and injudicious letters which Swinburne and he were exchanging on the subject of sadism adapted to Victorian educational and domestic life. Swinburne wrote much of this in French, addressing Houghton as 'Rodin', after Sade's schoolmaster with the mania for amateur surgery. At least Houghton was discreet, whereas some of the other recipients of Swinburne's juvenile fantasies were to put them to more sinister purposes.

Whatever the reason, patron and protégé drifted apart, though the absence of the final and abrupt break which ended others of Swinburne's friendships in no way mitigated the eventual bitterness. They continued to meet on reasonably amicable terms during the 1860s, yet in 1874 Swinburne wrote to John Morley deploring the use of Houghton as the reviewer of *Bothwell* in the *Fortnightly Review*: 'I must confess that I do shrink from the rancid unction of that man's adulation, or patronage, or criticism.'[21]

*   *   *

After the convulsive fit of 1863, Swinburne left London for a long period of convalescence, first with the painter J. W. Inchbold at Tintagel and then, at the end of the summer, with Mary Gordon and her family at Niton on the Isle of Wight. He and his cousin had remained close in spirit since her visits to East Dene in their childhood. The fantasies of Victorian schools and their discipline, and the role of a younger boy played by Mary Gordon seem implicitly more bizarre than Swinburne's Sadean jokes shared with Houghton. Yet they were overtly far more respectable. At the age of twenty-six, Swinburne was about to discover that Mary, at twenty-three, had lost none of her enthusiasm for the theme.

The first evidence of this was Mary's venture into the writing of fiction, *The Children of the Chapel*, a story of Elizabethan England, which she wrote and published in 1864. Swinburne was her collaborator, at least to the extent of contributing a pastiche of a morality play which the children act in the last chapter. The rest of the novel, according to its title-page, was Mary Gordon's work, though she admitted the inspiration of her cousin here and there. Its sexual preoccupations, in modern terms, are with flagellation and transvestism. The punishments of the pupils are spaced out at intervals of about twenty pages but it is the final chapter which would be most likely to chill the blood of twentieth-century child psychologists. There is a lingering description of the young hero being dressed as a girl for the play – the echo of *Mademoiselle de Maupin* seems distinctly audible. No detail of tight corset and rouge is omitted, the dresser pronouncing the boy to be 'the sweetest little lady that ever was seen'. Other voices join in the sexual taunting: 'Ha, dainty lady, hast thou lost thy roses? Mind she doesn't faint. Oh, see her beauty! . . . How the great ladies will envy him!' Worse still, for sensitive modern inhibitions, the boy has been compelled to dress as a girl against his will. Meanwhile, the master, whose idea the whole thing has been, 'would have stripped and whipped him then and there'.[22]

Unlike the overt sexuality of Swinburne's poetry, Mary Gordon presented the age with a wholesome romp in which the amusing subjects of discipline and dressing up retained their pre-Freudian innocence. In 1871 there was to be a criminal prosecution, whose more scandalous details Swinburne gleaned from Simeon Solomon. Two young men, Boulton and Park, were arrested while plying for hire in female dress among female prostitutes. The Victorian jurors heard the evidence and acquitted them, ignoring medical witnesses who hinted at sodomy. To dress in the clothes of the other sex was not a sinister aberration but a high-spirited caper, little different from the antics of a pantomime dame or principal boy.

A young German aristocrat, identical in age to Mary Gordon, a Professor of Medicine at Strasburg, had already begun to give his attention to the same subject matter which characterized her fiction, not least the topic of fetishism. When the Baron von Krafft-Ebing concluded his studies with the publication of the *Psychopathia Sexualis* in 1886, some readers were able to look at *The Children of the Chapel* and its genre with new insight. In retrospect, Mary Gordon's romp in the final chapter was a bizarre parallel to a romp of a more explicit kind, reserved for Leopold Bloom in *Ulysses*:

Tape measurements will be taken next your skin. You will be laced with cruel force into vicelike corsets of soft dove coutille, with whalebone busk, to the diamond trimmed pelvis, the absolute outside edge, while your figure, plumper than when at large, will be restrained in nettight frocks, pretty two-ounce petticoats and fringes and things....[23]

Not surprisingly, when the survivors of the age of innocence found the wholesome high spirits of a children's story impugned as a brothel burlesque, they showed little tolerance of Joyce or other perpetrators of the literary slander.

Swinburne and Mary Gordon remained in close correspondence during the autumn of 1864, when he was once again in Cornwall. This was the occasion when he wrote to her describing his lodgings at a schoolhouse and the birching of the pupils which he overheard. 'I could have wished for your company yesterday night', the letter began as he related his Cornish experiences.[24] Even his most straightforward letters to her were garbed with images or memories of their shared interest. Swinburne described himself as 'thrashed and licked' by the sea, a cut on his foot being 'worse than any ever inflicted by a birch'.[25] The three following letters to her were pre-occupied by the recollection of a school birching.[26] In short, there was hardly one piece of correspondence in which the subject was not somehow raised between them.

Mary Gordon was an enthusiastic partner and audience in the literary treatment of Swinburne's obsession. Given his instinctive gift for fantasy and hoax, it might be doubted whether he actually overheard anything in the schoolhouse, perhaps inventing the entire account merely to please her, as he was pleasing Lord Houghton and others by his fabrications of this sort. What is certain is that he returned to London at the end of October and became 'a frequent guest' at the Gordons' house in Chelsea during the winter afternoons. It was there that he read to the appreciative young woman the chapters of his novel, which appeared posthumously as *Lesbia Brandon*, and which Gosse believed was unfit ever to be pubished at all. Many years later, Mary Gordon wrote vaguely about the book for the benefit of a readership who would know nothing of its actual contents:

> I do not know what was the plot of the story, but I recollect some of the characters – one being the bright loveable schoolboy he delighted in portraying, in constant scrapes, but noble and honourable through all; and a tutor, who bid fair to be the 'villain of the piece'. There was a description of a bathing-place under the rocky cliffs, taken no doubt from the scenes of his Cornwall scrambles.[27]

Only by detailing Mary Gordon's enthusiasm for Swinburne's own obsessions is it possible to see why she was an eager audience for *Lesbia Brandon*, whose surviving chapters were at length published in 1952. The hero of the book is a schoolboy, Herbert Seyton, in the care of his sister, Margaret, Lady Wariston. A tutor, Denham, is appointed to the household. He loves the girl with a desperate and at first frustrated ardour, which he expresses by beating the boy with frequent severity. Lady Wariston is also loved by Lesbia Brandon, an unrequited passion. Even before the dénouement of the novel there are distinctly incestuous overtones. Yet the climax, in which Denham shoots himself and Lesbia Brandon dies of poison, both for love of Margaret, is precipitated by a bizarre discovery. Denham is the illegitimate son of the father of Herbert and Margaret, by the mother of Lesbia. He is thus half-brother to them all.

So far as the novel has a plot, it is in the development of lesbian, sadistic or incestuous passions of one character for another. The story is set in the patrician Northumberland circles which Swinburne knew at first hand, with an almost Brontëesque feeling for the wild moorland and sea and an enthusiasm for the adventures of riding and swimming. That Mary Gordon should still have responded favourably to the book, however, is surprising.

Lesbia's love for Margaret is obliquely described, being roused in the first place by seeing Herbert dressed as a girl for the purposes of a charade and falling victim to his effeminate appeal. In conventional Victorian terms, Lesbia is presented, reflecting Mary Gordon's role as Swinburne's younger schoolboy, as a girl who 'wanted all her life to be a boy ... and must needs have a boy's training and do a boy's lessons'. The question of whether Lesbia should be 'switched for her false quantities' in Latin verse is decided in the negative.

The bisexual nature of the novel's sadism is evident when Denham appears to be tormenting Margaret in the person of her brother. He beats Herbert and dreams of Margaret, wishing to:

> scourge her into swooning and absorb the blood with kisses; caress and lacerate her loveliness, alleviate and heighten her pains; to feel her foot upon his throat, and wound her own with his teeth; submit his body and soul for a little to her lightest will, and satiate upon hers the desperate caprice of his immeasureable desire; to inflict careful torture on limbs too tender to embrace, suck the tears off her laden eyelids, bite through her sweet and shuddering lips.[28]

If nothing else, the novel reveals that Swinburne's obsessions were not purely masochistic, as a reading of his letters might suggest. Putting himself into the mind of Denham, he contemplates the prospect of birching Margaret as well as her brother. 'To have seen her eyes also overflow, her lips tremble and her limbs heave with exquisite and hopeless pain, would alone have quenched the violent thirst of his mingling passions.'[29] Perhaps Swinburne toned down some of these descriptions in reading the novel to Mary Gordon, though it seems more likely that such outbursts were allowable in the character of Denham, whom she describes in terms of melodrama as the 'villain of the piece'.

* * *

Apart from such *jeux d'esprit* as *La Fille du policeman*, Swinburne had begun to take the craft of fiction seriously in 1862–5. Before starting the chapters of *Lesbia Brandon* he had written a complete and revised novel in 1862, whose definitive title was *Love's Cross-Currents: A Year's Letters*. It was in no way as likely to scandalize the Victorian reading public as *Lesbia Brandon* would have done. Yet it was impossible to find a publisher for it. In 1877, Swinburne described it as a book 'which had failed, as the anonymous work of an unknown writer, to find favour in the sight of any publisher'.[30] Part of the difficulty was that he intended to publish it anonymously, and insisted on this to William Michael Rossetti. Yet Moxon's, even after *Atalanta* and *Chastelard*, were not interested. 'I am at a loss to know whence the squeamishness of Moxon arises,' wrote Joseph Knight to Swinburne in February 1866, having tried without success to find a publisher on Swinburne's behalf.[31] The novel eventually appeared, with some revisions, under the pseudonym 'Mrs H. Manners', in the *Tatler* in 1877, and then in volume form with further revisions in 1905.

Written in the form of letters, the general impression of the story is of an imitation of *Les Liaisons dangereuses* devoted to two illicit romances within the bounds of a sprawling mid-Victorian family. Reginald Harewood woos his second cousin Clara, two years his senior, the wife of Ernest Radford, a zoologist with a plodding interest in bones and an ungrateful passing resemblance to Sir Walter Trevelyan of Wallington. At the same time, Clara's brother, Frank Cheyne, is in passionate pursuit of Reginald's half-sister Amicia. Neither affair ends in seduction, the chief interest of the novel being in the intricate play of character, the wit of the style and the lively presence of the sardonic duenna, Lady Midhurst, as manipulator of her descendants. 'As to being in love, frankly, I don't believe in it,' she informs Amicia, adding later, 'I wish to heaven there were some surgical process discernible by which one could annihilate or amputate sentiment.'[32]

Unlike the notorious Marquise de Merteuil of *Les Liaisons dangereuses*, Lady Midhurst seeks to retain the sexual and marital *status quo* rather than to subvert it, though for reasons just as cynical. Like many other elements in the novel, her character is a reflection less of Swinburne's reading of French fiction than of his interest in the contemporary writing of George Meredith. Lady Midhurst in her intrusive prurience recalls Lady Blandish, the *voyeuse* of *The Ordeal of Richard Feverel*, with her enthusiasm for spying on adolescent boys stripped for bathing. In her caustic descriptions of men and women, she anticipates Mrs Mountstuart Jenkinson in *The Egoist*. Having separated the youthful lovers, Lady Midhurst describes her reception by Clara and Radworth. 'The poor man calls aloud for an embalmer; the poor woman cries pitifully for an enameller. . . . She would have me racked if she could, no doubt, but received me smiling from the tips of her teeth outwards and with a soft pressure of the fingers.'[33] As for the unfortunate Frank, who had importuned Clara so hopefully: 'Dismissal was legible all over him.'[34]

In his fiction, Swinburne follows Meredith's prescription for comedy, given in the prologue to *The Egoist*, as a game played 'with human nature in the drawing-room of civilised men and women'. Much of the excellence in *Love's Cross-Currents* lies in its skill at depicting character through speech. Referring to her dreary zoologist husband, Clara writes: 'Ernest has taken to insects now; *il me manquait cela.*'[35] Reginald and Frank fall into schoolboy slang with a verve which is rare in serious Victorian fiction: 'I've got a sister, I believe she's a clipper, but I don't know. . . . Isn't she a brick. . . . But do you know she hates my governor like mad. . . . Well, she says my sister is no end of a good one to look at. . . . I never saw such a stunner as she is. She makes a fellow feel quite shut up and spooney.'[36]

Before dismissing Swinburne's fiction as unduly dependent on Meredith, it is fair to add that when *Love's Cross-Currents* was written, Meredith had published only his first two novels, neither of which influenced Swinburne's fiction as strongly as the later ones might have done. *The Egoist*, however, was not published until 1879, two years after Swinburne's pseudonymous appearance in the *Tatler*.

Perhaps the failure to find a publisher for this first and comparatively innocuous novel deterred Swinburne from a literary career which might have eclipsed all but the best of his poetry. True, the habitual references to school punishments occur in the first section, discussed by Frank and Reginald, but in the main body of the story Swinburne writes an adult comedy of manners. It may have been the horror of Moxon's and other publishers at the amoral style of his book which persuaded Swinburne that, for the future, fiction might as well be the medium for moral subversion. Certainly by 1864 he had embodied this in *Lesbia Brandon*. It hardly seemed there could be a hope of publication for this second novel, though Chatto went so far as to set up part of it in type in 1877 and printed galleys. Thereafter, Swinburne abandoned hope, though in 1878 he still insisted that he meant to finish it.

So much attention seems to be claimed by the sexual oddities of Swinburne's fiction that his more orthodox enthusiasms are liable to be overlooked. 'There was a strange grave beauty and faultless grace about her . . . pureness of feature, ample brilliant hair, perfect little lips, serious and rounded in shape, and wonderful unripe beauty of chin and throat.'[37] Such was the description of Amicia at eight years old, a writer's tribute perhaps to 'Boo', who was attracting Swinburne's close attention in the same year.

There is also the appreciation of Clara's beauty, later in the same novel, an affirmation of Swinburne's response to the erotic beauty of mature women and possibly to that of Lizzie Rossetti in particular:

She has a throat like pearl-colour, with flower-colour over that; and a smell of blossom and honey in her hair.... Her fingers leave a taste of violets on the lips.... Her hair and eyelashes change colour in the sun.... She has clear thick eyebrows that grow well down, coming full upon the upper lid, with no gap such as there is above some women's eyes before you come to the brow. They have an inexplicable beauty of meaning in them, and the shape of the arch looks tender.... She has the texture and colour of rose-leaves crushed deep into the palms of her hands.[38]

Such accounts convey the impression of intense erotic preoccupation with a particular model of female beauty, a detailed enthusiasm of a type rare in Victorian fiction. The same is true in the second novel, when Swinburne describes first Margaret and then Lesbia. The account of Margaret is a prolonged and subtle praise of her beauty, the whole of the first page being devoted to the colour of her eyes. By contrast, the hero of the novel is dismissed as being merely a male version of his sister.

When Herbert falls in love, hopelessly, with the beautiful lesbian who gives her name to the novel's title, there is a further loving appraisal of feminine beauty. In this case, the reference to 'the profound pallor of complexions at once dark and colourless' parallels William Michael Rossetti's tribute to Janey Morris, who may have been at least part of the inspiration for Swinburne's Lesbia.[39] Similarly, the character of Miss Leonora Vane Harley, otherwise Susan Farmer, parallels Fanny Cornforth, otherwise Sarah Cox. She is the beautiful but vacuous courtesan in the novel, the companion of the old satyr Linley, who has some resemblance perhaps to Monckton Milnes. Yet Swinburne was quick to distinguish the ethereal if perverse beauty of his heroines from the sham beauty of Miss Harley, otherwise Farmer. 'She was a woman made to kiss, to resist, to laugh at, and to leave.'[40]

As to Swinburne's identification of himself with the masochistic heroes, Herbert Seyton and Reginald Harewood, that is a matter of record. Yet the seriousness with which he undertook it is open to some doubt. The interest of the reader moves easily away from Herbert and his ordeals to the figures of the beautiful and perverse women with whom the novel seems principally concerned. The consequence of this concern is that one of the motifs running clearly through his fiction and his poetry at this time is the ever fascinating subject, to the European late romantics, of lesbianism.

*   *   *

It seems something of an anti-climax, perhaps, that Mary Gordon should have emerged from the sexual complexities of *Lesbia Brandon* and her relationship with 'Cousin Hadji' to marry Colonel R. W. Disney Leith, a professional soldier with a distinguished record of active service in India. They were engaged at the time that Swinburne was eagerly reading Mary the chapters of *Lesbia Brandon*, and they were married a few months later, in 1865. Disney Leith was then forty-six and his bride was twenty-five. The marriage ran its conventional course until Disney Leith's death in 1892, Mary confining her interest in flagellation to the novels which she wrote and producing a thriving brood of children. Swinburne had reason to think that she regretted her desertion of him for the military hero and, certainly, following her husband's death, she returned to their mutual enthusiasm.

The twentieth century has, by turns, regarded its immediate predecessors either as moral freaks, furtively indulging perverse eroticism under various camouflages, or as sexual ignoramuses blundering in the darkness which preceded the dawn of Freudian enlightenment. Both are half-truths. What distinguishes the Victorians from ourselves, in this respect, is neither total innocence nor universal furtiveness. Within the society of Swinburne's lifetime there coexisted extremes of innocence and conscious sexual perversity which the enlightenment has subsequently reduced to a general mediocre knowingness.

The products of Dr Vaughan's Harrow or the convicts of Norfolk Island needed little instruction in homosexuality. No degree of 'innocence' could conceal from Kate Joynes the need to consummate physical passion with her own sex. Those to whom such matters were merely academic might still have found them graphically described in such cases as that of Mary Hamilton, 'The Female Husband', in the back numbers of the *Gentleman's Magazine*. Men of Swinburne's tastes and education were more than well informed. He obliged Monckton Milnes with a sadistic fantasy in which a girl's virginity is taken by a dildo, and confessed, during his affair with Adah Menken, that the rear view of a callipygean Venus was the sure means of erecting any man. It offered, after all, the means for most of the important Sadean pleasures.[41] At the other extreme, unwittingly obliging such admirers, the young women of fashion began to adopt the narrow waist, with its emphasis upon the fullness of hips, and the absurd exaggeration of the bustle.

Even among men and women of education, a good deal that was neatly docketed in a later age as lesbian, or sado-masochistic, or paedophile, went unremarked as such. The elopement of Sarah Ponsonby with Eleanor Butler in 1778 and their half-century of fame as the ladies of Llangollen seemed an idyll of friendship far removed from the bedroom intimacies of Gautier's heroines or Baudelaire's 'Femmes damnées'. Nor, for instance, was it necessarily deplorable that grown men should find girl-children attractive and exciting. Millions of Victorians saw with their own eyes that little girls sold themselves in the streets of London, making the nature of that excitement plain to the world. Dostoevsky, in his magazine *Vreyma* for March 1861, records a harrowing episode of being accosted by a ragged and hopeless girl of six in the Haymarket. Yet this tableau of juvenile lost souls was no reason for suspecting the motives of E. W. Benson with little Minnie Sidgwick, or those of the Reverend C. L. Dodgson with other little girls. Lack of selfconsciousness in such attachments enabled Francis Kilvert to recount his own feelings for a pre-pubescent schoolgirl in terms which his successors would certainly hesitate to confide to paper. He describes going ten miles in the spring of 1870 merely to find an excuse for kissing her, though the tone of flirtatious conspiracy between them is perhaps more important than the actual deed. 'Janet kept on interrupting her work to glance round at me shyly but saucily with her mischievous beautiful grey eyes. Shall I confess that I travelled ten miles over the hills for a kiss, to kiss that child's sweet face.'[42]

In this moral and emotional climate, if Swinburne chose to pay court to Jane Faulkner when she was ten or eleven, there was nothing necessarily sinister about it. As for Kilvert, no child could have been more safely entrusted to any man. Much was therefore allowed, in an age that accepted purity of motive, which was outlawed in a new century where the inevitability of physical sexual impulse was to become an article of dogma. In literary terms, the distinction of view is exemplified by two novels. Miss Wetherell's *Queechy* (1854) was a popular and pious account of devotion between interesting little girls and men old enough to be their fathers but who became their husbands instead. The contrary and no less popular view was put a century later by Vladimir Nabokov in *Lolita*.

It was not difficult for Swinburne and Mary Gordon to indulge an interest in discipline without provoking suspicions, or even to maintain a playful charade of a girl playing a junior boy to the man's older boy. More to the point, though Swinburne savoured the full sexual and Sadean implications of this, it is at least possible that Mary played their lifelong game without considering that there was anything remotely indecent or even odd about it. Indeed, she insisted on the 'brother-and-sister' quality of their relationship, which had made marriage or sexual affection unthinkable. Of course, the Victorian press made no attempt to hide the age-old truth that the beating of one partner by another might be a concomitant of sexual pleasure. On 12 July 1863, for instance, *Lloyd's Weekly London Newspaper* reported the trial of a well-known *madame,* Sarah Potter, on charges arising from the flogging of three girls, Agnes Thompson, Catherine Kennedy and Alice Smith, at her brothel in Albion Terrace, King's Road. When it was revealed that the performances took place in 'The Schoolroom', the court echoed to the laughter of spectators at the absurdity of the comparison. There was, to most observers, a world of difference between such brothel exhibitions and the interest in discipline which Swinburne and Mary Gordon shared.

Even when the mask of moral enthusiasm slipped, innocence was not necessarily injured. Five years after his encounter with Janet, Parson Kilvert recorded an incident involving another schoolgirl, whose clothes had been pulled above her waist as she slid from a swing. He remarked that she wore no drawers and that the area of her body revealed was 'plump smooth and in excellent whipping condition'.[43] The observation appears with none of the Freudian awareness or sinister prurience which must have attached to it fifty or sixty years later. After all, most Victorian men and women knew perfectly well that there was nothing pleasurable in such things. If anything, they had the fascination of the macabre, to those whose memories reached back to the sinister consequences of courts-martial hearings in the 1830s. Many floggings were carried out within public hearing at such barracks as St George's, Charing Cross. At the time of Swinburne's birth, some men, like Marine Thomas Ramsby, received injuries so appalling that they died of them.

Even to Swinburne the subject belonged in part to the proofs of manhood and in part to the domain of the macabre. It was related, in some degree, to the enthusiasm for witnessing public executions. Indeed, Monckton Milnes shared both interests. He was one of a select party who went to Courvoisier's execution and prompted a companion, Thackeray, to write a famous abolitionist essay, 'Going to See a Man Hanged'. To have suggested that there was pleasure in hanging would have seemed to sensible men and women one step more absurd than the aphrodisiac claims of beating. Yet here too the Marquis de Sade had insisted that to be hanged and cut down at the last moment was an ecstatic experience, caused by compression of the spinal nerves.[44]

If Swinburne's contemporaries showed uneasiness over the true nature of physical discipline and execution, it was through a wistful jocularity. George Meredith, deserted by his young wife, ventilated his misogyny in 1859 throughout *The Ordeal of Richard Feverel*, often in wry comedy. Yet it is doubtful whether, a century later, he would have employed such terms for his facetiousness as: 'The old Saxon understood women, he did. And he affirmed that the best way to continue their warm admirer was to keep the bit well in their mouths and lay on the whip now and then.'[45] The phenomenon of *equus eroticus* was to be dealt with twenty-seven years later by Krafft-Ebing, yet anticipatory echoes had already been woken by a scandal in the Gordon family. In 1855 Emilie Frances Gordon was fined £5 for relieving her excitement by thrashing her horse. *The Times*, on 6 April, endeavoured to stimulate its readers' enthusiasm by suggesting a heavier sentence. 'We cannot but say that a few months' imprisonment, with a few private whippings, administered by the hand of the stoutest woman in Hampshire would have constituted a much more fitting punishment.'

The concealment of motives in such outbursts was in part the consequence of the lack of any fixed vocabulary of sexual behaviour. Such categories as 'sadist', 'masochist' and even 'homosexual' were not imported into the language until the end of the century. Among other terms for homosexuals, Swinburne even resorts quaintly to 'Platonist'. The term 'lesbian' existed as a geographical description, no more offensive than 'Cretan' or 'Athenian'. Even in 1915 it was still so finely balanced between its two meanings as to afford Ronald Firbank one of his polished improprieties in *The Artificial Princess*.

> 'Tell me, Sir Oliver,' she demanded, 'have you ever been to Greece?'
> 'More than once,' Sir Oliver dryly replied, 'I even married, *en secondes noces*, a Lesbian. . . .'
> 'A native of Lesbos. Just fancy that!' the Baroness marvelled, appraising a passing débutante, a young girl in a mousseline robe of palest Langue de chat.[46]

Sexual inversion was no subject for amusement to the Victorians. Only in the favourite topic of educational discipline was an adult enthusiasm and vindictiveness tempered by boisterous jocularity. No prosecution followed the appearance of *The Whippingham Papers*, including three pieces by Swinburne. Had he risked issuing his long poem *The Flogging Block*, it would certainly have been regarded as a curiosity. That it would have seemed worthy of prosecution, being entirely sexless, is far from certain. Seven years before Swinburne's death, for example, there appeared a piece of fiction by an author who was to be as famous as he. It catches the vindictiveness and the sardonic amusement of Swinburne's work as 'Etoniensis', not least in the aftermath of the beating.

> In a quarter-of-an-hour Bradshaw returned, walking painfully, and bearing what to the expert's eye, are the unmistakable signs of a 'touching up', which, being interpreted, is corporal punishment.
> 'Hullo,' said White, as he appeared, 'what's all this?'
> 'How many?' inquired the statistically minded Kendal
> 'It's all through you, you idiot,' he snarled, 'I got twelve.'
> 'Twelve isn't so dusty,' said White critically.[47]

The language of the publication is sonorous: '*Whack, rap, swish!* went the weapons of justice.' Between the same covers appears a paedophile's beauty parade of girls between the ages of ten and fifteen, and an older, wasp-waisted girl wielding a whip. 'The long lash leaped out and swung round her as she circled the whip-haft over her head.'[48] After so much solemn invocation of Freud, Krafft-Ebing and the Marquis de Sade, we at last confront the Victorians – including Mary Gordon and Swinburne – on their own ground. The publication, put carefully into the hands of the nation's children, is *The Captain*, 'A Magazine for Boys and Old Boys'. The fiction, with its chortling accounts of 'touching up' and the appearance of limping victims, is 'Bradshaw's Little Story'. Its author was the young P. G. Wodehouse.

Chapter 6

Poems and Ballads

ONE afternoon, towards the end of the 1860s, the young Henry James went to the National Gallery to view Titian's 'Bacchus and Ariadne', a painting which he had seen before and particularly admired. He described to his brother William how he was standing before the great canvas when he became aware of a little man beside him, talking vivaciously to a companion. The little man had a most remarkable shock of auburn hair, 'perched on a scarce perceptible body'. Henry James recognized him, from his photograph, as Swinburne. 'I thrilled ... with the prodigy of this circumstance that I should be admiring Titian in the same breath with Mr Swinburne – that is in the same breath in which *he* admired Titian and in which I also admired *him*.'[1]

The revelation of Swinburne's alcoholic excesses and his sexual oddities is apt to obscure the greater and far more sensational role in which he appeared as the apostle of a young and revolutionary culture. By the third decade of the Victorian period it was natural to feel that the major figures of the past quarter of a century had spent their creative force. Even Pre-Raphaelitism was eighteen years old by the time that Swinburne published *Poems and Ballads*. Whether or not Swinburne was to be a greater poet than Tennyson, he was certainly very different. For better or worse, the literary initiative had passed to a new generation of which he was the pre-eminent representative. The unrequited loves of 'Locksley Hall' and *Maud*, or 'Enoch Arden' and 'Aylmer's Field', had been expressed in terms as decorous as the language of Anthony Trollope or Mrs Gaskell. Swinburne brought a new and passionate lyricism to his erotic brooding on scented hair and the 'flowers' of a heroine's nipples, to supple nudity and physical love-making.

As it happened, he admired Browning and much of Tennyson. Yet his young contemporaries saw in him a literary and political revolutionary, whose anathemas were directed both against the effete autocracy of Napoleon III and against the homespun moralizing of *In Memoriam*. To an incredulous twentieth century, Gosse recalled Swinburne and his disciples in the early 1860s:

Swinburne in the studio of some painter-friend, quivering with passion as he recited 'Itylus' or 'Félise' or 'Dolores' to a semicircle of worshippers, who were thrilled by the performance to the inmost fibre of their beings. It used to be told that at the close of one such recital the auditors were found to have slipped unconsciously to their knees. The Pre-Raphaelite ladies, in particular, were often excessively moved on these occasions, and once, at least, a crown of laurel, deftly flung by a fair hand, lighted harmoniously upon the effulgent curls of the poet.[2]

Even Matthew Arnold conceded that Swinburne was 'the favourite poet of the young men at Oxford and Cambridge'.[3]

Whether his audience thrilled to the erotic cruelty of 'Dolores' or the lesbian passion of 'Anactoria', rather than to Swinburne's hypnotic performances, may be doubted. His importance was as a symbol of genteel rebellion by the middle-class young, who did not always inquire too closely into some of the subjects which constituted that rebellion. 'He was not merely a poet, but a flag,' said Gosse, 'and not merely a flag but the Red Flag incarnate.'[4]

The crusade over which the flag flew embraced all the arts, its banners proclaiming that the pure creative process must free itself of the petty considerations of bourgeois moralizing. Defending Meredith's poetry in the *Spectator* in 1862, Swinburne had insisted: 'If some poetry, not without merit of its kind, has at times dealt in dogmatic morality, it is all the worse and all the weaker for that.'[5] His clear-cut views upon what later became known as 'Art for Art's sake' were so evident that he presented a ready subject for caricature. One of the guests at the dinner to mark Dickens's departure for his American tour in 1867 was George Augustus Sala, whose facility for mildly sadistic pornography and whose capacity for drinking were both a match for Swinburne's. 'George Augustus Sala got very drunk as usual,' noted Hardman, 'and conducted himself with great indecorum.'[6] While still able to stand and articulate, Sala had delivered a brisk survey of modern verse, comparing Swinburne and Martin Tupper, the most remorselessly dogmatic poet of his kind. Sala gave thanks for poetry 'in the name of the clever (but I cannot say moral) Mr Swinburne, and of the moral (but I cannot say clever) Mr Tupper'.[7] It was a succinct expression of the general view.

Swinburne acquired an easy fame, or notoriety, in the 1860s from the reputation of his poetry, from the photographs which his admirers were able to buy, even from his portrayal in popular fiction. He was greatly annoyed by the caricature of him in Mortimer Collins's

Two Plunges for a Pearl in 1871, but a more memorable portrayal was in Meredith's *Sandra Belloni*. The novel first appeared in 1864 as *Emilia in England*, containing the character of a red-headed youth who was 'of the blood of dukes and would be a famous poet'.

It was also to Swinburne's advantage, as the figurehead of an artistic movement, that his associations were more than merely literary and parochially English. He allied himself, in this respect, with both the writing of France and the paintings of his own contemporaries. With William Michael Rossetti he produced *Notes on the Royal Academy Exhibition, 1868*, in which he championed the painting of Dante Gabriel Rossetti and Frederick Sandys. He also wrote a short poem to accompany Sandys's 'Cleopatra Dissolving the Pearl', which appeared as an illustration in the *Cornhill*. Sandys returned the compliment by taking Swinburne's 'St Dorothy' as the subject for his own painting of that title.

In the Royal Academy exhibition, Swinburne particularly commended the eroticism of female beauty in such paintings as Rossetti's 'Lady Lilith'. He responded readily to the sensuous self-indulgence, the voluptuous indolence of the girl slouching in her chair and languidly drawing her splendid mane of hair through her comb.

Clothed in soft white garments, she draws out through a comb the heavy mass of hair like thick spun gold to fullest length; her head leans back half sleepily, superb and satiate with its own beauty; the eyes are languid, without love in them or hate; the sweet luxurious mouth has the patience of pleasure fulfilled and complete, the warm repose of passion sure of its delight. Outside, as seen in the glimmering mirror, there is full summer; the deep and glowing leaves have drunk in the whole strength of the sun. . . . For this serene and sublime sorceress there is no life but of the body; with spirit (if spirit there be) she can dispense. Were it worth her while for any word to divide those terrible tender lips, she too might say with the hero of the most perfect and exquisite book of modern times – *Mademoiselle de Maupin* – '*Je trouve la terre aussi belle que le ciel, et je pense que la correction de la forme est la vertu.*'[8]

Swinburne wrote, in part, for those who would depend upon his description, rather than upon a visual reproduction, for the subtler qualities of the picture. Yet his pure portraiture offers an ideal of feminine beauty which is particularly his own, whether the woman is broodingly sensuous or merely sulky, whether proud or merely impatient. In the same exhibition, for instance, he dwelt upon his friend Sandys's picture 'Proud Maisie', a portrait of an imperious

young woman pulling a strand of her hair between her teeth.
Swinburne was moved by her 'rich, ripe, angry beauty', and by the
promise of sexual ferocity as 'she draws one warm long lock of
curling hair through her full and moulded lips, biting it with bared
bright teeth, which add something of a tiger's charm to the sleepy
and couching passion of her fair face'.[9] The fierce, animal quality of
such girls was also a preoccupation of his poetry at the time. In 'Laus
Veneris', for instance, the male victim falls prey to the girl, as
panther, 'Is snapped upon by the sweet mouth and bleeds,/His head
far down the hot sweet throat of her.' For better or worse, such
enthusiasms were far removed from the Tennysonian lament of the
pious lover in poems like 'Locksley Hall'.

> O my cousin, shallow-hearted! O my Amy, mine no more!
> O the dreary, dreary moorland! O the barren, barren shore!....

In his energetic dismissal of such earlier poetry, of what Alfred
Austin called 'idylls of the farm and the mill, of the dining-room and
the deanery', Swinburne stirred the unease of his elders, even
before the controversy over *Poems and Ballads*.[10] On the publication of *Atalanta in Calydon*, Tennyson himself had written to
Swinburne, generously praising his metrical invention. Yet even in
a poem so comparatively innocuous as this, Tennyson was caught
between personal reservations over the work and a desire not to
seem fossilized in his attitude to artistic developments. 'I had some
strong objections to parts of it,' he confessed to Swinburne, 'but
these I think have been modified by a re-perusal, and at any rate I
daresay you would not care to hear them.'[11] Browning, too, had
expressed his reservations over such of the poems which made up
Poems and Ballads as he had heard Swinburne recite before publication. 'I thought them moral mistakes,' he told Monckton Milnes,
'redeemed by much intellectual ability.' Browning hoped that such
pieces were not typical of the forthcoming book.[12] Ruskin was more
forthright, even though expressing his sympathy to Swinburne. 'I
cannot help you, nor understand you,' he wrote, adding the hope
that the young poet might eventually see the error of his ways and
that time would effect 'a change in the method and spirit of what you
do'.[13]

To Swinburne, secure and confident in the admiration of contemporaries, such warnings were the querulous mutterings of an older
generation, some of whom he admired in his turn but few of whom
could be expected to welcome wholeheartedly the change which

was coming. At best, they seemed paternal and solicitous; at worst, they sounded like men of established reputation anxious to maintain their own positions while not seeming to be out of step with the new fashion.

If Swinburne were to be alarmed by warnings of any sort, they were more likely to be those which came from his friends and near-contemporaries. George Meredith was no prude in this matter, his own novel *The Ordeal of Richard Feverel* having proved unacceptable at first to the circulating libraries. Yet he wrote to Swinburne suggesting tactfully and persistently that some expurgation of *Poems and Ballads* might be wise.

> As to the Poems – if they are not yet in the press, do be careful of getting your reputation firmly grounded; for I have heard 'low mutterings' already from the Lion of British prudery; and I, who love your verse, would play savagely with a knife among the proofs for the sake of your fame; and because I want to see you take the first place, as you may if you will.[14]

Even Dante Gabriel Rossetti had grown uneasy over the effect of Swinburne's poems, collected in a volume, upon the general readership of the 1860s. He found some relief in the fact that the poet chose to issue the comparatively unobjectionable *Atalanta in Calydon* in the previous year, thus forestalling the worst criticism, or at least delaying it for the time being.

> I really believe on the whole that this is the best thing to bring out first. It is calculated to put people in better humour for the others, which, when they do come, will still make a few not even over particular hairs stand on end, to say nothing of other erections equally obvious. I tremble for the result of your reading Baudelaire's suppressed poems, the crop of which read I expect you to be in fine flower, not to say fruit, by the time I reach London. If so, and these new revelations are to be printed too, I warn you that the public will not be able to digest them, and that the paternal purse will have to stand the additional expense of an emetic presented gratis with each copy to relieve the outraged British nature.[15]

In 1864, William Michael Rossetti had found a copy of the rare first edition of Baudelaire's *Fleurs du mal*, which contained the poems later known as *Les Epaves*. These had been condemned as obscene by the French courts when the first edition was the subject of a prosecution. As Dante Gabriel judged, these pieces were the only stimulants lacking to make *Poems and Ballads* the most outrageous collection of its kind. William Michael, knowing his friend's enthusiasm for Baudelaire, made him a present of the book in the autumn of 1864.

Dante Gabriel Rossetti was to grow increasingly uneasy over the manner of Swinburne's poetry during the remainder of the decade. By 1870 he could remain silent no longer. He was not one of those who objected to Swinburne's expressed hatred of the French emperor, the hope of seeing 'Buonaparte the bastard/Kick heels with his throat in a rope.' Yet, when Swinburne chose to ridicule Napoleon III, and Christ by implication, in 'The Saviour of Society', even Rossetti could no longer keep his misgivings to himself.

I cannot but think absolutely that a poet like yourself belongs of right to a larger circle of readers than this treatment of universal feelings can include. You know how free I am myself from any dogmatic belief; but I can most sincerely say that ... I do myself feel that the supreme nobility of Christ's character should exempt it from being used – not as a symbolic parallel to other noble things and persons in relation with which dogmatists might object to its use – but certainly in context of this kind with anything so utterly ignoble as this.[16]

Rossetti wrote at length, imploring his friend, 'Do, do, my dear Swinburne, withdraw these sonnets,' and concluding, 'This is my birthday, by the bye. Do make me the birthday gift I ask of you.'[17]

So far as some of the pieces intended for *Poems and Ballads* were concerned, Swinburne was writing for a less fastidious audience than Rossetti represented in his later protest. Among his correspondents there had appeared George Powell, an Etonian and Oxonian Welsh squire who shared Swinburne's curiosity about institutional sadism. Powell, the proprietor of Nant Eos, near Aberystwyth, encouraged Swinburne's interest in the punishment of his successors at Eton, and his ambition to obtain a photograph of the flogging-block. He was also the recipient of Swinburne's complaints about the after-effects of drinking bouts. Ignoring Samuel Butler's easy assumption that 'The man with a headache does not pretend to be a different person from the man who got drunk', Swinburne complained of what he called vaguely 'bilious influenza', and swore to Powell that the sickness he suffered was God torturing him with all the deliberate relish of a cosmic Marquis de Sade.[18]

While Powell encouraged their mutual Sadean interest, which was to colour so much of *Poems and Ballads*, Charles Augustus Howell provided another morbid influence to counterbalance the gentle and benign reproaches of the Rossettis. Howell, described bluntly by Gosse as 'an arrant rascal', and regarded by William Morris as a thief, was an Anglo-Portuguese, three years younger than Swinburne.[19] His reputation was obscure and, in some views, distinctly shady. He was reputed to have been a diplomat, a diver for treasure, and even to have lived as a sheik in north Africa. For the time being he followed the more mundane occupation of secretary to Ruskin and, as an acquaintance of the Rossettis, he had superintended Lizzie's exhumation and the retrieval of Dante Gabriel's poems from his wife's coffin.

More positively than Powell, this new friend encouraged Swinburne's sadistic writing, both in poetry and prose. After writing 'Dolores', the litany of 'Our Lady of Pain', which was to cause more bother than any other piece in *Poems and Ballads*, its author wrote gleefully to Howell, 'Tu le vois, Justine, je bande – oh! putain, que tu vas souffrir!'[20] The friendship grew warmer, Swinburne composing flagellation fantasies for which he invited Howell to find illustrations, and also to respond with similar pieces of his own. Swinburne, even signing himself 'A. F. de Sade', contributed his recognizable share of material, as he had done in his correspondence with Monckton Milnes.

Unfortunately, Howell lacked both the wealth and the gentlemanly instincts of Monckton Milnes. When times grew hard for him, in the 1870s, he sold Swinburne's foolish and injudicious outpourings to the pawnbroker in whose house he lodged. To his dismay and anger, the poet found himself politely but firmly held to ransom by George Redway, a bookseller into whose hands the papers came. They would be returned in exchange for the copyright of one of Swinburne's more respectable works. It was not, technically, blackmail since Redway had bought the manuscripts and they were his property. In moral terms, however, Swinburne's indiscretion had laid him open to the blackmailer's art. Howell himself was to come to as bad an end as most Victorian popular moralists could wish. He was picked up from the gutter outside a Chelsea public house in April 1890. He died of 'pneumonia' in hospital a few days later. T. J. Wise added with relish that the true cause of death was that he had been found in the gutter with his throat cut and a ten-shilling piece wedged between his teeth.[21]

*   *   *

Within this web of strangely contrasting friendships, Swinburne prepared his major volume of poems for publication. Baudelaire, particularly in the condemned poems of *Les Epaves*, was the last, and potentially the greatest, influence upon him. Among these pieces, Edmund Gosse considered 'Les Femmes damnées' as having the most obvious appeal for Swinburne.[22]

> A la pale clarté des lampes languissantes,
> Sur de profonds coussins tout impregnés d'odeur....

It is the supreme Baudelairean portrayal of lesbian love, the lazy passion of Delphine and Hippolyte in a setting of casual opulence more specifically detailed than the suggestiveness of *Mademoiselle de Maupin.*

> In a faint glimmering where the lamps burn low,
> Sprawled on deep cushions that are rich with scents,
> Hippolyte dreams of such intense caressing
> As lifts the veil of her young innocence.
>
> Eyes clouded by the shock of experience,
> She looks like a traveller for a long-lost sky,
> Head turned to the blue horizons
> Of a morning that has long passed by.
>
> Slow tears falling from deadened eyes,
> Fatigue and weariness and pleasure's sadness,
> Her arms subdued, like weapons cast aside,
> Showing in all a fragile loveliness.
>
> Lying at her feet, calmly but full of joy,
> Delphine with eager eyes gloats over her,
> Like a strong animal that guards its prey,
> Once having used its teeth to mark her there.
>
> Beauty in strength kneels before beauty frail
> And in her pride voluptuously savours
> The wine of triumph, moving to the other girl
> As if to take the reward now due as hers.
>
> She seeks out in the eyes of her pale victim
> Those silent anthems sensual pleasure sings,
> That gratitude, both endless and sublime,
> Which eyes express as vividly as sighings....

Swinburne fell eagerly upon the theme of lesbian passion both in his fiction and, for instance, in such poems as 'Anactoria', the address of Sappho to her lover. Yet, as so often in the collection of *Poems and Ballads*, the subtle and pungent eroticism of Gautier and Baudelaire becomes the petty sadism of biting and scratching as a substitute for the greater expression of sexual passion. In such terms he makes the most famous lover of her own sex speak.

> Ah that my lips were tuneless lips, but pressed
> To the bruised blossom of thy scourged white breast!
> Ah that my mouth for Muses' milk were fed
> On the sweet blood thy sweet small wounds had bled!
> That with my tongue I felt them, and could taste
> The faint flakes from thy bosom to the waist!
> That I could drink thy veins as wine, and eat
> Thy breasts like honey! that from face to feet
> Thy body were abolished and consumed,
> And in my flesh thy very flesh entombed!

It is tempting to dismiss even the extravagance of the last four lines as a ludicrous echo of the Cannibal Club charades at Bertolini's Hotel, rather than a consuming passion of the ancient world. The truth is, of course, that Swinburne had deliberately chosen a grander manner of utterance, appropriate to an admirer of Aeschylus, rather than the more obviously modern and intimate tone of Baudelaire. As the poet of eroticism, Swinburne achieved the violence of love at the cost of losing the subtlety of Baudelaire's private glimpses in such pieces as 'Tristesses de la lune'.

> To-night the moon is more languidly dreaming,
> Like a beautiful woman on cushions reclining
> With a caress for the contours of her breasts, discreet
> And light, in the moments before sleep....

Nor does Swinburne attempt, for instance, the lingering appreciation of a particular woman's beauty in the close, confidential style of Baudelaire in 'Les Bijoux'.

> My beloved was naked, and, knowing my taste,
> Wore on her only her sonorous jewels,
> Giving her triumph and splendid opulence,
> Like Moorish slave-women in their happiness....

Swinburne's nearest approach to such loving description is, perhaps, not in his poetry at all but in his accounts of the individual women who sat as models to Rossetti or Sandys.

Baudelaire was demonstrably a late, powerful influence upon Swinburne's poems collected in 1866, yet this applied only in respect of some of Baudelaire's subject matter. Swinburne's essay in the *Spectator* of 6 September 1862, for instance, shows an enthusiasm for Baudelaire's poetry of sexual appreciation but not much for his other great theme of fascination and revulsion in the face of metropolitan or urban landscapes, in 'Le Spleen' or 'Le Crépuscule du soir'. So far as Swinburne's critics were concerned, it was a sufficient lapse of moral taste to have allied himself with Baudelaire's interest in morbid sexuality. Merely to have avoided the other moral excesses was hardly a sign of sobriety.

*   *   *

Into *Poems and Ballads* Swinburne put sixty-two poems, which represented his major output in the first thirty years of his life. He had, of course, published *Atalanta* and *Chastelard*, but it was upon his collected individual poems that he was most likely to be judged as the successor of Tennyson and Browning. In the light of the indignant response to the volume, it has to be conceded that about a dozen of the poems dealt with subjects which were unlikely to find favour in the drawing-rooms of the 1860s. Indeed, represented with sufficient vividness they would hardly have been more welcome a century later. 'Phaedra' deals with the incestuous passion of the heroine for her stepson; 'Les Noyades' describes the fate of a man and a woman tied in a naked embrace to be drowned for their crimes; 'Anactoria' is Sappho's violent declaration of lesbian passion; 'Hermaphroditus' and 'Fragoletta' celebrate the parallel theme of bisexualism; 'Dolores' becomes the litany of sadism.

> Cold eyelids that hide like a jewel
>   Hard eyes that grow soft for an hour;
> The heavy white limbs, and the cruel
>   Red mouth like a venomous flower;
> When these are gone by with their glories,
>   What shall rest of thee then, what remain,
> O mystic and sombre Dolores,
>   Our Lady of Pain?

Not only reading but reading aloud was a pastime of the mid-Victorian family, making it doubtful whether its members would relish chanting Swinburne's assurances that his goddess was the child of Priapus by Libitina. Nor would such readers be likely to feel Swinburne's enthusiasm for some of his idol's aphrodisiac charms.

> Could you hurt me, sweet lips, though I hurt you?
>   Men touch them, and change in a trice
> The lilies and languors of virtue
>   For the raptures and roses of vice;

> Those lie where thy foot on the floor is,
>   These crown and caress thee and chain,
> O splendid and sterile Dolores,
>   Our Lady of Pain.

Had Swinburne prepared a collection of sixty-two poems of which a dozen were in this vein while the rest consisted of lyric virtuosity coupled with unexceptionable Tennysonian moralizing the matter would have been more straightforward. But even in such poems as 'A Ballad of Life' and 'A Ballad of Death', with their Pre-Raphaelite pictorialism and their almost Spenserean lushness, there were passages detailing a girl's breasts and nipples in a manner calculated to bring a family reading to an abrupt halt.

> Ah! that my tears filled all her woven hair
> And all the hollow bosom of her gown –
> Ah! that my tears ran down
> Even to the place where many kisses were,
> Even where her parted breast-flowers have place,
> Even where they are cloven apart....

At the same time, in other poems of the collection, Swinburne showed himself to be the supreme lyric poet to whom no objection could be taken. Readers sheltered by their ignorance of its origins were enchanted by 'Itylus'. It took its place in the *Golden Treasury* of F. T. Palgrave, recommended reading for those innocents who never need be told that it was about a girl who was raped and whose tongue was cut out, and her sister who avenged this by killing her own son and making his father eat him in a stew. Similarly, those who did not delve too deeply into a poem like the 'Hymn to Proserpine: After the Proclamation in Rome of the Christian Faith', were able to savour its poetic accomplishment in the terms which seemed most attractive to them.

Thou hast conquered, O pale Galilean; the world has grown grey from thy
   breath;
We have drunken of things Lethean, and fed on the fullness of death.
Laurel is green for a season, and love is sweet for a day;
But love grows bitter with treason, and laurel outlives not May.
Sleep, shall we sleep after all? for the world is not sweet in the end;
For the old faiths loosen and fall, the new years ruin and rend.
Fate is a sea without shore, and the soul is a rock that abides;
But her ears are vexed with the roar and her face with the foam of the tides.
O lips that the live blood faints in, the leavings of racks and rods!
O ghastly glories of saints, dead limbs of gibbeted Gods!

Aeschylean or not, Swinburne had shown himself capable of a rhetoric as well as a lyricism which clung in the minds and memories of his readers. There was, as it were, an ineradicable force to the rhythm of such poems as 'The Hymn to Proserpine', as well as a power of language. This, like the elegaic cadences of 'Itylus' with all their plaintive insistence, made him, in the literal sense, the most memorable poet of his generation.

By contrast with the exuberance of language and the intoxication of rhythm which he showed, the idylls of Tennyson in his middle fifties seemed lame and insipid. Swinburne's verse had power and drama, a natural attraction for the young men of his own generation. There was a modernity of subject as well as technique, a style of description in such poems as 'Laus Veneris' which might as easily have belonged to the twentieth century as to the nineteenth. Here, at least, the caricature of Swinburne as a facile lyricist with nothing to say was easily proved false.

> Outside it must be winter among men;
> For at the gold bars of the gates again
>   I heard all night and all the hours of it
> The wind's wet wings and fingers drip with rain.
>
> Knights gather, riding sharp for cold; I know
> The ways and woods are strangled with the snow;
>   And with short song the maidens spin and sit
> Until Christ's birthnight, lily-like, arow.

In the description of wind and weather, the verses have a terse and contemporary quality which reminds one, say, of:

> The empty winds are creaking and the oak
> Splatters and splatters on the cenotaph.

From such instances it might be hard to decide which of the two was more recent, though one is Swinburne and the other Robert Lowell's 'The Quaker Graveyard in Nantucket'.

*   *   *

Apart from considerations of the excellence or novelty of Swinburne's poems, there was the practical difficulty of finding a publisher for a collection which included such dark gems as 'Dolores' and 'Anactoria'. Moxon's had published *Atalanta* and *Chastelard* but their representative, J. B. Payne, had refused to take on *Love's Cross-Currents*. This was in part because Swinburne wished to publish the novel anonymously, or at least pseudonymously. At the same time, there was a growing nervousness on the part of the firm as to where their young prodigy might be leading them.

It was not common for a Victorian publisher of repute to find himself prosecuted for the obscenity or the blasphemy of anything he issued. Yet the original Edward Moxon had stood in the dock of the Central Criminal Court in 1841 charged with blasphemous libel for his edition of the *Poetical Works of P. B. Shelley*. It was hardly a typical case. Henry Hetherington, an avowed atheist, had been sent to gaol for a blasphemous publication and had thereupon laid an information against Moxon, the most eminent publisher in question, for issuing *Queen Mab* unexpurgated. Moxon was convicted but merely required to find sureties for future good behaviour. None the less, his successors in the firm remembered his example.[23]

To have chosen a firm other than Moxon might have been difficult for Swinburne. In 1864, Dante Gabriel Rossetti had done his best to interest Alexander Macmillan in publishing *Atalanta*, *Chastelard* and the individual shorter poems. The reply was unpromising. 'I certainly thought it a work of genius,' Macmillan explained, 'but some parts of it were very *queer* – very. Whether the public could be expected to like them was doubtful.'[24] By September, the matter was decided. 'Don't swear more than you can help,' wrote Rossetti to Swinburne, announcing Macmillan's rejection of the poems, 'I mentioned the St Dorothy as an unobjectionable poem, but Mac had some funky reminiscences of the allusions to Venus, so it really seemed a bad lookout.'[25]

It seemed that if *Poems and Ballads* was to be issued, Swinburne would have to swallow his indignation over *Love's Cross-Currents* and make his peace with Moxon's. Monckton Milnes, after Macmillan's rejection, had done his best to interest John Murray in the poems, but without success. Even Moxon's, proposing to issue the book in the spring of 1866, remained cautious. As a test of public reaction, 'Laus Veneris' was first issued as a booklet on its own. It was arguably the mid-point of Swinburne's work in its power to offend susceptible readers and therefore a good indicator of likely trouble. But 'Laus Veneris' produced no paeans of outrage, simply because it was not to the moderately offensive poems but to those which were most so that the critics reacted.

A final warning voice was raised to Swinburne in the gentle and maternal reproof of Pauline Trevelyan. News of Swinburne's conduct had reached Wallington in letters from Josephine Butler, better known for her campaign against the Contagious Diseases Acts, and from William Bell Scott. Swinburne protested to Pauline Trevelyan that such reports were slanderous and without the least foundation. Half convinced, she begged him to be more careful and more discreet in the future, not least over the reputation which his published poems would give him.

If it is only for the sake of living down evil reports, do be wise in which of your lyrics you publish. Do let it be a book that can be really loved and read and learned by heart, and become part and parcel of the English language, and be on every one's table without being received under protest by timid people. There are no doubt people who would be glad to be able to say that it is not fit to be read. It is not worth while for the sake of two or three poems to risk the widest circulation of the whole. You have sailed near enough to the wind in all conscience in having painted such a character for a hero as your Chastelard, slave to a passion for a woman he despises. . . . Don't give people a handle against you now. And do mind what you say for the sake of all to whom your fame is dear, and who are looking forward to your career with hope and interest.[26]

But what place could there be for such gentle and anxious wisdom in the new moral and cultural rebellion of which her dear Algernon was the figurehead? By the virtuous standards of Wallington, *Chastelard* had sailed close to the wind, and *Chastelard* would prove mere pap for infants by contrast with what was coming next. Pauline Trevelyan was, at least, spared the sorrow of reading *Poems and Ballads* in all its violent, erotic splendour. She and her husband set off for Europe in April 1866. By early May she was gravely ill at Neuchâtel and there, on 13 May, she died. Their old friend Ruskin, who sat beside her bed on that day, reported that one of her last thoughts was for Swinburne, about whom she asked anxiously, inquiring if Ruskin thought him capable of the evil attributed to his conduct. He earnestly reassured her on this point. The last struggle began, the rattle in her throat growing fainter over an hour or more, until Swinburne's 'good angel' lay dead, leaving him to his critics and his own dark gods.

*   *   *

Of the trial publication of 'Laus Veneris' Swinburne later remarked, 'Moxon, I well remember, was terribly nervous in those days.'[27] The booklet was issued in January 1866 and, as time passed without the appearance of hostile criticism or of policemen with warrants for the arrest of the publishers in the aristocratic calm of Dover Street, the firm's courage was reinforced. *Poems and Ballads* was printed and announced as due for publication in May. Then there was a silence. Swinburne discovered a large number of misprints in a pre-publication copy and there was a delay while these were attended to. It was July before the volume was ready at last.

In the meantime, Swinburne had had one useful piece of publicity when Monckton Milnes, now Lord Houghton, took the chair at the Anniversary Dinner of the Royal Literary Fund on 2 May. He insisted that the reply, to the toast of 'Literature', should be given by Swinburne. Here, in full view of the press and its readers, the young poet was proclaimed as 'The representative of that future generation. . . . He alone, of his age, has shown the power to succeed in the highest walks of poetry.'[28] Swinburne drank in the praise and made a spirited reply, presenting a literary manifesto which dared his listeners in the fashionable elegance of Willis's Rooms in St James's to disagree that, by implication at least, Swinburne was the new messiah of literature and Baudelaire had been his prophet. He need not have worried about the reception of his speech. His audience, including Anthony Trollope, Charles Kingsley and Leslie Stephen, cheered his oration repeatedly and the evening ended in the agreeable warmth of personal triumph. Swinburne's behaviour on such occasions was to prove unpredictable, however, and not merely to be determined by the amount he had drunk. He was subsequently at a dinner where someone was so unwise as to ask him to reply to a toast on behalf of 'The Press'. The expectant guests were unnerved to see Swinburne get to his feet, fix them with a gaze of fury, and shriek at them: 'The Press is a damnable institution, a horrible institution, a beastly institution!' Exhausted by this outburst, he sank back into his chair and closed his eyes, as if lapsing into instant unconsciousness.[29]

Such public scandals lay in the future. For the time being, the triumph of Swinburne's latest appearance was a prelude to the publication of his book, which was at length issued in July. Copies were sent out for presentation or review, including one to Victor Hugo. It was late in the month and the first major reviews of the book would be in the weekly papers on 4 August. On that day, Swinburne went to Moxon's and met J. B. Payne. The two men walked down Dover Street together and along Piccadilly.

Swinburne stopped to buy a copy of the *Saturday Review*. He glanced at it and burst at once into shrill anger and hysterical distress. Payne, naturally anxious to avoid a scene in the street, shepherded the shrieking poet into a café and tried to calm him with a cup of tea. It was, by any of Swinburne's standards, a futile restorative. His language and manner sent the waiters scurrying for shelter, while Payne begged him to continue his expletives in French, for the sake of all concerned.

Then Swinburne showed him the cause of the outburst. It was a review of *Poems and Ballads* by John Morley. Morley was almost Swinburne's opposite, a level-headed journalist who edited the *Fortnightly Review* and the *Pall Mall Gazette*. Chief Secretary for Ireland and Lord President of the Council, he combined the roles of Liberal politician and biographer as author of the standard *Life of Gladstone*. As a literary critic he was most influential in editing the English Men of Letters series. In his *Saturday Review* article, he was the sensible, intelligent adult reproving a dirty-minded nursery prodigy. The review was acute and devastating with the verve and precision of a skilled prosecutor. It was all the more damning because Morley professed to dislike prigs and puritans as much as Swinburne. But the phrases of condemnation stood out starkly. 'At all events he deserves credit for the audacious courage with which he has revealed to the world a mind all aflame with the feverish carnality of a schoolboy over the dirtiest passages in Lemprière. It is not every poet who would ask us to go hear him tuning his lyre in a stye.' There was worse to come. Swinburne was 'either the vindictive and scornful apostle of a crushing iron-shod despair, or else he is the libidinous laureate of a pack of satyrs'.

Morley was no middle-aged reactionary, being an almost exact contemporary of Swinburne. His common sense, moreover, was his most deadly weapon.

If he were a rebel against the fat-headed Philistines and poor-blooded Puritans who insist that all poetry should be such as may be wisely placed in the hands of girls of eighteen, and is fit for the use of Sunday schools, he would have all wise and enlarged readers on his side. But there is an enormous difference between an attempt to revivify among us the grand old pagan conceptions of Joy, and an attempt to glorify all the bestial delights that the subtleness of Greek depravity was able to contrive.

The review continually hinted at 'the mixed vileness and childishness' of Swinburne's enthusiasms without specifying the nature of 'the unnamed lusts of sated wantons' in which he revelled. Yet for all his dismissal of philistine and puritan squeamishness, Morley never quite severed his attachment to their values.

The only comfort about the present volume is that such a piece as 'Anactoria' will be unintelligible to a great many people, and so will the fevered folly of 'Hermaphroditus', as well as much else that is nameless and abominable. Perhaps if Mr Swinburne can a second and a third time find a respectable publisher willing to issue a volume of the same stamp, crammed with pieces which many a professional vendor of filthy prints might blush to sell if only he knew what they meant, English readers will gradually acquire a truly delightful familiarity with these unspeakable foulnesses; and a lover will be able to present to his mistress a copy of Mr Swinburne's latest verses with a happy confidence that she will have no difficulty in seeing the point of every allusion to Sappho or the pleasing Hermaphroditus, or the embodiment of anything else that is loathsome and horrible.

For all his protests of support for Swinburne in the battle against unenlightened Grundyism, Morley was as fearful as the puritans themselves that such poems as 'Faustine' might become the subject of 'a drawing-room discussion'. If Morley took such exception to the book, Swinburne had little to hope from the gauntlet of the weekly critics. On the same day, Robert Buchanan, foe of Swinburne and the Pre-Raphaelite poets alike, denounced *Poems and Ballads* in the *Athenaeum*. He found the book redolent of every disreputable locale, the poems themselves showing 'evidence of having been inspired in Holywell Street, composed on the parade at Brighton, and touched up in the Jardin Mabile'.[30] As for their author, added Buchanan, 'Here, in fact, we have Gito, seated in the tub of Diogenes, conscious of the filth and whining at the stars.' Gito was the homosexual favourite in the *Satyricon* of Petronius and it was perhaps as well for J. B. Payne that his companion chose to look first at the *Saturday Review* rather than the *Athenaeum*. Buchanan concluded that even apart from the morally repulsive subject matter, Swinburne had not the least ability as a poet. The resulting pieces were therefore 'prurient trash'.

Throughout the autumn of 1866, Swinburne was the subject of reviews, similar or worse. The *Pall Mall Gazette* described the book under the title of 'Swinburne's Folly', on 20 August, and the *Globe* on 29 November accused him of 'poetic Billingsgate of the choicest description' when he attempted to defend his poems. Yet even on 4 August it was clear that a storm of quite unexpected ferocity was about to engulf Swinburne and the firm of Moxon. To the hostile reviews were added rumours which were far more disturbing. The book was to be dealt with in *The Times* by Eneas Sweetland Dallas, whom Rossetti mocked amiably in a limerick

> Poor old Dallus!
> All along of his phallus,
> Must he come to the gallows?[31]

According to Sir William Hardman, who knew Dallas well, the latter 'detests the youthful poet [Swinburne] and his works.... He had written a crushing review for *The Times,* in which both Poet and Publisher were held up to the execration of all decent people. The article was in type, when a private hint was given to Moxon, in order that he might, if so inclined, disconnect himself from the bawdry'.[32] It was also rumoured that Dallas's review would be accompanied by a demand, presumably in an editorial, requiring the prosecution of the publisher of *Poems and Ballads.*

Payne and his partners at Moxon's might have braved a single assault of this kind. Yet the attacks of the weeklies and the threats of *The Times* were next reinforced by a separate demand that the Attorney-General should indict the firm for obscene libel, a demand which came this time from J. M. Ludlow, one of the leaders of the Christian Socialist movement.[33] Memories of *Queen Mab* and the conviction of Edward Moxon in 1841 were vividly recalled. If *Poems and Ballads* became the subject of an obscenity prosecution, it seemed very likely that the verdict would go against the book. In 1876, in one of the literary feuds which characterized his middle years, Swinburne as contributor got the *Examiner* sued for a libellous piece denouncing Robert Buchanan. Charles Russell, Buchanan's counsel, began to read out passages from *Poems and Ballads* to the jury. 'Mr Justice Archibald thought that there had been quite enough of that. There could be no doubt that they were poems written in a style that was very much to be deprecated.'[34] Russell then added that Swinburne had degraded his poetry 'by loading it with a beastly sensualism, and by adopting the indecent garbage of the French Baudelaire'.[35] This was a view commended by Mr Justice Archibald in his summing-up, when he remarked that if *Poems and Ballads* 'had not been written at all, or had been committed to the flames it would have been much the better'.[36] On 5 August 1866, Payne anticipated such judicial condemnations in his own case. He informed Swinburne that Moxon had now withdrawn the book from circulation.

*   *   *

Swinburne himself had received his share of obloquy, his postbag bringing threats of castration and branding, as he told Howell. Yet he had been quite unprepared for any action so precipitate as Payne's, taken 'without consulting, without warning, and without compensation', as he insisted.[37] The Rossetti brothers hurried round to Dover Street and endeavoured to make Payne resist the demands for the book's suppression. 'They reported on their return that the publisher was distracted with terror of the Public Prosecutor, and desired nothing so much as to be rid of the poet and all his friends.'[38]

In the whole matter, as Swinburne later remarked, Lord Houghton strove to remain neutral. But Houghton was on holiday at Vichy and such advice as he might have given in this crisis was not available. The poet turned instead to Lord Lytton, to whom he wrote on the day after his book's withdrawal. Four days later, on 10 August, he had accepted an invitation to stay with Lytton at Knebworth and warned him of the problem over his book.

> I have no right to trouble you with my affairs, but I cannot resist the temptation to trespass so far upon your kindness as to ask what course you would recommend me to take in such a case. I am resolved to cancel nothing, and (of course) to transfer my books to any other publisher I can find. I am told by lawyers that I might claim legal redress for a distinct violation of contract on Messrs Moxon's part, but I do not wish to drag the matter before a law court.[39]

On 17 August, Swinburne went down to take counsel at Knebworth. 'He looks 16,' wrote Lytton, 'a pale, sickly boy, with some nervous complaint like St Vitus' dance.'[40] During the next week, Lytton set about the task of finding a more courageous publisher than Moxon to take on the book. It was of no use applying to such firms as Macmillan or John Murray, who had been reluctant enough even before the storm of hostile reviews. Yet, within a week, acting through his friend Joseph Knight, Lytton had produced a willing successor to Moxon. This was John Camden Hotten, 'that somewhat notorious tradesman', as Edmund Gosse described him.[41] To match Hotten, Swinburne chose as a go-between in matters of business the melancholy, sinister figure of Charles Augustus Howell.

The lists of 'Useful and Amusing Books' or 'Popular and Interesting Books' issued by Hotten from his premises at 74–5 Piccadilly seemed, superficially, conventional enough. There were Shakespeare and military history, the Book of Common Prayer, death-warrants of the famous, cookery books, *Joe Miller's Jests,* the works of Mark Twain and Nathaniel Hawthorne. But he was not the publisher of all these, merely the retailer, and the books which he actually produced were a more selective and curious batch, advertised with circumspection.

One of Hotten's specialities was contemporary American literature, which had the great advantage that it was ill protected by the law of international copyright. Hotten, ever the happy pirate, looted it eagerly, fastening on Walt Whitman and Nathaniel Hawthorne and even publishing Mark Twain's collected journalism as *Eye Openers* before it appeared in the United States.[42] Yet Hotten had an even more risky line of business, which he ran with great discretion from his Piccadilly premises, supplying the wealthy with erotica while avoiding conflict with the law. His publications in this line included Payne Knight's *Worship of Priapus,* John Wilkes's condemned poem *An Essay on Woman,* and a collection of Thomas Rowlandson's copulatory cartoons under the title of *Pretty Little Games.*[43]

Poems and Ballads, as well as Swinburne's other books taken over from Moxon, would be published openly, though Hotten and Howell must have seen how useful Swinburne could be to the more private side of the business. Among these masterpieces, there was one species which outsold the rest, represented by titles like: *The Merry Order of St Bridget: Personal Recollections of the Use of the Rod* by Margaret Anson and *Flagellation and the Flagellants: A History of the Rod* by the Reverend William Cooper, BA. Both books were, in fact, the work of James Glass Bertram, a marine economist whose public reputation rested on a very different title: *The Harvest of the Sea: A Contribution to the Natural and Economic History of the British Food Fishes.* A retired subaltern of the Queen's Royal Regiment, St George H. Stock, produced a novel *The Romance of Chastisement,* while Hotten himself claimed to have found seven more books in the library of the late and great social historian, H. T. Buckle. These were said to include *An Exhibition of Female Flagellants, Madame Birchini's Dance,* and *Lady Bumtickler's Revels: A Comic Opera.* The claim that they had been found in Buckle's collection was rubbish, according to Hotten's customer and friend Henry Spencer Ashbee. None the less, they were duly published under the portentous collective title of 'The Library Illustrative of Social Progress'.[44]

Given the voracious public appetite for erotic – or at least curious

– literature of this sort, it is easy to see why Hotten and Howell should have regarded Swinburne as such a marketable author. He had already supplied Howell with some extremely injudicious manuscripts. These, or specimens of the same kind, were soon to be in Hotten's hands. Already the public row over *Poems and Ballads* ensured a good sale for the poet's literary work. When it came to 'Revelations of the School and Bedroom', as *The Romance of Chastisement* was sub-titled, Swinburne would be an able and possibly enthusiastic partner in that special genre. If he should prove reluctant, or if his fame should encourage him to seek a more reputable publisher than Hotten for his poetry, he could be faced with the revelation of his secret literary life. From the first, Hotten held him fast and had no intention of letting him go.

*   *   *

Poems and Ballads, reissued in September, met with Ludlow's continuing demand for a prosecution. Ruskin refused his support for this and the threat faded. Indeed, the counter-attack had already begun, led by young men of the 1860s for whom Swinburne's poetry was the poetry of their generation. One young Oxonian, describing *Poems and Ballads* to Edmund Gosse, remarked, 'It simply swept us off our legs with rapture.'[45] Their Cambridge contemporaries, determined not to be outdone, joined hands and marched forward, clearing the pavements before them as they shouted the morally offensive stanzas of 'Dolores' or the politically unnerving lines of 'A Song in Time of Revolution' into the unwilling ears of their elders.[46] *Poems and Ballads,* recalled Gosse, 'took the whole lettered youth of England by storm with its audacity and melody'.[47]

Even in print, the hostile critics had by no means won the battle outright. When the book was reissued by Hotten, Henry Morley came to its defence in the *Examiner* of 22 September. He wrote of his reservations, which included Swinburne's almost fetishistic preoccupation with girls' eyelids, but on the central moral question his stand was unambiguous.

In the *Poems and Ballads* there is the same stern blending of pain and wrath with the delights of wantonness. The theme is not one to be sung *virginibus puerisque,* but shall it therefore not be sung? Shall a young poet be praised for the frivolous songs of love and wine that satisfy conventional ideas of decorum, but condemned for fastening upon the inmost life of such themes, painting such uttermost delights as they claim to have in them only to show the rottenness within?

On 6 October, Lord Houghton, having returned from his stay at Vichy, also wrote to the *Examiner* in Swinburne's defence, while the *Sunday Times,* the *Westminster Review,* and *Fraser's Magazine* remained favourably disposed. The lettered youth of England, as Gosse called them, included not only young men at Oxford and Cambridge but their less affluent contemporaries elsewhere. In London, for instance, the young Thomas Hardy was overwhelmed by the power of Swinburne's verse, to the point of reading it as he walked the streets with book in hand, 'to my imminent risk of being knocked down'.[48]

In October, Swinburne himself replied to his detractors in *Notes on Poems and Reviews,* which he wrote at Hotten's suggestion and which he described as notes on individual poems that had been severely handled by the critics. Yet the theme which ran through his pamphlet was summed up by the quotation from Théophile Gautier's *Albertus,* which he included in it.

> Mothers of families I hereby warn
> That I do not write for their girl-children,
> For whom one cuts up bread and butter:
> Mine is a young man's poetry.

To men like John Morley, who had complained in veiled terms about the lesbian or hermaphrodite implications of poems like 'Anactoria', Swinburne suggested that the obscenity they saw in it was a mere reflection of their own minds. 'What certain reviewers have imagined it to imply, I am incompetent to explain, and unwilling to imagine. I am evidently not virtuous enough to understand them. . . . I have not studied in those schools whence that full-fledged phoenix, the "virtue" of professional pressmen, rises chuckling and crowing from the dunghill, its birthplace and its deathbed.'[49] Moreover, Swinburne inquired, if the loves of Sappho were so shameless and abominable, how was it that her surviving poems were on the syllabuses of England's great schools, where sternly moral pedagogues enforced the learning of them with the aid of the birch and other disciplinary sanctions? Was there not, somewhere, a strong and nauseating whiff of hypocrisy in all the simulated outrage over 'Anactoria' and her sisters?

In this, at least, he raised a question calculated to embarrass Victorian educators and critics. A modern novel which dealt graphically with straightforward copulation between husband and wife would have led to a successful prosecution. The current penalty for selling something stronger, like *Fanny Hill,* was two years' imprisonment.[50] On the other hand, Sophocles's *Oedipus Tyrannos,* whose hero murdered his father and then fathered children himself on his own mother, was published by the Clarendon Press in Greek 'For the Use of Schools'. The vices of the Roman Empire, homosexual, lesbian, and sadistic, which would have raised demands for prosecution in English, were available in the original Latin of Martial and Juvenal. Swinburne had trespassed by crossing, as it were, the language frontier and making such material available to those who had not received the accredited passport of a classical education.

The Victorian attitude to such matters had been conditioned by publications like the *Family Classical Library,* a derivative of Bowdler's *Family Shakespeare.* When Charles Badham produced a volume of Juvenal's satires for this he confessed in his introduction that he had deliberately mistranslated indelicate passages. When Juvenal complains in his first satire that the triumphal statues of upstarts are fit only to be urinated upon, 'Cuius ad effigiem non tantum meiere fas est', Badham translates coyly: 'Whose titled effigies one's choice compel/ For purpose that we care not here to tell.'[51] As for the erotic delights which Swinburne strove to emulate in his own poetry, these too fell victim to the translator's ingenuity when, for instance, the Bohn Library produced Martial in English. 'Quod ut superbo provoces ab inguine,/Ore adlaborandum est tibi' appeared as 'But for you to raise an appetite in a stomach that is nice, it is necessary that you exert every art of language.' As earlier commentators had recognized, however, *inguine* is not 'stomach' but 'genitals', and *ore* is not 'language' but 'tongue'.[52] The Loeb Library, with its scholarly texts running parallel in Latin or Greek and English, found an even neater solution. When the material became objectionable, it ceased to use English and translated instead into Italian, as though into a language more suited to moral degeneracy.

To make matters worse for those who wished the classical heritage to consist of manly bloodshed and political rhetoric, the first systematic excavations at Pompeii had begun in 1748. The discoveries of Joaquin de Alcubierre and his successors at the site matched Swinburne's view of the ancient world rather than that offered by the *Family Classical Library.* In 1900, in an obscenity prosecution, the Common Serjeant was obliged to utter a warning on such matters. 'In towns buried from the corrupt times of the

Roman Empire, now disinterred or in the course of being disinterred, there are discovered pictures of the most lewd and filthy character. Nobody would think of destroying those pictures, but to sell photographs of them in the streets of London would be an indictable offence.'[53]

In the light of such sentiments during the Victorian period, it was in vain for William Michael Rossetti to protest on Swinburne's behalf that a classic and pagan influence from the antique past was a perfectly proper inspiration for modern poetry. He praised the 'amazing candour and beauty' of 'Anactoria' and 'Hermaphroditus', yet admitted that 'The statue in the Louvre, and the Lesbian loves of Sappho are not germane to the modern mind.'[54] At the same time Dante Gabriel was confessing to Tennyson that while he thought the press attacks on *Poems and Ballads* had been 'coarse and stupid', and though he would take no part against his friend, he shared the more intelligent reservations over the poems which had caused most trouble.[55]

Swinburne responded with passion to the self-righteous anger of his detractors, and to the moral sermonizing of the reviews. But as the autumn progressed, a crueller and unanticipated weapon appeared in the ranks of the enemy: ridicule. On 15 September the *Spectator* published 'The Session of the Poets', by 'Caliban', describing an evening with the great poets of the age which culminated in a burlesque row between Swinburne and Tennyson.

What was said? what was done? was there prosing or rhyming?
    Was nothing noteworthy in deed or in word? –
Why, just as the hour of supper was chiming,
    The only event of the evening occurred.
Up jumped, with his neck stretching out like a gander,
    Master Swinburne, and squeal'd, glaring out thro' his hair,
'All Virtue is bosh! Hallelujah for Landor!
    I disbelieve wholly in everything! – There!'

With language so awful he dared then to treat 'em, –
    Miss Ingelow fainted in Tennyson's arms,
Poor Arnold rush'd out, crying *'Saecl' inficetum!'*
    And great bards and small bards were full of alarms;
Till Tennyson, flaming and red as a gypsy,
    Struck his fist on the table and utter'd a shout:
'To the door with the boy! Call a cab! He is tipsy!'
    And they carried the naughty young gentleman out.

The identity of 'Caliban' remained secret for the time being, though he was eventually revealed as no other than the same Robert Buchanan who had condemned Swinburne's poetry as 'prurient trash' in the *Athenaeum* review, and who now ridiculed himself as well as other poets in the lampoon, so that his identity should not be guessed.

Later still, even the most shocking pieces in *Poems and Ballads* were treated not as moral outrages or even as errors of sexual decorum. They were derided instead as literary fakes, the natural prey of heartless parody. The best of the parodies, A. C. Hilton's 'Octopus', took as its target the least likely poem, the celebration of the beautiful sado-masochistic goddess 'Dolores'. In Hilton's case, however, the poem is addressed to an octopus at the Crystal Palace Aquarium and catches the rhythm and imagery of Swinburne's original with cruel skill.

> Wast thou born to the sound of sea-trumpets?
>   Hast thou eaten and drunk to excess
> Of the sponges – thy muffins and crumpets,
>   Of the seaweed – thy mustard and cress?
> Wast thou nurtured in caverns of coral,
>   Remote from reproof or restraint?
> Art thou innocent, art thou immoral,
>   Sinburnian or Saint? . . .
>
> Ah! thy red lips, lascivious and luscious,
>   With death in thy amorous kiss!
> Cling round us, and clasp us, and crush us,
>   With bitings of agonised bliss;
> We are sick with the poison of pleasure,
>   Dispense us the potion of pain;
> Ope thy mouth to its uttermost measure
>   And bite us again![56]

Far from the laughter of parody and the fury of literary controversy, two figures had remained in the background, sad and uncomprehending. They were, of course, Admiral and Lady Jane Swinburne. They had, as Houghton noticed, begun to get proud of their wayward son and had praised him excessively whenever his work fed their 'longing desire to be pleased', as the admiral put it. Now, as they expressed it to Ruskin, there was only sorrow and pain for them in seeing dear 'Hadji's' name attached to eager exploitations of sexual perversity. Ruskin wrote a gallant letter to admiral

Swinburne, defending Swinburne against the worst accusations and urging him to read again certain passages and see if he could not find beauty there. The admiral's tone was of confused and pathetic gratitude to this influential friend of his son, to whom he recalled Algernon's childhood reverence and piety, and looked wistfully forward to some moral reformation.

It was never more than a hope. The world had, as it were, proclaimed the young poet to be of the devil's party. With little to lose by way of moral reputation, it was left to him to prove that the world was right.The gentle voice of Pauline Trevelyan had been stilled by death. The Swinburne parents were entering an anxious and bewildered old age. It seemed at last that Swinburne was free to consent to his own destruction.

Chapter 7

A Scandal in Bohemia

ON 10 November 1866 *Punch* had dismissed Swinburne from its notice with leaden humour. 'Having read Mr Swinburne's defence of his prurient poetics, *Punch* hereby gives him royal licence to change his name to what is evidently its true form – SWINE–BORN.' During the ten years which followed, Swinburne also renounced *Punch,* or rather the society which it served, in both word and deed. The earnest platitudes of Tennyson he called 'vomitorial rot', and suggested that the law of indecent exposure should be put into force against such poems and their author.[1]

His own poetic allegiances were firmly maintained. In April 1867 he read in the French press that Baudelaire had died. Without hesitation he set to work on a grand elegy, 'Ave Atque Vale: In Memory of Charles Baudelaire', which was to appear eventually in his *Poems and Ballads: Second Series* in 1878.

> Shall I strew on thee rose or rue or laurel,
>> Brother, on this that was the veil of thee?
>> Or quiet sea-flower moulded by the sea....
>> Or wilt thou rather, as on earth before,
>> Half-faded fiery blossoms, pale with heat
>> And full of bitter summer....

Baudelaire's forbidden erotic themes were gently woken in such lines as:

> Where the sea sobs round Lesbian promontories
> The barren kiss of piteous wave to wave....

Above all, it was the morbid eroticism, as contemporaries thought it, the decadence of Baudelaire, which Swinburne celebrated.

> Sleep; and if life was bitter to thee, pardon,
>> If sweet, give thanks; thou hast no more to live;
>> And to give thanks is good, and to forgive.
> Out of the mystic and the mournful garden
>> Where all day through thine hands in barren braid
>> Wove the sick flowers of secrecy and shade,

Green buds of sorrow and sin, and remnants grey,
  Sweet-smelling, pale with poison, sanguine-hearted,
  Passions that sprang from sleep and thoughts that started,
Shall death not bring us all as thee one day
  Among the days departed?

It was one of Swinburne's grandest occasional poems, a final tribute to the man whom he revered as the sublime poet of the modern age. Unfortunately, he had no sooner written it than he suffered the most embarrassing setback which could befall any writer of elegy. Baudelaire was still alive.

Premature reports of death were comparatively common, and this one was based on a progressively exaggerated report of the French poet's illness. It would not have been seemly to say much about the elegy during its subject's lifetime, but Baudelaire obliged his admirer by dying in the following August. The poem was brought out of store and published in the *Fortnightly Review* for January 1868.

Swinburne's international sympathies served his reputation well. In Paris, in 1869, the *Rappel* called him England's greatest living poet. He informed Dante Gabriel Rossetti of this, inviting Tennyson and company to go and hang themselves. In the United States, where *Poems and Ballads* had been issued by G. W. Carleton as *Laus Veneris and Other Poems and Ballads,* his fame or notoriety rivalled that in England. English reviews, including John Morley's, were reprinted and the *New York Times* roundly condemned the lasciviousness of the poems on 3 November 1866. In consequence, the book sold out one printing after another. William Winwood Reade, author of *The Martyrdom of Man,* wrote, 'To Algernon Swinburne, Pagan, suffering persecution from the Christians ... greeting ... your book is making a furore in this continent. No new volume of Tennyson has ever made more talk.... The publisher has sold 6,000 and is now printing the seventh.'[2]

London had, of course, the indisputable advantage over New York of Swinburne as a public self-advertisement. Edmund Gosse recalled Algernon, then in his thirties, appearing in public as 'a hypertrophied intelligence.... His vast brain seemed to weigh down and give solidity to a frame otherwise as light as thistledown.'

In the streets he had the movement of a somnambulist, and often I have seen him passing like a ghost across the traffic of Holborn, or threading the pressure of carts eastward in Gray's Inn Road, without glancing to the left or the right, like something blown before a wind ... if I stood a couple of yards before him silent, he would endeavour to escape on one side and then on the other, giving a great shout of satisfaction when at length his eyes focused on my face.[3]

If Swinburne had difficulty in bringing Gosse into focus, it was because he had now become what Gosse bluntly described as 'a drunkard'.[4] Gosse saw, for instance, the arrival of a cab in Cheyne Walk, from which the 'delicately dressed' figure of Walter Pater descended, complete with lemon-yellow kid gloves. He was followed by Swinburne, who fell out of the vehicle on hands and knees, his top-hat rolling away in the gutter. Pater appeared presently in the drawing-room. Swinburne was escorted elsewhere to be cleaned up and sobered down.[5]

Performances of this kind were not confined to private visits among his friends, nor even to more formal occasions, such as Mrs Sabine Greville's house-party, where Swinburne made a determined dash for the sherry and was soon 'wild-drunk', as Lord Burghclere reported.[6] On 2 December 1866, Arthur Munby dined at the Arts Club in Hanover Square, he and Swinburne being members. He saw Swinburne, 'obviously drunk ... waving his arms ... talking loud and wild'.[7] He was shaking hands indiscriminately, ordering a cab and then cancelling it, until with glazed eyes he announced that he must 'make a call' and tottered downstairs to the lavatories. Presently another club member, Walter Severn, came upstairs crying , 'What a sad business! Here is Swinburne come into the club again, dead drunk!' And he described the scene with Swinburne prostrate downstairs.[8]

Munby and others saw the same performance with minor variations during the years which followed, Swinburne 'belching out blasphemy and bawdry' for the edification of other members.[9] His favourite subjects, described in a loud and high-pitched voice, were lesbianism and the act of sodomy, variously practised. A year to the day after the first performance, however, Munby saw one of the wilder outbursts, Swinburne leaping about the club drawing-room, flinging up his arms and blowing kisses, while continuing to swear violently.[10]

To make matters worse, Swinburne acquired a drinking-companion of a kind far removed from his other friends. This was Charles Duncan Cameron, introduced to him by Burton. Cameron had been British Consul in Abyssinia, at the Emperor Theodore's hill-top capital of Magdala. Believing that the British Foreign Office had insulted him, Theodore seized the few Europeans at Magdala and imprisoned Cameron in chains. He was even said to have stretched him on the rack. In April 1868 a British expeditionary force, commanded by Sir Robert Napier, the future Lord Napier of Magdala, reached the foot of the rock. Watched by G. A. Henty for *The Times* and Henry Morton Stanley for the *New York Times,* the 33rd Foot, the Duke of Wellington's Own, stormed Magdala. Cameron was set free and the Emperor Theodore shot himself with an ornamental pistol which had, ironically, been a present from Queen Victoria. In London, Cameron was received as a hero by the press, and by Swinburne as a worthy successor to Burton.

Cameron was an imposing figure who drank in consequence of his ordeals, while Swinburne drank to keep him company. The ex-consul also had the recommendation of believing that England would be convulsed by armed revolution within a few years. It was Munby again who reported the extraordinary behaviour of this pair. On 2 June 1869, he recorded that Swinburne had brought Cameron to dine at the Arts Club. They both got very rapidly drunk and created 'a scandalous noise', both in the dining-room and in the hall beyond it. Worse still, the other diners were dismayed to see them get up and perform indecent embraces together for the entertain- ment of all present. 'The Committee have called on Swinburne to resign,' Munby added.[11]

As it happened, Swinburne contrived to remain a member of the club for a year longer. In August 1870 he resigned, in order to save the committee the embarrassment of expelling him. Once more, it was Cameron's company which had driven him to a final act of indecorum. They had both got drunk again and Swinburne had gone to the cloakroom to find their hats when the time came to leave. Unable to distinguish his own among the rest, he had seized the other members' hats, one by one, tried them on, and then thrown them on the floor when he found they would not fit. After a while, he burst into a great rage and began a wild dance, stamping on the silk top-hats and crushing them beyond repair. It was this affront which had moved the committee to its inflexible decision. 'A sad case,' remarked Munby, 'Swinburne seems to have no conscience, no sense of shame at all.'[12]

The most urgent question had nothing directly to do with con- science or shame. It was a matter of whether Swinburne could survive much longer the insults to his physical health which his drinking habits represented. By the spring of 1867 he was writing repeatedly to his friends to cancel appointments or merely to complain that he was too ill to go out. Bilious attacks, fainting fits and 'bilious influenza' were accompanied by diarrhoea, whose cause was evidently inflammation of the bowel from excessive drinking. By 1868, Gosse recalled, Swinburne at thirty-one 'was dejected in mind and ailing in body; the wonderful colours of youth were now first beginning to fade out of his miraculous eyes and hair'.[13] He complained of 'illness hardly intermittent during weeks and months'.[14] He was, in short, killing himself. A man could not always live in the excitement of poetic inspiration, and outside that rare atmosphere the tedium of life was only to be borne by the aid of some other stimulation or sedative.

Dr George Bird, who was both friend and physician, was sometimes able to keep his patient from the bottle for short periods. On 12 May 1868, for instance, he wrote to Swinburne's idol, Mazzini, 'Dr Bird is most glad to say that for five days past Mr Swinburne has avoided "the perilous stuff" and is consequently very much improved in body and mind.'[15] Yet for all that Bird and others could do, Swinburne's health continued to deteriorate. Most alarming of all, he began to have 'fainting fits' at times when he might have been expected to be entirely sober. On 13 July 1867, at Lord Houghton's breakfast party in Upper Brook Street, as the host recorded, 'Swinburne fell down in a fit ... he was looking wretchedly ill before.'[16] A doctor was fetched, who pronounced that there was no immediate danger, though Houghton took the precaution of telegraphing Admiral Swinburne at Holmwood. The poet had had a similar attack at the house of Karl Blind shortly before, so that there was now real alarm. In the following year, 1868, there occurred his most famous collapse, in the reading-room of the British Museum. Edmund Gosse, who was an assistant librarian there, recalled the sight of his idol being carried out: 'I shall not lose that earliest, and entirely unanticipated, image of a languishing and pain-stricken Swinburne, like some odd conception of Aubrey Beardsley, a *Cupido crucifixus* on a chair of anguish.'[17]

On receiving Houghton's telegram, Admiral Swinburne hurried to London by the next train. He went straight to Upper Brook Street, where Swinburne was still recovering, and arranged the patient's removal to his rooms at Dorset Street, Portman Square. There he was examined by two doctors who suggested, tactfully, that a more regular life and diet was the answer. The admiral returned to Holmwood with the prodigal on the following day.

This was a routine frequently repeated during the next ten years.

Swinburne's health would deteriorate to the point of collapse and then some thoughtful friend would summon the old admiral. The patient would be fetched back to Holmwood, nursed back to health by his family, and would then break loose and return to his former metropolitan life. Though he recovered quickly at first, subsequent convalesence seemed more protracted. In 1871, when Admiral Swinburne had once again to fetch his son home, either envisaging a long stay at Holmwood or weary of the repeated crises, he packed up the contents of Swinburne's lodgings, put them in a warehouse and disposed of the London accommodation. Matters were much worse on that occasion; both the Swinburne parents were ill themselves and were obliged to send his old nurse to find him at first. He was known to be ill from drinking, as Lady Swinburne told Dante Gabriel Rossetti, yet the old nurse could find him nowhere. He had gone off with John Thomson, who was both his secretary and his intermediary in dealings with flagellation brothels. There was something grotesque in the charade of Swinburne, now thirty-four years old, being hunted through London by his old nanny, while writing to his parents and refusing to give them his present address, like a troublesome nursery child who has hidden to vex his elders.

At length Admiral Swinburne recovered sufficiently to set out in search of his son. He was duly brought back to Holmwood, where he remained for three months. He must not 'take lodgings in town', wrote Lady Swinburne fretfully to Rossetti, urging him that only at Holmwood could her son overcome 'his fearful propensity'.[18] Yet Admiral Swinburne was over seventy and, in the nature of things, his son could hardly expect to be looked after like a child for many years longer.

The truth was, as Swinburne himself admitted, that the periods of convalesence at Holmwood, or at the home of his Gordon cousins, The Orchard, at Niton on the Isle of Wight, and with Jowett in Scotland or Cornwall, were both physically beneficial and creatively stimulating. In 1871, Henry Kingsley, who had seen him only at home, found it hard to imagine that Swinburne's town life could possibly be as wild as rumour indicated.

The Swinburnes and ourselves are neighbours and friends. The Admiral and Lady Jane Swinburne have bought Holmwood, old Lady Stanley of Alderley's home. They are very agreeable neighbours to us, for they have the best library of its size I have ever seen. I believe Algy is very eccentric in London, but I never see him there. Here he is a perfectly courteous little gentleman.[19]

Swinburne certainly affected old-world mannerisms of courtesy in his nervous bowing and gestures of politeness, but he also contrived to convey an improbable impression of sobriety. He had convinced himself that he drank very moderately and that the habit was not really responsible for his problems. When Edmund Gosse saw Swinburne getting drunk at dinner, he pretended that, through some oversight, there was no more wine in the house. Swinburne approached Mrs Gosse secretively and asked if Edmund really thought he could be 'so little of a gentleman as to drink more than was good for me'.[20] In this, at least, his childishness manifested itself in an extraordinary capacity for innocent self-deception.

After Swinburne's collapse in the British Museum, he was sent to convalesce in September at Etretat, on the Normandy coast between Le Havre and Fécamp. The village, with its lines of new villas on the chalk cliffs, had become fashionable in the previous decade, and George Powell had taken a farmhouse there. On their arrival, the pair renamed this dwelling the Chaumière de Dolmancé, in honour of the hero of Sade's *Philosophie dans le boudoir.*

One morning, soon after his arrival, Swinburne went down to the beach alone, walked to the eastern end, the Porte d'Amont, stripped off his clothes and plunged into the sea. He had little knowledge and no experience of the area but within a short while he felt the undercurrent of the tide beginning to carry him more and more strongly out to sea. Much of Swinburne's swimming actually consisted of floating, since he lacked the bodily strength for continuous vigorous exercise. He discovered after a brief struggle that he was no match for the force of the tidal current. He preserved his energy by floating with the tide, and began to shout for help and utter high-pitched screams.

The cries were heard by a man at the semaphore station, who scrambled up a chalk rock to gain a view of the victim. He saw Swinburne being carried faster and faster in the current, disappearing out to sea beyond the eastern point of Etretat, the cries growing fainter and more distant. Swinburne himself was possessed by two thoughts, one of annoyance at not having completed his book of poems *Songs Before Sunrise,* and the other an ironic reflection that he was to be drowned at just the same age as Shelley.

The man from the semaphore station had no boat and was unable to reach the floating figure. Fortunately, he saw one of the fishing-smacks from the village and was able to hail it, directing it towards the cries and the shrieks. Swinburne was hauled from the water by Théodule Vallin and his crew, and brought aboard.

The weather was glorious; the poet's body was rubbed by the horny hands of his rescuers, and then wrapped in a spare sail, over which his mane of orange-ruddy hair was spread to dry, like a fan. He proceeded to preach to the captain and his men, who surrounded him . . . in rapturous approval, the doctrines of the Republic, and then he recited to them, 'by the hour together', the poems of Victor Hugo.[21]

Another fishing-smack had set out from Etretat as the news of the poet's peril spread along the beach, though it was too late to take part in the rescue. However, it was perhaps only appropriate that the figure in the bows of this second craft should have been that of the eighteen-year-old Guy de Maupassant. In the days that followed, Maupassant made the acquaintance of Swinburne and Powell, being invited twice to lunch at the Chaumière de Dolmancé. Though he admired Swinburne's poetry, he thought the two men grotesque. At the first visit to the farmhouse, he found the luncheon table surrounded by displays of bones, including the flayed hand of a parricide which still had dried blood and muscles adhering to the bones. A pet monkey, 'Nip', took pride of place in the house. On the second visit, he was told that the meal would consist of roast monkey – not Nip, but another animal specially obtained from a dealer in exotic animals at Le Havre. The smell and taste of the meal was, as Maupassant reported, appalling.[22]

It was also at Etretat that Swinburne was observed by another acquaintance, Julian Osgood Field, who became one of his odder companions in London. Field had been educated at Harrow and Merton College, Oxford, and took to the life of a professional swindler effortlessly. His addresses included Park Lane, the Grosvenor Hotel and Her Majesty's Prison, Wormwood Scrubs. At Etretat, according to Field, Swinburne was the object of passion of 'a remarkable American lady. She was a very small woman with big flashing eyes: a widow, very rich, from Cincinnati.'[23] On discovering Swinburne's identity, 'she threw herself at him with all the vigour with which her late spouse had packed pork and piled up pieces'.[24]

Perhaps the amorous widow might have been deterred by the birches and bitings, the Sadean amusements and sexual interchange which characterized Swinburne's erotic paradise. Yet she took care to ascertain the nature of some of his extravagances and duly harped upon them. 'She "read up" for Swinburne, and with a very wicked look in her eyes would recite to him some of his naughtiest lines. The effect was grotesquely funny of this eager lady looking passionately into the half-frightened eyes of the very unwilling little poet.'[25]

Though Field's uncorroborated word ought not to be relied upon too heavily, he concedes that Swinburne escaped this particular admirer and came unscathed from Normandy. In the following year it was at Vichy, rather than Etretat, that Swinburne undertook his convalescence, in company with the painter Frederic Leighton and his own friend Sir Richard Burton. With Burton he visited Clermont-Ferrand and scaled the Puy de Dôme, recovering his health once more through rest and exercise. 'This place is doing me great good,' he told his sister Alice. 'I was rather spent with the heat in London . . . and now Burton says he never yet saw me so fresh and well.'[26]

It was not to last for long. When the month of August 1869 was over, Swinburne moved to the Hôtel Castiglione in Paris. He had arranged a meeting with Gautier and, he hoped, Flaubert. Yet the address at which he was to meet them, 2 rue Lafitte, was the object of a pilgrimage in its own right. It was the apartment of Frederick Hankey, '*the* Sadique collector of European fame', as Swinburne described him, who had been the supplier of Fryston and other collections.[27] It was here, as Swinburne told George Powell, that he had been privileged to see the Pradier statue of two girls engaged in mutual cunnilingus. There was also a vast library of erotic literature, described by the Goncourt brothers in their *Journal* for 7 April 1862. It consisted of heavily illustrated volumes, sumptuously bound, the bindings ornamented in gold with 'phallus and vagina, women's buttocks and whips, death's heads and instruments of torture'. Hankey was distinctly sadistic rather than masochistic. He shocked the Goncourts by his account of attending the execution of a girl in London, with prostitutes to amuse him during the process, and having bribed the executioner to fix the condemned woman's skirt higher to increase the eroticism of the scene. He was most annoyed to discover that she had been reprieved.

At the time of Swinburne's visit, Hankey had just published *L'Ecole des biches*, a semi-realistic account of the lesbian and heterosexual performances put on in his apartment. As he told the Goncourts, the police might grow troublesome over the use of women in sadistic displays but he invited them to see the step-ladder to which his victims were attached on such occasions and even described one of his recent triumphs. This involved his friend Gaiffe and Mademoiselle Tagliafico, the daughter of a singer. Gaiffe, on

Hankey's instructions, had compromised the girl. Hankey had pretended to discover this, and had then confronted her with the alternatives of being revealed to her family and the world for what she was, or else accepting her fate.

Hankey had a more immediate interest for Swinburne, as one of the greatest authorities on the brothels of London and the range of sexual tastes for which they catered. Not only did he know of houses where girls were divided into classes for clients who wished to treat them as schoolchildren, or where clients were beaten like children in their turn, he also named some of the customers. They included Monckton Milnes and senior army officers from the House Guards. According to one rumour, the Prince of Wales himself had patronized a house in Church Street, Chelsea. It might seem unlikely, but Mary Jeffries, who owned it, certainly provided sexual entertainment for the King of the Belgians on his visit to England.[28]

Swinburne, naturally predisposed towards the practices in such establishments, must have found Hankey a convivial source of information. There exists an unpublished paper of Hankey's describing the flourishing trade in London on the part of these brothels. Some had direct and distinct aristocratic connections, one was conducted by a woman who had been 'governess in a titled family', another by Mrs James, a former maid of Lord Clanricarde. There was also, as Swinburne had cause to know, one 'in the Regents Park, a lovely villa which is presided over by a well educated lady, well versed in the birchen mysteries'.[29]

* * *

Whatever the more obvious drawbacks to Swinburne's sadomasochistic obsession, it was at least some diversion from the consumption of brandy in lethal quantities. Indeed, it was possible to imagine that if only the right woman could be found for him – a marriageable version of Mary Gordon, perhaps – it might be possible to reverse the decline in his health and state of mind.

Dante Gabriel Rossetti and Burton were partners in the attempt to bring Swinburne to bed with the famous actress Adah Isaacs Menken. She was a few years older than Swinburne and had been several times married, one of her husbands having been the pugilist John Carmel Heenan who fought his famous and bloody bareknuckle contest against Tom Sayers in 1860. Born in New Orleans, Adah Menken had earned both fame and notoriety in the title role of *Mazeppa*, a drama adapted from Byron's poem. Its first performance had taken place in the United States, at Albany, in 1861. The actress appeared with cropped hair and her figure revealed in skin-coloured costume and tights, strapped helplessly on a galloping horse.

In 1864, *Mazeppa* opened in London at Astley's in Horseferry Road. Combining a stage with a circus ring in front of it, the famous theatre was ideally suited for this particular display. Decorously covered in close-silk web, the illusion was none the less of Adah Menken, strapped naked on the horse, and the illusion was strengthened by the management of Astley's in advertisements for the play which suggested a far greater degree of nudity. A new piece of sheet-music, vividly illustrated, appeared as *The Menken Gallop*. For satirists in search of an easy target there was none better.

> Here's half the town – if bills be true –
> To Astley's nightly thronging,
> To see 'the Menken' throw aside
> All to her sex belonging,
> Stripping off woman's modesty
> With woman's outward trappings –
> A bare-backed jade on bare-backed steed,
> In Cartlich's old strappings![30]

Though the actress had cultivated Rossetti's acquaintance and given him the use of her private box at the theatre, she still seemed an unlikely choice as wife or mistress for Swinburne. Yet the association was more easily contrived than might have been supposed. In the first place, Adah Menken had ambitions to be a poet herself, having written some pieces for which she sought a publisher. Moreover, Swinburne was widely thought to have taken her as the model for 'Dolores', and by 1865 she was certainly using this name to sign some of her letters. 'Adah Isaacs Menken was to a certain extent the origin of *Dolores*', wrote Swinburne's friend Arthur Symons.[31] More to the point, Dolores was the name which she had been given at birth, whereas Adah Isaacs Menken was a mixture of stage pseudonym and her first husband's name.

Friends took Swinburne to Astley's and pointed out the erotic charms of Dolores strapped naked on a horse. Then the actress herself was approached and it was suggested to her that she might undertake Algernon's sexual education. According to one account, Rossetti paid her £10 to do this, but Adah Menken was no whore, and anyway was earning £100 a week for her part in *Mazeppa*. The consequence, at any rate, was that Swinburne received a visit at his Dorset Street rooms, late one night in December 1867. When he opened the door, according to Field's account, he was confronted by a 'handsome boyish-looking American lady, sweetly smiling', who said, 'Well, I guess I've read your poems and just love them: and I've come over here from Paris on purpose just to love the poet!'[32]

Whatever the words, which Field added were reported to him by Swinburne but which were in fact 'far more realistic and Zolaesque than I can possibly chronicle', Adah Menken spent that night at Dorset Street, as well as many more nights between then and February 1868. Swinburne revealed little of his bedroom activities with Menken, except to express general satisfaction with her and to describe her to Powell in January 1868 as 'my possessor'. They were photographed together, and copies of the picture were displayed for purposes of publicity. Adah Menken was shown seated with Swinburne gazing down at her with an air of resignation, a pose made necessary by the fact that she was somewhat larger than he. There was some private hilarity over the whole thing and Burne-Jones rather unkindly burlesqued their passion in a series of cartoons, *Ye Treue and Pitifulle Historie of ye Poet and ye Ancient Dame*.

Swinburne made no complaint, though he was hardly appreciative of Adah Menken's habit of sitting on the edge of the bed in the early winter morning, swinging her handsome legs and reading her poetry to him. Indeed, he seemed immensely flattered and proud at the liaison into which he had been drawn. It was his mistress who broke the whole thing off. She informed Rossetti, according to Gosse, that it was difficult to get Algernon 'up to scratch', and she was not enthusiastic over the first sadistic overtures. 'I can't make him understand that biting's no use!'[33]

The great passion was over, and Adah Menken returned to Paris, whence she had come in the previous October, to appear again in *Mazeppa*. She had also been photographed there, in a more intimate pose than with Swinburne, sitting upon the knee of Dumas the elder. It was there, too, that she died in the following year, allegedly the victim of the same bowel inflammation, caused by excessive drinking of brandy, which brought on Swinburne's 'bilious influenza'. Her poems, at least, survived her, being published in London soon after her death. Swinburne himself had dismissed her from his affections, though on hearing of her death he managed a reference to 'my poor dear Menken'.[34]

Promiscuous though she might have been, and exotic in her sexual suggestiveness, she was too conventional for him. The only ultimate satisfaction for Swinburne was to be found in the brothels of the 1860s and, more specifically, in the establishment which Hankey referred to as being in Regent's Park, but which was actually in St John's Wood. His introduction to the place was the work of his secretary, John Thomson, who had also played the part of a go-between in the affair with Adah Menken. Thomson was 'a big-hearted young fellow, with a fat baby face and large spectacles', whose mother owned a house in Bloomsbury where Swinburne's acquaintance Savile Clarke lodged.[35] Both Edmund Gosse and Clarke's friend, George Sims, concur in their accounts of the fateful introduction of Swinburne to Thomson.

One night, going in late, Savile Clarke went down into the kitchen to get some hot water for the whisky that he and Swinburne desired to take as a nightcap. Clarke, finding the kitchen door ajar, went in and was astonished to see a fat-faced boy of about sixteen sitting in front of the fire and reciting 'Paradise Lost' from memory to the blackbeetles.

He went upstairs and fetched Swinburne down, and they spent the night listening to the boy, who appeared to know all the English poets, ancient and modern, by heart.

Swinburne took an interest in the boy and had him constantly with him, and it was while he was Swinburne's secretary that poor John first met Adah Isaacs Menken, the actress and poetess, with whom he fell madly in love.[36]

Thomson's passion for Adah Menken never got further than taking her and her poems to John Camden Hotten, arranging for what was to prove their posthumous publication. Yet Thomson, during his association with Swinburne, lived at the brothel at 7 Circus Road in St John's Wood, a suburb which was, as Sims remarked, 'then playfully referred to as "The Grove of the Evangelist"'.[37] Thomson was a literary journalist in later life, dramatic critic of the *Despatch* and author of a column known as 'Waifs and Strays'. In the 1860s, however, the boy was both secretary to Swinburne and evidently a partner of some kind in the brothel. The establishment was run, according to Gosse, by two golden-haired and rouge-cheeked ladies who charged a good deal of money for their services. The *madame* was a respectable elderly woman who accepted the payments, while Hankey added to the list 'two very young girls', who were visitors to the house.[38]

Thomson's part in the proceedings may well have been the writing of invitations to established clients, one of which was appended

by H. S. Ashbee to Hankey's manuscript account. It takes the form
of a letter announcing the arrival of 'a new governess' who would
display her talents in 'the schoolroom' on the following Sunday. The
letter concludes with a drawing of a birch and the promise that 'The
gate will be open at 2.'[39] Such was the copy written either by
Thomson or by some other supernumerary. The house was known
to A. E. Housman as Verbena Lodge, though he was too young to
have gathered much about it in the 1860s. Indeed, the closer connection in this respect is with George Augustus Sala's anonymous
novel of 1881, *The Mysteries of Verbena House: or, Miss Bellasis
Birched for Thieving.*

Swinburne, like the majority of clients, was impelled to Circus
Road by childish and masochistic obsessions. Such houses were also
the scenes of sadistic displays in which the women were the victims.
Hankey recalls one willing partner, 'quite of the lowest order', who
consented to such ordeals, though the reason seems to have been
that she was drunk almost to the point of insensibility. After the trial
and imprisonment of Sarah Potter in 1863, a good deal of information about her brothels was published in *Mysteries of Flagellation*. It
duplicated much of the material associated with the house in Circus
Road, though adding the account of one witness, Bridie Stephens,
who had been present when an outraged husband brought his
unfaithful young wife to the Wardour Street brothel to be beaten,
that being the condition of forgiveness.

As with the extravagances of Hankey's behaviour, the goings-on
at Circus Road and in similar establishments provoke two reactions.
The first, typified by the Goncourts in Hankey's case, is of shock,
horror, and disgust. Towards Swinburne there might also be a sense
of uncomprehending pity. Max Beerbohm belongs in this category,
to the extent that after Swinburne's death he assured Edmund
Gosse that the drunkenness, or 'toping', as he lightly called it,
should be described because it would make readers feel more
indulgent towards the poet. Of the sexual oddity, no one in the
future must ever hear.[40]

The second reaction, quite contrary to the first, is to dismiss the
whole thing as a joke, much as Burton had treated Hankey's
demand for a girl's skin. After the *grand guignol* of the fantasies
composed by Swinburne and others, it may come as an anti-climax
to suggest that the proceedings in Circus Road probably resembled
nothing so much as the sauna baths of a century later. Though it
seems unkind to deride Swinburne's accounts of victims reeling

about in bloodstained clothing, he actually compared such acts in reality with the contemporary Russian use of the birch in bathing.[41] The girls of Circus Road were unlikely to risk the consequences of inflicting serious damage on their clients. Nor would the house have survived long if those clients had emerged into St John's Wood like the walking wounded of Swinburne's fantasies. Money, which was the common denominator, was more easily extracted for a charade, an erotic game, a sexual romp in which the guests were guaranteed some form of satisfaction while having no amorous demands made upon them by the girls. Whether or not Swinburne was impotent, as Walter Raleigh later assumed, it was certainly a sport for the sexually unambitious. Indeed, as Raleigh wrote, there was 'nothing very awful about it'. Nor, according to another of Gosse's correspondents, John Bailey, was it unusual. 'Swinburne's peculiarity was not so peculiar', to judge by the success of Circus Road and similar establishments all over London.[42]

The golden-haired young women with rouged cheeks did so well out of Swinburne and his companions that they closed up the house for a while and went off to Paris. It was during this interval, in the winter of 1867–8, that Rossetti and his friends endeavoured to guide Swinburne into a more orthodox alliance with Adah Menken. After the failure of this, Swinburne returned to the 'schoolroom', informing Houghton that their favourite girl at the brothel had returned from France in high feather, and also promising George Powell an introduction to the establishment.[43]

During this period, one other woman was looked to as the means of saving Swinburne from the grotesque routines of Circus Road. She was Mathilde Blind, a young poetess who was the stepdaughter of the revolutionary Karl Blind, and the sister of Ferdinand Cohen who had died in prison after an attempt to assassinate Bismarck. She was infatuated by Swinburne, who expressed admiration for her poetry and her family's revolutionary faith. But he ignored her devotion and the opportunities created for him to propose marriage to her.

There was, apparently, little that could be done to save him from himself. George Sims told Gosse that after the failure of Adah Menken's gallant attempt to bring Algernon 'up to scratch', he used to be seen by a park-keeper in Regent's Park, walking in the mornings from Dorset Street to Circus Road, among the trees and shrubs. He would pause and scribble down verses which he had been composing as he walked and which were triumphant songs of liberty and republicanism. Then he walked on to the expensively furnished villa, where young women would recreate for him the atmosphere of the nursery at East Dene.

The cure, when it came, was obvious though unforeseen. Swinburne's fantasies remained with him for the rest of his life, but the visits to the brothel ended in the following year. Neither self-disgust nor sudden maturity broke him of the habit. The grasping old woman who acted as *madame*, and the calculating young women, who measured their clients' ecstasies in pounds and shillings, evidently decided that their victim was entirely ensnared. Their demands for money grew exorbitant and, as Gosse reported, there was apparently a quarrel which resulted in Swinburne withdrawing his custom from them. It was one thing to be beaten like a child, but to be made a fool of over money by such creatures as these was quite intolerable.[44]

So far as the nursery or schoolroom games had drawn his attention away from drink, they had done him less harm than the 'toping' which Beerbohm viewed with such tolerant amusement. As Whistler had already discovered and as Watts-Dunton was to find out in the future, it was actually possible to talk Swinburne out of drinking, provided that his mind could be kept occupied. In the years which followed the break with the Circus Road ladies, however, there were too few friends to do the talking and too little to keep him occupied.

The period during which he patronized the brothel certainly coincided with less 'bilious influenza' than was subsequently the case. From 1869 until 1871 matters became more serious until Admiral Swinburne made his routine journey to fetch the ailing Algernon back to Holmwood. The passing of Consul Cameron, who retired to Switzerland and died there in 1870, threw Swinburne into the equally raffish society of young men who frequented a small café in Rupert Street, Soho, called the Solferino. One of these was Julian Field, whose career as swindler was founded upon an extremely simple technique. His prey was elderly ladies in reduced circumstances to whom he presented himself as a rich young gentleman able to lend them money on favourable terms. He would arrange the loan himself with an ordinary moneylender at the usual extortionate rate of interest. The lady would sign the mysteriously worded papers, undertaking responsibility for the debt, and then Field would disappear taking all or most of the money with him.

Field recalled Swinburne's drunken and hysterical enthusiasms, the sight of him 'running out at night into the street, throwing up his hat in the air and dancing before buses in the maddest and most dangerous way, singing, and clapping his hands'.[45] He was also the subject of jokes by his new acquaintances, who teased him over the fact that his idol Landor dropped his aitches. Swinburne, glaring terribly at his tormentor, shouted, 'Well, and what the 'ell's that got to do with you if 'e 'appens to 'ave that awful 'abit?'[46]

His drinking habits were in danger of becoming a public joke. One evening, in the Solferino, he was shown a cartoon of himself from *Vanity Fair* with the title 'Singing before Sunrise'. Annoyed but not yet comprehending the artist's meaning, he asked, 'What the —— does the —— villain mean by that?' To Field's amusement a young man from the Foreign Office explained: 'Boozed before breakfast.'

> Hearing that, Swinburne jumped up from the table, tore the cartoon to pieces, and danced a hornpipe on it in the middle of the restaurant, much to the surprise of a party of elderly Italian gentlemen who looked dirty and sullen enough to be Carbonari. Then Swinburne shrieked to me, 'Tell that —— what I did with his —— paper!'[47]

It was after his return from Holmwood in 1871 that he eventually found rooms at 3 Great James Street, near Bedford Row in Bloomsbury. He lived here, while in London, until the great crisis of health and spirit in 1878 and the fateful advent of Theodore Watts-Dunton. Edmund Gosse recalled the 'rather empty rooms on the first floor of an old house in Great James Street, which used to remind me of one of Dickens's London houses in "Great Expectations" or "Little Dorrit"'.[48] Yet Gosse's memories, at first hand, were still of Swinburne 'the little gentleman'. He was impressed, for instance, by the way in which when they returned from an evening spent together, Swinburne had 'simply sat back in the deep sofa in his sitting-room, his little feet close together, his arms against his side, folded in his frock-coat like a grasshopper in its wing-covers, and fallen asleep.'[49]

During the 1870s, however, the growing impression which Swinburne gave was of solitude, loneliness and even of drinking by himself. He was seen 'sitting very erect at the London Restaurant in Chancery Lane eating asparagus slowly, vacantly, but with peculiar distinction'.[50] The experience of those who visited him at Great James Street was rather more unnerving than Gosse's had been. The young George Moore arrived with an introduction from

Swinburne and his sisters Alice and Edith, by George Richmond, 1843.

East Dene Villa, Bonchurch, by G. Brannon, 1836.

Sir John Swinburne,
after the painting by
F. Ramsay.

Victorian Eton.

The author of *Poems and Ballads*.

Pauline, Lady Trevelyan, by William Bell Scott, 1846.

Benjamin Jowett, a photograph by Julia Margaret Cameron.

'The sole remark likely to have been made by Benjamin Jowett about the mural painting at the Oxford Union: "And what were they going to *do* with the Grail when they found it, Mr Rossetti?"', by Max Beerbohm.

William Bell Scott, John Ruskin and Dante Gabriel Rossetti.

Lady Lilith, by Dante Gabriel Rossetti.

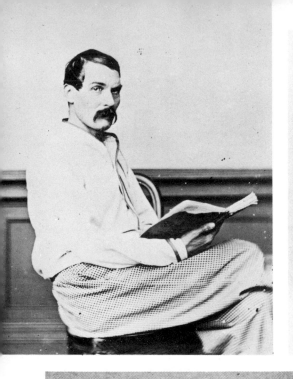

ABOVE LEFT Sir Richard Burton.

ABOVE RIGHT Richard Monckton Milnes, 1st Baron Houghton.

Swinburne and Adah Isaacs Menken.

Proud Maisie, by
Frederick Sandys,
c. 1867.

Swinburne (*right*) and Theodore Watts-Dunton in the garden of
The Pines, Putney.

Swinburne in 1900, by R. P. Staples.

William Michael Rossetti. He entered the old house through an archway, like the chambers of the Temple.

I opened a door and found myself in a large room in which there was no furniture except a truckle bed. Outside the sheets lay a naked man, a strange, impish little body it was, and about the head, too large for the body, was a growth of red hair. The fright that this naked man caused in me is as vivid in me to-day as if it had only occurred yesterday ... and the idea of sitting next to that naked man, so very like myself, and explaining to him that I had come from William Michael Rossetti frightened me nearly out of my wits. I just managed to babble out, 'Does Mr Jones live here?' The red head shook on a long thin neck like a tulip, and I heard, 'Will you ask downstairs?' I fled and jumped into a hansom.[51]

Moore's reception was at least more serene than that which Swinburne accorded to Theodore Watts-Dunton, the self-appointed ministering angel of his later years, when he went to Great James Street for the first time with a letter of introduction. Having tapped at the door and heard sounds within, he entered.

He found Swinburne stark naked with his aureole of red hair flying round his head, performing a Dionysiac dance, all by himself in front of a large looking glass. Swinburne perceived the intruder, he rushed at him, and before Mr Watts-Dunton could offer any explanation or deliver his letter of introduction, he was flying in panic helter-skelter down the stairs, and was driven by the enraged Corybant off the premises.[52]

By no means all his time was spent in the solitude and growing squalor of Great James Street. He had found both secretary and companion in John Thomson of the Circus Road *ménage*, and companionship also in the painter Simeon Solomon. While the Swinburne parents inquired anxiously for the address of their ailing son, he was with Solomon, being regaled with the delights of Solomon's homosexual experiences, which he did not appreciate, and Solomon's enthusiasm for the subject of flagellation, which formed a fertile interest. Apart from other considerations, Swinburne was seeking an illustrator for his 'schoolroom' fantasies and Solomon was among the artists most likely to oblige him.[53] At one time, it had been hoped that Burne-Jones might prove a sympathetic partner, but these expectations were not fulfilled in Swinburne's case.

The friendship with Solomon lasted until 1873, when the painter was arrested for soliciting in a public urinal near Oxford Street. He was sentenced to eighteen months' imprisonment, though this was suspended and police supervision was imposed. It was the end of Solomon, who lost both reputation and income, ending his days as a pavement artist and dying in 1905. Swinburne turned savagely against him, even before Solomon, like Howell, sold his letters. Repeatedly, Swinburne appeared determined to show that, eccentric as his dealings with women might be, it was with the opposite sex that he was exclusively preoccupied. Sado-masochism, far from being effeminate in his view, showed a hardihood and masculinity which was beyond the normal relation of the sexes.

His allegiance to the Divine Marquis was absolute, overcoming even his attachment to libertarian or revolutionary causes. In 1876 he was in much the same predicament as Houghton had found himself in during 1865 at the time of the punitive acts carried out by the British army in Jamaica. In Swinburne's case the issue was the suppression by its Turkish rulers of a rebellion in Bulgaria. Liberal England was outraged by reports in the *Daily News* of women and children massacred by the Turks, as well as women not only massacred but raped and even tortured beforehand. In the House of Commons, Disraeli humorously dismissed such accounts by remarking that it was the invariable custom in Turkey to despatch offenders quickly and without preliminaries. To the queen, he replied that the reports of such atrocities were 'not authenticated', despite the eye-witness reports of journalists.[54]

Any sympathy which Swinburne might have had with the subject race was dispelled in a letter to Houghton on 21 January 1876. *The Times* had reported that one Turkish leader, Sadick Bey, had gone from village to village, violating more than a hundred girls. Swinburne pointed out gleefully that Sadick – or Sadique – Bey must be a reincarnation of the Marquis de Sade. Only one form of violation could be appropriate to such a man and to a country which had given its name to the term 'buggery'. *The Times* also mentioned 'various tortures not unknown to the Justinian code'.[55] With no trace of compassion for the victims of the repression, his correspondence during the following year makes much of the heroic deeds of Sadick Bey (*ci-devant* Marquis). Indeed he was led to support his sexual amusement by striking political attitudes in favour of Turkey and against the Russians, as the manipulators of political unrest for their own expansionist purposes. Towards the end of 1876 he composed, though he did not publish, 'A Ballad of Bulgarie', ridiculing Gladstone, Ruskin, Bright, the Liberals and the pacifists who sought an end to Turkish reprisals. For Swinburne, it was Sadick

Bey who had achieved total liberation, in a manner which even his eighteenth-century predecessor had rarely known except in fantasy.

If his writings are taken at face value, Sade had demonstrated that eroticism is a more powerful force in politics than any other. Swinburne, in early middle age, appeared to be the proof of it, at least in so far as the inspiration of his political thought was concerned. To see Italy set free was sublime, though not as sublime as the ecstasies of Sadick Bey. In 1874, Swinburne referred to Mill's essay *On Liberty* as 'the text-book of my creed as to public morals and political faith'. Yet there was more than one Victorian definition of freedom, including that of Swinburne's Balliol contemporary T. H. Green. Green condemned entirely the notion of freedom as mere lack of restraint and demanded instead that it should be a positive power of doing or enjoying something worth doing or enjoying. To Swinburne, the overthrow of authority was liberty, whether that authority was exercised by King Bomba at Naples or by the prudes and puritans of the Victorian press. The delights of the Marquis de Sade in theory and Sadick Bey in practice represented this freedom in its absolute form.[56]

During his convalescence at Holmwood, the 'perfectly courteous little gentleman', as Henry Kingsley thought him, passed the time by composing praises of Sade and Sadick Bey and showering them upon his correspondents. He also devised 'The Bogshire Banner', which reads almost like a Rabelaisean parody of the Barsetshire novels of Trollope. Among ecclesiastical dignitaries devised for the diocese of Arseborough, and for Rossetti's amusement, were Bishop Athanasius Buggeridge and his relations, Bishop Tollywegg, and such laity as the Hon. Monica Friggins and her cousin, Mr Suckling Cunter. Thanks are given at Mount Scrotum for the recovery of the Dowager Duchess from an attack of gonorrhoea, while, 'The prayers of the congregation were last Sunday desired in Arseborough Cathedral for Viscount Fitzarse, who is suffering from syphilis, contracted at Poxford.'[57] For George Powell's amusement, there was an account of Dean Buggeridge in town and his visit to Quimlico.[58]

Until his disgrace, Simeon Solomon was also favoured with these accounts. In return he supplied Swinburne with details of flagellation from *Peter Spy* and with an account of his amusements with a young French model, whom he persuaded to ask people for copies of Sade, while also teaching her the choicest passages from the Marquis's work.[59] Solomon was an eager recipient of such material as Swinburne sent, though reminding him from time to time that he was not really attracted by the charms of women. Dante Gabriel Rossetti, however, seemed to tire rapidly of Bogshire and the schoolboyish obscenity of Swinburne's other parodies of such poets as Elizabeth Barrett Browning. The strain which these uninspired indecencies put upon their friendship was indicated by the warning sarcasm of Rossetti's replies. He congratulated his correspondent on having occasionally managed to avoid an affront to 'the most sacred associations of early life', and went on to refer scathingly to the unremitting and scatological improvisations of Bogshire as 'a touch of genius that takes one's breath away'.[60]

That Swinburne had imperilled his friendship with Dante Gabriel Rossetti was apparent in 1872 when, after Rossetti's attempted suicide, William Michael wrote and asked Swinburne not to attempt to see his brother again. Yet the material of this sort with which he plagued his friends and correspondents had also brought him trouble of another kind. He had sent to Hotten, either directly or through the willing agency of Charles Augustus Howell, outlines and material for flagellation literature. He certainly supplied Hotten with an illustration of the Eton flogging-block, as well as literary material for illustration. The publisher retained these as well as a number of other similar effusions with which his willing poet provided him. Early in 1873, however, Swinburne had quarrelled with Hotten over payments and copyrights, and had presumably decided that, with the public outcry over *Poems and Ballads* subdued, it was time to transfer his work to a more reputable firm.

Hotten had no intention, it seemed, of letting him go. Swinburne, though protesting to Howell that there was nothing whatever to be ashamed of in the compromising papers which Hotten held, was clearly nervous about the outcome. He asked Howell to make sure that Hotten would show the papers to no one. In return, he even offered to write material for the new edition of *Flagellation and the Flagellants*.[61] Swinburne was adamant that he had never, by written or verbal contract, given Hotten the right to publish his works in perpetuity. William Michael Rossetti intervened on Swinburne's behalf and assured him that Hotten meant to fight over the matter and had insisted that Swinburne had agreed to the publication by him of all future works.

It was a delicate business, in the light of the compromising and indiscreet erotica. *Flagellation and the Flagellants* had been published quite openly in its first edition in 1870, as a pseudo-scholarly work with a number of highly-coloured interpola-tions, such as 'Birch in the Boudoir'. If Hotten incorporated Swinburne's fantasies in a new edition, even putting the poet's name to them, there was little that could be done to prevent him. Brave hopes of transferring *Atalanta* and other books of verse to Chapman and Hall seemed utterly frustrated by Hotten in February 1873.

Two developments followed, one planned and one fortuitous. First, the negotiations with Hotten passed from the uncertain hands of Howell to those of a businesslike solicitor. This was Theodore Watts, who as Theodore Watts-Dunton superintended Swinburne's declining years. While the lawyer dealt briskly with Hotten, Swinburne wrote anxiously to Howell about the recovery of his manuscripts. The worst thing about publication was that he had included himself by name as a victim of the block. Not only would this move some readers to disgust, it would move others to gales of laughter at the spectacle of the pretentious literary youth making such a public fool of himself at last.

But though, as he complained, God was torturing him with insomnia as well as bilious influenza, a belief not the least incompat-ible with Sadean atheism, providence came to his aid in the matter of Hotten. First there were rumours that Hotten, perhaps sensing intimations of mortality, was to be received into the Catholic Church. Then, on 14 June 1873, he died suddenly at the age of forty-one. He was buried in the Victorian Valhalla of Highgate Cemetery, where the booksellers of London put up a monument to his memory. Swinburne had escaped the worst, and he allowed the firm to continue as his publisher. Control of the business passed into the hands of Hotten's partner, Andrew Chatto, who with W. E. Windus founded a famous publishing house. It was not in Swinburne's nature to learn from experience, yet he had survived the years after *Poems and Ballads* with less damage to health and reputation than he had had reason to expect.

Chapter 8

'What Could be Done
With and *For* Algernon?'

AT a quite different level, the ten years which followed the
publication of *Poems and Ballads* marked a no less important
change in Swinburne's literary character. Georges Lafourcade
remarked that, in 1868, 'The publication of *William Blake* and *Ave
Atque Vale* marks the end of the Pre-Raphaelite and Baudelairean
phase in Swinburne's development.'[1] Had not the poet himself, on 9
October 1866, written to William Michael Rossetti, the most earnest of his intimate friends, to indicate that mere self-indulgence was
not enough? 'After all, in spite of jokes and perversities ... it is nice
to have something to love and believe in.... It was only Gabriel and
his followers in art (l'art pour l'art) who for a time frightened me
from speaking out.'[2]

The essay on Blake was dedicated to William Michael Rossetti
and, though dealing with the virtues of art for art's sake, discussed
repeatedly the beliefs which were manifest in Blake's poetry. A
stronger personality than Rossetti's was needed to improve upon
this and direct the poet's wayward impulses into the service of some
great cause. It required a man of commanding moral authority who
was yet intelligent and sophisticated enough to manage Swinburne
in this respect. There were few such figures in the background of his
life. In the event, at a date which Gosse put as early as March 1867, a
group of his acquaintances met at the house of George Howard,
Lord Carlisle, to discuss the problem of 'what could be done *with*
and *for* Algernon'.[3] The precise day of the meeting is uncertain and
it seems that Swinburne had not at this time met the most famous of
those who gathered at Lord Carlisle's London house, Giuseppe
Mazzini. At sixty-two, Mazzini's life of service to the cause of Italian
independence and European democracy was almost over. Yet he
had been Swinburne's idol, whose picture had ornamented the
young man's rooms at Balliol. Apart from Mazzini's creation of the
Young Italy and the Young Europe movements, he combined

political activism with a natural interest in literature. His first political essay, at the age of twenty-one, had been 'Dante's Love of
Country'. Byron had been one of his political inspirations in his cell
at Savona in 1830. As an exile in England, he had contributed essays
on Byron, Goethe, George Sand, and Carlyle to the *Westminster
Review* and other periodicals. In short, his appeal for Swinburne was
that of a leader dedicated to the new order in Italy and Europe,
while escaping that cultural philistinism endemic among political
zealots.

One other member of the group which met to discuss Algernon's
future was perhaps even more important than Mazzini. This was
Benjamin Jowett, who though he was not to begin his famous period
as Master of Balliol until 1870 was already well assured of entering
into his kingdom in the near future. It was Jowett who saw that the
answer to Swinburne's problems might lie in harnessing his
enthusiasm to one of those idols, like Landor, or Hugo, whose
worshipper he so easily became. Mazzini and the Italian cause
seemed likely to exercise the most powerful appeal.

Swinburne, in the wake of the *Poems and Ballads* scandal, had in
any case begun to write poetry in support of the Italian cause. In
1866-7 he was occupied with 'A Song of Italy', as well as 'Ode on
the Insurrection in Candia'. Though the latter poem referred to the
rebellion of the Cretans against Turkish domination, it was entirely
in sympathy with Mazzini's design for European freedom. Mazzini
himself had fallen out with the leaders of independent Italy by 1867
and, to that extent, might be regarded as a democrat first and Italian
patriot second. He was shown a copy of Swinburne's poem on the
Cretan rebellion, and expressed 'admiration of the spirit and form
of it'.[4] The discussion of Swinburne's future with Carlisle, Jowett
and Karl Blind proved fruitful. 'Accordingly Mazzini, informed of
the promise and situation of the young poet, promised to take
intellectual charge of him.'[5]

In practice it was to be a rather distant supervision. Though Dr
Bird dutifully informed Mazzini of the extent of his patient's consumption of brandy, it would have been absurd to expect the ageing
political leader to play the role of moral nursemaid to his young
admirer. Swinburne himself sent Mazzini a copy of *Atalanta in
Calydon* late in 1865. Mazzini replied on 10 March 1867, having
also by that time read the 'Ode on the Insurrection in Candia'.
However, Mazzini mingled with his praise a hope for his disciple's
moral improvement and a judicious reproof for *Poems and Ballads*.

Don't lull us to sleep with songs of egotistical love and idolatry of physical beauty: shake us, reproach, encourage, insult, brand the cowards, hail the martyrs, tell us all that we have a great Duty to fulfil, and that, before it is fulfilled, Love is an undeserved blessing, Happiness a blasphemy, belief in God a Lie. Give us a series of 'Lyrics for the Crusade'. Have not our praise, but our blessing. You *can* if you choose.[6]

On 30 March, Swinburne received his true reward, an invitation to meet Mazzini at Karl Blind's house. On the following day, the rapture of the occasion still in his blood, Swinburne described the occasion to his mother. Mazzini entered the crowded room and saw the unmistakable figure of the young poet. He walked straight across to him and was perhaps disconcerted when Swinburne went down on his knee before all the other guests and kissed Mazzini's hand. Mazzini, never having seen him before, none the less remarked 'I know *you*', and insisted on Swinburne reading 'A Song of Italy', while holding the poet's hand between his own. The letter which arrived at Holmwood thrilled with the excitement of the meeting. Swinburne announced:

He says he will take me to Rome when the revolution comes, and crown me with his own hands in the Capitol. He is as ready to go in for a little joke such as this or a bit of fun, and talk about anything that may turn up, as if he was nobody. He is a born king and chief and leader of men. You never saw such a beautiful smile as his. He is not the least bit discouraged or disheartened – and I don't know how anyone could be who had ever seen his face. . . . He is clearly the man to create a nation – to bid the dead bones live and rise.[7]

For the future, Mazzini was 'my Chief', and Swinburne swore to his mother that he would obey instantly if his leader were to say, 'Go and be killed because I tell you'.[8]

The news of Algernon's new cult of Mazzini was not received with enthusiasm by his parents. On 10 April he wrote to his sister Alice, asking her to reassure Lady Swinburne 'concerning my Chief and myself; he is not at all likely to despatch me on a deadly errand to Rome or Paris, nor have we Republicans any immediate intention of laying powder-mines under Windsor Castle'.[9] In more serious terms, he declined to write to 'Mimmie' about his new friend. 'I love her and him too much to write to the one about the other when I see it is hopeless to make the one share my love for the other.'[10]

A few weeks later, after further private meetings with Swinburne, Mazzini went abroad. Indeed, he was abroad for much of the time during which he had nominal 'intellectual charge' of the poet.

Unwelcome to the new regime in Italy, as he had been to the old, Mazzini was eventually imprisoned for some months at Gaeta in 1870. He continued to send messages for Swinburne through his other correspondents. When Swinburne heard that Mazzini had fallen ill late in 1867, he remarked to William Michael Rossetti that he would willingly have followed the example of one of Mirabeau's admirers who wished to have the blood transfused from his own body into that of his ailing hero. However, as Swinburne hastily added, such extreme remedies were not necessary in Mazzini's case.

The political romance of the revolutionary leader and the poet was marred by two considerations. First there was Swinburne's own realization that writing poetry to order, for whatever political cause, was not his *métier*. Writing to his mother in May 1867, he remarked of Mazzini that 'all he wants is that I should dedicate and consecrate my writing power to do good and serve others exclusively; which I can't. If I tried I should lose my faculty of verse even.'[11] Ruskin had offered the same advice and, though Mazzini stood far above Ruskin, the problem was the same.

On Mazzini's side, there was the increasing difficulty of trying to exert moral control, of whatever sort, over Swinburne. The stories of drunkenness were common, though the charade of the Circus Road brothel was almost presently not revealed. Yet news of the affair with Adah Isaacs Menken certainly reached Mazzini, accompanied by rumours to the effect that Swinburne was planning to satisfy public curiosity by going on the stage with her. 'I did not ask Swinburne about the stage or the double photograph,' wrote Mazzini, 'I really cannot play the part of spiritual father to him except when he himself offers means and opportunity.'[12] As to the poetry, Mazzini seemed to want the one thing which Swinburne could not do, or could do only at the cost of losing his poetic ability. 'I wish very much that he would write something,' Mazzini complained, 'giving up the absurd immoral French art for art's sake system.'[13] It seemed, after all, that Swinburne must renounce Théophile Gautier and the bible of aestheticism, *Mademoiselle de Maupin*, perhaps even Baudelaire and the lamplit lesbian embraces. Whatever Sade may have thought, to accomplish the revolution of political liberalism was no longer compatible with rebellion in the fields of art and sex.

In terms of Swinburne's conduct, Mazzini went further, believing that the poet would solve the problem himself by dying in the very near future. 'He will not last more than one or two years,' he wrote in 1870 and, in the following spring, 'My faith in his improvement is very weak.'[14]

As it happened, Mazzini himself died on 10 March 1872 in Pisa, still firmly believing that Swinburne's life was coming to its end. Swinburne lamented that 'I have lost the man whom I most loved and honoured of all men on earth', writing almost pityingly to his parents as to those who were not privileged to have shared in the worship of a moral colossus.[15] Having written the letter, he evidently drank alone until it was time for him to go to an evening party. This was being given by Dr Westland Marston, father of Swinburne's friend the blind poet Philip Marston, at Northumberland Terrace in Chalk Farm. It was a crowded, literary occasion, according to Arthur Munby, who witnessed the arrival of Swinburne, hopelessly drunk in his misery. It was whispered that the wretched poet was 'overcome by Mazzini's death', and they concealed him downstairs in the servants' quarters until he could be sobered up sufficiently to be sent back home.[16]

*   *   *

Of those who met at Lord Carlisle's house in 1867, it was not Mazzini who was to play the major role in Swinburne's life but Benjamin Jowett. Jowett, while admitting that Mazzini as a young man might have believed in the 'moral dagger' of assassination, none the less esteemed him highly, though more rationally than Swinburne. 'He was a very noble character, and had a genius far beyond that of ordinary statesmen.'[17] In this shared enthusiasm, as in so many other things, Swinburne and Jowett found common ground. Professor of Greek and future Master of Balliol though he might be, Jowett had stood firm in the face of the attempt to prosecute him for heresy over *Essays and Reviews*; he had applauded Mazzini's defence of Rome and swore that he had 'raised the Italian character by it'; he was no prude, and his admiration of the ancient world was as unfettered as, though rather more innocent than, Swinburne's. Aristophanes' jocular references to the seduction of boys were not to be cut from Oxford productions of Greek comedy. Only the insistent advice of John Addington Symonds alerted Jowett to the danger he would be in, and persuaded him to cut out an essay on 'Greek love' from his translation of the *Symposium*.[18] His was pre-eminently the unembarrassed mind of scholarship.

In the year before Mazzini's death, the relationship between the great patriot and Swinburne was still one of sympathy, though on Mazzini's side rather more detached. As for the issue of Italian unity, it was hardly one which could be kept warm after the acquisition of Venice in 1866 and Rome four years later. So it was that, in 1871, Jowett became active in his old pupil's life again. In the long vacation he invited Swinburne to Scotland, to that most Victorian of Oxford institutions, a reading party. At Tummel Bridge, Pitlochry, the party assembled in August. These gatherings in Scotland had been a familiar sight for thirty years past, an earlier Balliol reading party having been celebrated by A. H. Clough in one of his poems of social comedy, *The Bothie of Tober-Na-Vuolich: A Long-Vacation Pastoral*, in 1848. The medley of patrician athleticism, well bred indolence and casual scholarship is skilfully evoked in its lines.

It was the afternoon; and the sports were now at an ending.
Long had the stone been put, tree cast, and thrown the hammer....
Be it recorded in song who was first, who last, in dressing.
Hope was first, black-tied, white-waistcoated, simple, His Honour;
For the postman made out he was heir to the Earldom of Ilay....
Hope was first, His Honour, and next to his Honour the Tutor.
Still more plain the Tutor, the grave man nicknamed Adam,
White-tied, clerical, silent, with antique square-cut waistcoat
Formal, unchanged, of black cloth, but with sense and feeling beneath it;
Skilful in Ethics and Logic, in Pindar and Poets unrivalled;
Shady in Latin, said Lindsay, but *topping* in Plays and Aldrich....[19]

In the opening of his long poem Clough catches precisely the atmosphere of the select and patrician summer party, the model for Jowett's, to which Swinburne attached himself as a distinguished guest. Swinburne made much of his 'visit to the master of Balliol... who would have told me so ten years hence when I was rusticated, and *all but* expelled!'[20] The arrival of the poet among the summer visitors caused something of a sensation at Tummel Bridge, where holidaymakers strove for a glimpse of him, as they had done for a sight of Wordsworth or Tennyson. In the end, greatly to Swinburne's amusement, they packed the local church in large numbers on Sunday morning, mistakenly believing that they would be certain of seeing him there. Amusement apart, their belief shows the extent to which he muted or even suppressed his Sadean atheism in his published work.

The visit to Scotland was a success, Swinburne and Jowett

enjoying one another's company thoroughly. A sufficient time had elapsed between their period as master and pupil for them to meet on grounds of agreeable equality. Jowett had his reservations about modern poetry, including some of Swinburne's, yet he was an acute critic and valued in Swinburne a remarkable degree of classical scholarship. For the next fortnight there was swimming, and walking to Glencoe and the western Highlands. Swinburne volubly deplored what he considered to be Queen Victoria's erection of a memorial to Prince Albert's virility in the form of a stone phallus, but in general he behaved himself well.

In the following year, 1872, he went to Tummel Bridge earlier in the summer and stayed longer with Jowett. He joined in the physical exercises of the party, including the modest attempts at mountaineering which were considered appropriate to such vacation parties. 'I certainly am,' he wrote to his mother, 'and Jowett has remarked it to me, very much stronger and up to far more walking and climbing work than I was last year.'[21] Whether this was quite true seems doubtful. By the time that he wrote the letter, he had been with Jowett for almost three weeks and, with his usual powers of recuperation, had had longer to regain his strength than in the previous year.

Perhaps more obviously than any of Swinburne's other close acquaintances, Jowett sought to occupy the poet's mind. Ironically, the first task imposed in 1872 was that of assisting the Master in compiling a *Children's Bible*. It was less absurd than it seemed, for Swinburne's detailed knowledge of the Bible as a text had been, since childhood, repeatedly illustrated in letters and arguments, whatever his reservations about its philosophy. Jowett, while questioning the accuracy of some of Swinburne's Greek verses quoted in his work, none the less valued the poet's scholarship. In the great undertaking of translating Plato, the former pupil was at least a useful critic, if hardly a collaborator.

More than a dozen years after his first departure, Swinburne's steps turned towards Oxford and Balliol again, prompted by the renewal of an old friendship. He was frequently Jowett's companion at the Master's Lodging, as well as in Cornwall and at Torquay. It was at Torquay in 1874 that Jowett seemed most evidently to act as Swinburne's external conscience. Algernon, having sported verbally with Simeon Solomon over extravagant scenes of birching and furtive activities of other kinds, suddenly heard that the scapegrace painter with his obvious homosexual proclivities was also in the area. He wrote to Watts-Dunton, hoping very much that, if he did encounter Solomon, he would not be seen by Jowett in the company of so clearly disreputable a character. This delicacy of scruple on the part of a well known customer at the Circus Road brothel, the publicly proclaimed lover of Adah Menken, and the celebrated drunkard who partnered Consul Cameron's 'indecent embraces' at the Arts Club, says much for the nature of Swinburne's relationship to Jowett. W. H. Mallock, novelist and author of *The New Republic*, was an undergraduate at Balliol during the period of Swinburne's earlier visits. He was invited to dinner by Jowett and arrived to find that Swinburne was also to be present. Throughout the meal, Swinburne proved to be a subdued and disappointing conversationalist. After the meal, coffee was taken in the drawing-room, and presently Jowett left his guests to themselves. 'On Swinburne,' wrote Mallock, 'the effect of the Master's disappearance was magical. ... The words began to thrill me with the spell of his own recitation of them. Here at last I recognized the veritable genius who had made the English language a new instrument of passion.' Swinburne's enthusiasm, self-generating, reached a point of near paroxysm as he began to chant Sydney Dobell's description of a beautiful girl bathing. His voice, Mallock recalled, 'made the Master's academic rafters ring'. Then the door opened and Jowett's high pitched voice said, 'You'd both of you better go to bed now.' As though it were the nursery once again, the scourge of Church and State went quietly off to his room.[22]

It was difficult to imagine that the regime of the Master's Lodging could in itself do much for Swinburne. Mrs Knight, whose husband was the Master's butler, had instructions to unpack the bottles surreptitiously from Swinburne's luggage and put them out of harm's way until the visit was over. Yet by 1870 there were enough admiring young men in the college who were prepared to entertain the guest on his own terms. It was Mallock again who arrived at the end of an undergraduate lunch party at which the poet had been guest of honour. Swinburne was entertaining his young hosts with a recital from *La Soeur de la reine*. Then, having drunk some more port, he lay back in his chair and recited 'Dolores' and other pieces from *Poems and Ballads*. He asked for another glass to refresh himself after this, and promptly passed out in the rooms of his embarrassed host.[23]

Jowett was fully aware of the dangers of letting Swinburne out of his sight during the Oxford visits. One of the great counter-attractions for the poet was the company of Walter Pater at Brasenose and, indeed, that of the Greek scholar Ingram Bywater at Exeter. It was Bywater who told Gosse of the occasion when Jowett discovered that the wayward Algernon was missing from the Master's Lodging, tracked him to Bywater's rooms, 'swooped down on Swinburne and carried him of like an indignant nurse, with a glare at Bywater as he did so'.[24]

Yet Jowett had turned the Master's Lodging into an intellectual *salon* where Swinburne might feel at home. Among his more famous guests were Tennyson, Browning, George Eliot, G. H. Lewes, Ruskin, Matthew Arnold and Turgenev. He presided over these with easy self-assurance. Edwin Harrison, a Fellow of the College, reported: 'A "perpendicular" at the Master's last night ... dear old Jowler, simple, hospitable and genial; handsomer too than anybody in the room, man or woman.'[25] Young men of promise were also selected as undergraduate guests at certain dinners. It was on one such occasion that a future prime minister, H. H. Asquith, heard Swinburne in his middle years hotly defending the doctrine of tyrannicide in the face of Jowett's gentle teasing. Referring to the meetings of the Old Mortality, at which the morality of assassination had been debated many years before, Swinburne added, 'There was not one of us who would have questioned for a moment that sacred duty.'[26]

Social gatherings alone would hardly have deflected Swinburne from the 'racketing' career of his metropolitan life, as Gosse termed it. He and Jowett had a strong mutual interest in one another's work and it was on Jowett's advice, for instance, that Swinburne cut four thousand lines from his verse play *Bothwell*, upon which he was working at the time of the Tummel Bridge reading parties. Jowett, whose classical scholarship lay in broader sympathy with Athenian culture than with mere niceties of grammar, valued Swinburne's meticulous accuracy as reviser of his translations of Plato. It was this which gave rise to one of the best cameos of the two men together. Swinburne was staying at the Master's Lodging, reading through the proofs of *The Dialogues of Plato*.

One morning the Master was in his study going through with their authors the English essays which the undergraduates had sent in for his perusal and criticism: Swinburne was sitting, with the proofs of a Platonic dialogue, in a small adjoining room, the door between the two being open. It was the Master's habit sometimes to make rather withering remarks to these young essayists and to-day one of his most biting observations was interrupted by a joyful crow of laughter from the next room and Swinburne's exultant voice exclaiming, 'Another howler, Master!' 'Thank you, Algernon,' said the Master meekly, and gently closed the door.[27]

In many respects, Swinburne and Jowett were perfectly matched, whether in the more formal setting of Balliol or in the reading parties, first in Scotland and from 1874 at Great Malvern, where the poet would be, as Edwin Harrison remarked, the life and soul of the proceedings with his nightly impersonations of Sarah Gamp and general gaiety. Unlikely though it seems, he found in Jowett a reflection of his own high spirits in these meetings. It was precisely this quality of gaiety which, for Swinburne, constituted part of Jowett's appeal and which, as an instance, had led to Jowett playing the part of a Chinese executioner in a common-room charade.[28] On this evidence, there is every reason to accept such judgements as that of Sir Geoffrey Faber, who thought 'the poet himself found the society of the Master more continually to his taste than that of any other man he knew',[29]

The Swinburne of the Balliol reading parties and the worship of Mazzini was contemporary with the figure of the flagellation brothels and the solitary drinking. With Jowett and with men of a similar stamp, his mind was constantly occupied; alone in London he needed something to occupy him in addition to his literary work and found little except his own compulsions. It was a dilemma which William Bell Scott had predicted far back in Swinburne's youth as he surveyed the boy's effortless and privileged existence. Jowett and Mazzini between them had, moreover, steered Swinburne as a poet into the support of Italian unity. It was a cause which he regarded with natural sympathy but not one which had taken a central place in his earlier writing.

The impulse which Swinburne's two mentors gave to his work led to the appearance of a new collection of poems, *Songs Before Sunrise*, in 1871. *A Song of Italy* had been published separately but much of the new book was devoted to the theme of Italian unity. It was in many ways a dangerous subject. By 1868, when these poems were written, let alone by 1871, the unification of Italy was a subject of decreasing urgency and declining topicality. When Swinburne's collection appeared, the great cause was fast becoming a mere curiosity of European political history. Worse still, it was evident here, as in *A Song of Italy*, that poetic instinct had been sacrificed to a sense of political obligation.

By no means all the poems in *Songs Before Sunrise* are confined to

the question of Italy, the more general theme of political change
being evident in most of them. One of the most influential was 'The
Eve of Revolution', designed to rouse each of the major European
countries in turn.

> The trumpets of the four winds of the world
> From the ends of the earth blow battle....

Admirably democratic and undeniably humanitarian, such verses
were apparently doomed to give the impression of Swinburne
energetically but vainly trying to generate inspiration on a subject
which belonged to other men.

> I hear the midnight on the mountains cry
> With many tongues of thunders, and I hear
> Sound and resound the hollow shield of sky
> With trumpet-throated winds that charge and cheer....

Such pieces gave Gosse the feeling of a whirlwind let loose in a
vacuum and, certainly, it is hard to read them without concluding
that something has gone irremediably wrong with Swinburne's writing, and that Mazzini and Jowett had much better have left him
alone. Nor is there much improvement when Swinburne, in his
poetic tours of Europe, as in 'A Watch in the Night', tries to harness
his former Baudelairean eroticism to the new cause.

> France, what of the night? –
> Night is the prostitute's noon,
> Kissed and drugged till she swoon,
> Spat upon, trod upon, whored.
> With bloodred rose-garlands dight,
> Round me reels in the dance
> Death, my saviour, my lord,
> Crowned; there is no more France.

Yet the weakness which besets these poems is the deficiency
of imagination characteristic of political or 'committed' verse.
Trumpets are blown and support is rallied with a remorseless fre-
quency. Other men's example, if not their poetry, was conscripted
for the new order in such pieces as 'The Eve of Revolution'. When
Swinburne turned to Greece, it was in terms of sunlight upon
Thermopylae and Athens, the sea-wall of Salamis, and the grassy
plain of Marathon. The inspiration surely belongs to the famous
'Isles of Greece' verses in the third canto of Byron's *Don Juan*.
For all that, it was not only Swinburne and other enthusiasts for

the Italian cause who admired the poems. 'I hear what splendid things you have been reading to our friends in London,' wrote Dante Gabriel Rossetti from Hawkhurst on 22 March 1870.[30] In this observation, at least, much of the appeal of *Songs Before Sunrise* was indicated. The poems commended themselves most of all to those who were privileged to attend Swinburne's readings or 'performances' of his poems. He confessed that he detested the act of writing and was given to regarding speech or recital as the true poetic medium. Into these private appearances he put the bulk of his emotional energy. 'I have had so many readings, and reading to a company is just the most tiring thing I know,' he wrote to his mother. 'It leaves you next day hardly up to writing or reading either.... I don't wonder it killed Dickens.'[31] On the other hand, it is easy to see why Swinburne should have regarded the act of performance as inseparable from the writing of poetry, it was an experience for which brandy made a poor substitute. True stimulation was in 'The intoxicating effect of a circle of faces hanging on your words and keeping up your own excitement by theirs which is catching even when your own words on mere paper are stale to you.'[32]

There was, moreover, a purely aesthetic reason which made Swinburne's political poetry, so empty and bombastic to later generations, acceptable to his Victorian contemporaries. Read at such a level, *Songs Before Sunrise* may appear to be competent political rhetoric, addressed to an age which was conditioned to admire oratory. Even parliamentary oratory was regarded with unprecedented respect in the historical figures of Burke or Sheridan. For the splendour of his rhetoric no less than his convictions, Burke was the idol of John Morley. Sheridan's speech on the impeachment of Warren Hastings was regarded by Byron as the finest political speech in the history of England. The tradition of such rhetoric, strengthened by the prominence of Demosthenes and Cicero in the education of the nation's leaders, continued into the age of Gladstone. Even such comparatively subdued parliamentary speakers as Palmerston were capable of astonishing performances on the right occasion. On 24 June 1850, as Foreign Secretary, Palmerston rose to defend his conduct in guaranteeing the freedom of British citizens the world over, by force of arms where necessary. He began to speak at a quarter to ten, when the last flush of sun was fading from the summer sky. He sat down at twenty past two, as the short night ended with the first glimmering of dawn. He was heard, for four and a half hours, with the attention normally reserved for a great actor, and was cheered at the conclusion with a rapture generally accorded to a virtuoso musician.

To a world of contemporaries brought up upon such legends and examples, *Songs Before Sunrise* had an appeal quite distinct from the lyric passion of *Poems and Ballads*, not least when the pieces were read or performed by Swinburne. Those who received them merely as the printed word admired with respect rather than ecstasy, as they might have done Palmerston's speech.

In practice, many who thrilled to the revolutionary promise of *Songs Before Sunrise* belonged generally to the same group which had admired the rebellious eroticism of the earlier book. Yet even in terms of poetic achievement, the more private poetry of the later volume continued to show an intimate modernism which was beyond the scope of most writers in the 1860s, as in the verses 'Before a Crucifix'.

> Here, down between the dusty trees,
>   At this lank edge of haggard wood,
> Women with labour-loosened knees
>   With gaunt backs bowed by servitude,
> Stop, shift their loads, and pray....

Both the freedom of rhythm and the intensity or compactness of verbal description would make such versification seem in advance of much of the *Georgian Poetry* volumes in 1912–19 and not anti-quated by the poetic fashions of the 1930s.

Swinburne, having dedicated the volume to Mazzini as its princi-pal inspiration, decided to use it as the first means of freeing himself from Hotten and thereby began the squabble which ended only with Hotten's death. Legal opinion, consulted by Swinburne's advisers and by F. S. Ellis as the alternative publisher, pronounced that though Hotten had an indisputable right to the earlier works, he could not reasonably claim the right to publish books which Swinburne had not written at the time. In consequence, Ellis pub-lished the new collection while Hotten was put off for the time being by a clear warning that any action on his part would result in Swinburne demanding a complete disclosure of his accounts. Since it is suggested that some of these accounts referred to money taken from Swinburne on the basis of blackmail, Hotten conceded defeat in the matter of *Songs Before Sunrise*.[33]

If Swinburne believed that he had mended his ways in the

new collection, he was soon to find that there were reviewers of a different opinion. To abandon the loves of Sappho or Hermaphroditus did not automatically convey respectability upon the poet or his works. On 14 January 1871, the *Saturday Review* dismissed the reformed Swinburne and his supporters.

We may perhaps excuse little boys and girls who have felt admiration rather than disgust as they have watched a comrade roll himself in his miry puddle. But when educated men, and we may add women too, read with admiration the love poetry of Mr Swinburne – the most unnatural perhaps of all writers on love since Swift – we cannot repress our indignation. . . . As we opened Mr Swinburne's latest poem, we were prepared to find merely a second or third repetition of the old performance. We must do him the justice at once to admit that he is not indecent. Offensive, indeed, he is, as he always is; and silly, as he often is. . . . Much as he delights in what used in our younger days to be called blasphemy, he delights still more, if that were possible, in the reddest of Red Republicanism.

To live down the reputation of *Poems and Ballads* was difficult. Even when reviewers had finished reminding their readers that this was the poet of unspeakable loves and vile practices, their disapproval coloured any discussion of the political freedom which Swinburne advocated. Thus, for instance, the *Edinburgh Review* for July 1871 dismissed his demands for European liberty on the grounds that the freedom for which he argued was 'wholly negative, and as such it is necessarily delusive and false. True liberty has its root in law, in the higher principles of our nature, is indeed the moral reflex of the responsibility thence arising.' Whether this was a truer freedom than the removal of repression might be doubted, but it was certainly a more restrictive and anti-libertarian view which had been made fashionable by Swinburne's former companion in the Old Mortality, the philosopher T. H. Green.

In more specific terms, Swinburne's political views were clear, though perhaps not always consistent. He was pleased to hear of the execution of the Emperor Maximilian of Mexico, seeing in this the downfall of tyranny, though he supported the Confederacy in the United States Civil War, despite its system of slavery. There was, in his view, a divine right of secession. The Franco-Prussian War of 1870 filled him with uncertainty, since he naturally supported France but this meant wishing victory to the odious Napoleon III. However, the Prussian triumph, followed in its turn by the coming of the Third Republic in France brought the best of results from the worst of catastrophes. The death of the emperor, in exile at

Chislehurst, inspired Swinburne only with contempt for those who mourned his passing.

One of the criticisms of Swinburne's political poetry which came easily to the hand of the *Saturday Review* was that while other men had fought and died for the causes which he claimed to support, he himself had passed his life in ease and decadence. It was all very well for him to offer his life's blood for Mazzini, when the only blood he shed in reality was from injuries received in falling out of a hansom cab. In 1867, there came an opportunity for him to take a more direct part in political affairs. After a decade of renewed struggles for Irish independence, the Fenian movement had staged some of its most spectacular attacks on authority, led in many cases by Irishmen who had served with distinction as officers on both sides in the American Civil War. Attempts to seize Chester Castle, to start a general insurrection in Ireland and to blow open Clerkenwell prison ended in failure. Another attempt, to rescue two Fenian prisoners from a prison van in Manchester, succeeded. The two men escaped, but in the course of the attack a policeman was killed and the rescuers themselves were caught and condemned for his murder.

Throughout the year, the courage and idealism evident in Fenian prisoners on trial moved many Englishmen to campaign against their execution. In the case of those condemned at Manchester, Swinburne wrote his verses 'An Appeal to England', which appeared in the *Morning Star* on 22 November 1867. The theme of the poem was that political executions were alien to the tradition of England, but the prime minister, Lord Derby, insisted on regarding the crime as one of ordinary murder. The Fenians were executed on the following day.

Yet in consequence of this, Swinburne received an invitation from the national Reform League to stand for Parliament, his costs being guaranteed by the League. It was in August 1868 that he reported to his mother this 'offer of a seat in Parliament next session if I would only allow my name to be put up'.[34] It was to be a constituency on the Isle of Wight where, presumably, Swinburne might hope for election as a Radical Liberal candidate. The National Reform League had been formed to support the Reform Bill of 1868 and to urge such further measures as the abolition of the House of Lords. Its vice-president was Charles Bradlaugh, republican and atheist as well as a fellow member of the Cannibal Club. Swinburne's election to Parliament might well have provoked the constitutional crisis which Bradlaugh brought to the House of

Commons with his own election in 1880. As a republican and atheist it was absurd for him to swear allegiance to the Crown as a Christian. For all that, Bradlaugh was prepared to recite a form of words as the means to parliamentary activity. It was the Tory members who prevented him on the grounds of his words and deeds outside the House. There followed the political farce of Bradlaugh's being repeatedly expelled from the House and just as repeatedly re-elected by his constituents until he was at length permitted to take his seat.

Swinburne, with his well-advertised opinions on similar subjects to Bradlaugh's, might even have brought forward this crisis by a dozen years through his election to the Commons. It was not to be. He consulted Mazzini and upon his advice declined the offer, as he explained to his mother.

> Of course I felt myself flattered, but at first objected on the grounds that I was not fit or properly trained, and might be taking a better man's place – but most of my friends have been day after day urging and pressing me to accept. Still I don't think it is in my line.[35]

* * *

Apart from other considerations, Swinburne's reputation as a poet was now sufficiently widespread and impressive, despite the reproaches of the *Saturday Review*, to make any descent into the farmyard squabblings of the House of Commons seem absurd. Indeed, he had come to terms with John Morley, the author of the famous review of *Poems and Ballads* in the *Saturday Review*, who was now editor of the *Fortnightly Review*, one of the most influential periodicals of the late-Victorian period. It was in December 1866 that Joseph Knight introduced Swinburne to Morley. Even though no more than four months had passed since the review of *Poems and Ballads*, any quarrel between them was forgotten and Swinburne contributed regularly to the *Fortnightly* until 1892. For Swinburne, the periodical was both a guarantee of publication for his individual poems and essays and a useful source of income. In his later dealings with it the editor was not Morley but Frank Harris, who claimed that at some cost to himself he raised the rate of payment for Swinburne and Matthew Arnold to twenty-five pounds a page.[36]

Ready acceptance of his work by such periodicals was only one feature of Swinburne's established position as a poet, despite the hostility of reviews. Among his peers he was acknowledged as the leader of the new generation, Dante Gabriel Rossetti referring even to *Songs Before Sunrise* as 'The glorious poetry of your own which I heard last week', and confessing that such literary splendour 'made me meek indeed'.[37] Frank Harris, again, remembered coming across Swinburne's poetry in the United States in 1873, when its reputation there was at its height. 'My very soul was taken,' he wrote of the effect of the poems upon him, 'I had no need to read them twice.... I shall not forget them.... They flooded my eyes with tears, my heart with passionate admiration. In this state the old gentleman came back and found me, a cowboy to all appearance, lost, tear-drowned, in Swinburne.'[38]

As Harris discovered, Swinburne was no mere discovery of his own but a poet with a readership and reputation in America to match those in England, admired by Whitman and abominated by Emerson. In Europe too his poetry began to appear widely in German and in French. With the advent of the Third Republic, even the conservative Paris newspaper *Figaro* was ready to print his work. 'Not if I know it,' Swinburne replied.[39] For all that, he was keenly interested in the new generation of French poets including Stéphane Mallarmé who, like Baudelaire, was a translator of Edgar Allan Poe. Some of Swinburne's work was translated by Victor Hugo's son, François-Victor, and other poems by Augusta Holmès. Reputedly the daughter of Alfred de Vigny, and certainly the idol of George Moore and mistress of César Franck, she also inspired the passion of Saint-Saëns. Her career, as odd in its way as Swinburne's own, is graphically described in Laurence Davies's masterly study *César Franck and his Circle,* which reveals her as a singularly appropriate champion of the English poet in France.[40] As Swinburne's correspondence with George Powell shows, he had found a new attraction in the operas of Wagner, an interest which he shared with Augusta Holmès, who went so far as to compose her own operas in imitation of, and homage to, the great German master.

*   *   *

Quite apart from his secret fantasies, with which he regaled men like Howell and Hotten, Swinburne wrote his public poetry in at least two different genres. First he was the author of *Poems and Ballads* and *Songs Before Sunrise,* the poet of moral rebellion or political revolt. He was also, more prolifically, the poet of unactable and, in the end, unsaleable dramas. In the early 1870s he had been at work on the sequel to *Chastelard*, the second part of his massive trilogy based upon the life of Mary Queen of Scots. It was published under the title of *Bothwell* in 1874 and brought the story of the queen forward from the murder of Rizzio until the heroine's flight into England.

Inspiration had not entirely failed him but the sheer length of the verse drama was daunting to reviewers. *Bothwell* is some fifteen thousand lines long and, as Gosse remarked, ran to 532 pages. In simpler terms, it was several times the length of any Shakespeare play. Even the *Saturday Review* was obliged to admit that there was nothing indecent or shocking about the play and, to that extent, its reception was more favourable. Yet it was, as Gosse called it, 'a leviathan', and Swinburne admitted to Morley that the subject had got the better of him.

I find that to cast into dramatic mould the events of those eighteen months it is necessary to omit no detail, drop no link in the chain, if the work is either to be dramatically coherent or historically intelligible; while every stage of the action is a tragic drama of itself which cries aloud for representation. . . . Shakespeare alone could have grappled with it satisfactorily, and wrung the final prize of tragedy from the clutch of historic fact. But having taken up the enterprise I will not at least drop it till I have wrestled my best with it.[41]

The problem, as Gosse described it, was that Swinburne toiled onward at this 'mounting structure . . . without, for a long time, any clear conception of its limits. It dilated in bulk and material at every step he took.'[42] Jowett had suggested in August 1871 that the opening scene should be cut. Swinburne stayed in bed all the next morning, during the Tummel Bridge reading party, and worked upon his manuscript. He handed Jowett the revised version, which the Master scanned and found to be three lines longer than on the previous day.[43] Swinburne accepted Jowett's suggestion of cutting the play by four thousand lines, yet this hardly altered the impression of *Bothwell* as a manifestation of the author's ill ordered state of mind during the early 1870s.

For all that, the book sold well initially, though it was not possible to find an American publisher willing to take it on. By July 1874 Swinburne was even discussing with William Michael Rossetti the possibility of putting *Bothwell* on the stage. Since the play in its uncut form would have run for at least ten or twelve hours, he was willing for some cuts to be made, though nothing in his work was to be altered. An actress was chosen to play the part of Mary Stuart, but the production was not undertaken. Even heavily cut, the prospect of getting Swinburne's leviathan on to the stage was not to be contemplated.[44] By October 1875 the play had been cut to a size suitable for production and sent to Swinburne. In its condensed form he found it chaotic and incomprehensible, the necessary explanation of the plot being incompatible with a reduction of the drama to stage-length. There the matter ended.

The fate of *Bothwell* is more important in the story of Swinburne's life than the mere failure of an individual book. One of the central problems, as W. B. Scott and others believed, was that Swinburne's salvation might lie in having some great undertaking to occupy him. The truth was that he worked with great speed, regarding seventy lines of verse as a poor day's output.[45] At this rate, however spasmodic the work might be, his books of collected poems represented brief periods of spiritual exhilaration interspersed by long phases of inactivity. He had, of course, produced critical work on such authors as Blake and Byron but it was difficult to escape the sense, in his middle years, that some central work was missing. The verse dramas made up for this, though they seemed the fruit of labour rather than of inspiration, while the readership for these unactable monsters grew uncertain as the tastes of the Romantic Revival finally yielded to those of the later Victorians.

Ironically, there was one other literary form in which Swinburne might have achieved a fame to surpass that of *Bothwell* and perhaps even to equal *Poems and Ballads*. In the Meredithian chapters of *Love's Cross-Currents*, and for that matter *Lesbia Brandon*, he had shown more than a casual talent for writing fiction. Indeed, as his style indicates, he had precisely the type of subtle elegance in fiction which was to characterize the new age of Meredith or Henry James, and to mark the passing of the earlier Victorian manner. That he should have ignored this possibility is hardly surprising. In *Love's Cross-Currents* he had written a novel which might have caused little comment after Meredith's career but which was a remarkable literary innovation when Meredith had only just appeared as a novelist. Yet the book failed to find a publisher until its appearance under a pseudonym, in the *Tatler*, in 1877. With *Lesbia Brandon* the case was worse, though Swinburne thought it his most important unpublished work. By 1878, after Chatto's failure to issue it, there was little more that could be done. By comparison, however, the verse dramas on Mary Stuart seem a labour of futility, while the unwritten novels of Swinburne remain one of the great losses to an ideal Victorian literature.

Atalanta in Calydon, being modelled on the length and style of Greek drama, gave Swinburne's poetry a freedom from historical constraint as well as limiting the size of the work to one which could be sustained by imaginative flights of verse without the mere padding of narrative. During a visit to Jowett at West Malvern in the summer of 1875, he set to work on a successor to *Atalanta*, ten years after the appearance of the former play. This later drama, *Erectheus*, was written almost effortlessly, according to Gosse's account, and in this respect too contrasts clearly with the labour expended upon *Bothwell* and its kind.

The subject of the new play was the downfall of Erectheus, King of Athens, as described by Lycurgus the orator. Embroiled in war with Eumoplus and the Thracians, Erectheus inquired of the oracle at Delphi what he must do to obtain victory. The oracle replied that he would be victorious if he sacrificed one of his daughters before the great battle. Erectheus obeyed, won a great victory and was, in turn, destroyed by Poseidon the father of his antagonist Eumoplus.

Comparison with the story of Iphigenia was inevitable but, to Swinburne's annoyance, some readers and reviewers took the play as being merely a translation from Euripides rather than an original work. They were not entirely to blame. Euripides had written an *Erectheus*, subsequently lost apart from a fragment quoted by Lycurgus. On the other hand, Swinburne had little sympathy with Euripides, by contrast with his devotion to Aeschylus, whom he had tried to emulate in his own play.

Erectheus was, on the whole, politely and even respectfully received by contemporary critics. John Addington Symonds, for instance, acknowledged that it was 'constructed upon pure classic principles, and will bear the most minute scrutiny that the scholar can give'.[46] This, in essence, was the problem; *Erectheus* was commended for its scholarship and its fidelity to the forms of classical drama rather than for the headlong poetic exuberance which had characterized *Atalanta in Calydon*.

A greater undertaking than *Erectheus* also dated from the years immediately following the *Poems and Ballads* scandal. In 1869 Swinburne wrote to Dante Gabriel Rossetti, discussing that most popular of themes among mid-Victorian poets, the legends of King Arthur.[47] Rossetti himself was planning a poem about the quest for the Holy Grail, though it was never written. Morris had already shown his enthusiasm for such subjects. Swinburne, dismissing Tennyson's attempts as 'Idylls of the Prince Consort', and the 'Morte d'Albert', announced that he had begun a long poem of his own. It was to appear thirteen years later as *Tristram of Lyonesse*, occupying a good deal of his time after the completion of *Bothwell*.

Other considerations apart, Swinburne's style of living was costing far more money than his parents could afford to give him. By 1872 he wrote to John Morley that he was 'pressed to death' for money and he complained frequently of his lack of 'tin'.[48] *Tristram*, whatever its merits or defects, was written as a conscious means of paying bills. With his bank account overdrawn, his half-year's allowance spent and bills falling due, Swinburne consulted Thomas Purnell on the possibility of selling off bits of *Tristram* already completed in order to placate his creditors.

He had, of course, made the financial situation worse by spending large sums of money on drink and even larger ones to buy the favours of the Circus Road ladies and their professional sisters. Yet, ironically, his position deteriorated just as his reputation seemed most secure. Chapman and Hall were negotiating to bring out his works in a cheap collected edition in 1872, the same year in which Swinburne was asking Morley to send him cheques direct so that he could raise money at once by cashing them without having to put them through his bank account. On the other hand, the idea of a popular edition of his works, freely available and falling into the hands of the young and the innocent, amused him greatly, as he wrote to George Powell. 'The prospect of the widespread depravation which will ensue in our moral, religious and hitherto happy land is enough to make God wriggle in heaven and the Marquis stand erect in his grave.'[49]

At times, his reputation as an established figure in English literature was confirmed in unexpected ways. In 1874 he was informed, apparently by Jowett, that his poetry was much admired by Victoria's youngest son, Prince Leopold, then an undergraduate at Christ Church. Never one to allow mere political prejudice to interfere with literary appreciation, Swinburne at once pronounced the young prince to be 'a thoroughly nice boy, modest and simple and gentle, devoted to books and poetry, without pretence or affectation'. Three years later, when there was public grumbling about Leopold, one of his most enthusiastic defenders was the author of *La Fille du Policeman* and *La Soeur de la Reine*.[50]

Despite the more private excesses of which he was increasingly accused, Swinburne the established author seemed conscious of a position which he was obliged to keep up. He wrote to his mother of the younger poets who looked to him for a lead, much as he might have written about being the captain of his house at school. 'I have been gathering about me the circle of younger poets who are called *my* disciples. . . . They are very nice fellows and very loyal to me as their leader.'[51] As for the minor poets of the day who thought to be his rivals, Swinburne swore to Watts-Dunton in 1875 that they had rights to neither titles nor souls if men of his calibre required them.[52]

At times, as Gosse described it, Swinburne's growing self-esteem appeared utterly ludicrous. In 1878, when his consumption of brandy had reached even greater and more alarming proportions, Swinburne went to Glasgow to stay with his old friend John Nichol, who was still Professor of English Language and Literature. They went out one evening and, during the course of it, Swinburne became so drunk that there was nothing for it but to get a cab and take him back to the house. Nichol decided that in order to prevent Swinburne getting at such drink as happened to be in the house itself, he would carry him upstairs, put him into bed, and then lock him into the room. Having done this, Nichol was presently aware of sounds from the locked room, the impatient rattling of the door handle, and Swinburne's high-pitched voice, wailing, 'Oh! my God! And he a petulant provincial pedagogue, and I a poet of European reputation!'[53]

In 1867, Swinburne's American friend E. C. Stedman had received Bayard Taylor's description of the poet as 'a wilful, perverse, unreasonable spoiled child'.[54] It was a common enough reaction but at thirty years old, let alone during the following decade, it was hard to see how time and chance would permit the indulgence of 'childhood' to continue much longer. Swinburne's way of life depended on the existence of Holmwood as a refuge and on his father as the means of rescue. There was also, of course, the seaside home of the Gordons at Niton on the Isle of Wight, where he spent the summer of 1874 after a collapse which had brought him first to Holmwood and then to the soothing mental Aegean of childhood. Yet even if his aunt, Lady Mary Gordon, had been prepared to accept responsibility for him in the future, his lease upon the security of Niton was running out too.

In 1876, Swinburne had spent much of the year at Holmwood recuperating, though in October he claimed to have suffered a relapse through being poisoned by some Indian lilies which were left

in his bedroom. The victim sensed, with literary aptness, an echo of
the horrors of Jacobean tragedy in this affliction. He was still at
Holmwood, semi-convalescent, in the new year of 1877. There, on 6
March, he began to write to his friends – to Jowett first of all –
informing them of the death of Admiral Swinburne two days earlier.

The spoilt child, the prodigal son so regularly fetched home from
impending metropolitan ruin, was now the head of the family, a man
of forty with no apparent foundation to his life. There were places
for such men, as Charles Reade had shown in his novel *Hard Cash*
and in his campaign over the lunacy laws. Private asylums were
prepared to lock away sane men and women who were merely
drunkards or nuisances, provided a doctor could be persuaded to
sign the necessary form. True, Reade's campaign had exposed the
worst abuses and, in any case, Swinburne was in no immediate
danger so long as his mother was alive. After that, it was less certain
that he could be left to his own destruction.

Holmwood was, of course, to be sold. The family fortunes were
not sufficient to keep it going after the admiral's death. Lady
Swinburne would find her home elsewhere and, for Algernon, there
was nothing but a return to the lodgings in Great James Street. The
long childhood was, it seemed, at an end.

Chapter 9

'Dear Theodore,
What's Dunton?'

O NE of Swinburne's first and most revealing responses to his
father's death was to compose a pious funeral elegy, 'Inferiae',
lamenting that he 'whose heart fed mine has passed into the past'.
The young rebel who wished to see Napoleon III 'kick heels with his
throat in a rope', whose romps at Circus Road paid unworthy
homage to the Marquis de Sade, and who viewed the profanation
of Dulgarian women with unalloyed amusement, now struck a
Tennysonian chord of sombre platitude. 'Crossing the Bar' was
only the most obvious of parallels in Swinburne's mourning of a
father,

> Whose sail went seaward yesterday from shore
> To cross the last of many an unsailed sea.

As for the questions of religious faith and personal immortality, a
good Sadean would surely have a suitably irreverent answer for such
delusions. Swinburne, in the last verse of the poem, faltered.

> The life, the spirit, and the work were one
> That here – ah, who shall say, that here are done?
> Not I, that know not; father, not thy son,
>   For all the darkness of the night and sea.

In one respect, there was nothing new in this concession to the
existence of a spirit after bodily death. In 1865 he had written to
Seymour Kirkup that the transmigration of souls seemed a reason-
able doctrine.[1] In 1882, on the death of Dante Gabriel Rossetti,
Swinburne informed William Bell Scott that his strong inclination
was to believe in the survival of individual and conscious life after
bodily dissolution.[2] Indeed, his poem on Rossetti's death, 'A Death
on Easter Day', could hardly be read in any other sense.

> Albeit the bright sweet mothlike wings be furled,
>   Hope sees, past all division and defection,

And higher than swims the mist of human breath,
The soul most radiant once in all the world
Requickened to regenerate resurrection
Out of the likeness of the shadow of death.

In more general terms, he held no more than a creedless faith, as
he expressed it to Scott on this occasion. To William Michael
Rossetti, in 1869, he had remarked that no atheist, so far as he was
aware, would positively assert the impossibility of a creative intelligence in the universe, but that no creed could logically follow from
this.[3] In short, as a child of his time, Swinburne's beliefs ran parallel
to such non-dogmatic but intensely cultivated fashions as the new
'spiritualism'. A practice which guaranteed the most evident
personal benefits of orthodox religion while making few of its
demands contained an obvious appeal for all sorts and conditions of
men and women.

Despite his earlier views, Swinburne's poetry on occasions of this
kind had begun to assume a conventionality which seemed worthy
of Tennyson. Indeed, what distinguished them was, as Browning
remarked of two other debaters in 'Bishop Blougram's Apology',

... a life of doubt diversified by faith
For one of faith diversified by doubt.

To expect that Swinburne should present a consistent theology, or
even philosophy, was absurd. Such things were to be left to the
theologians and the philosophers. He, at least, could indulge the
luxury of inconsistency, being caustically anti-clerical or anti-theist
on one day and then pondering personal immortality the next, as the
mood took him. Indeed, it was not only his father's death which
preoccupied him in such considerations. Despite the nervous energy
and the volatile temperament, despite the undergraduate intem-
perance of his drinking habits and the adolescent enthusiasms, he
was forty years old in the year of Admiral Swinburne's death. He
had himself already reached the average age of death for the Victorian period. There was, of course, no reason why a man of his
social standing and comparative wealth should not be preserved far
beyond forty. Early mortality among the urban poor was the cause
of the low average figure. Yet the *enfant terrible* of the 1860s
appeared, with little warning, to find himself in the declining
decades of his life. For the first time, the past seemed more important than the future.

*   *   *

Yet the 1870s as a decade showed Swinburne at his most vigorous, argumentative and malicious. For all his meditations on religion and immortality, he fastened upon Tennyson the sanctimonious philosopher with merciless ridicule. Swinburne, with his ear for rhythm and cadence, had a genius for parody. He chose as his target, in 1870, Tennyson's poem 'The Higher Pantheism', with its pompous and remorseless justifying of God to the lover of nature.

> God is law, say the wise; O Soul, and let us rejoice,
> For if He thunder by law, the thunder is yet His voice.
> Law is God, say some; no God at all, says the fool,
> For all we have power to see is a straight staff bent in a pool;
> And the ear of man cannot hear, and the eye of man cannot see;
> But if we could see and hear, this Vision – were it not He?

Swinburne's version of this, 'The Higher Pantheism in a Nutshell', catches both the metre and tone of the poem, though ridiculing most effectively of all the owl-eyed solemnity of Tennyson's popular philosophizing.

> One, who is not, we see; but one, whom we see not, is:
> Surely this is not that: but that is assuredly this.
> What, and wherefore, and whence? for under is over and under:
> If thunder could be without lightning, lightning could be without thunder....
> Parallels all things are: yet many of these are askew:
> You are certainly I: but certainly I am not you.
> Springs the rock from the plain, shoots the stream from the rock:
> Cocks exist for the hen: but hens exist for the cock.
> God, whom we see not, is: and God, who is not, we see:
> Fiddle, we know, is diddle: and diddle, we take it, is dee.

In similar terms, Swinburne parodied Browning in 'John Jones', and Elizabeth Barrett Browning in 'The Poet and the Woodlouse'.

Though he was not engaged upon the composition of such poems as had caused so much controversy in 1866, Swinburne had been reading and admiring the poetry of John Donne during 1876. By the following year, influenced to some extent by Donne's style, he had translated a number of the poems of Villon. As he warned Norman McColl, a few of these were fit for publication and others were not. 'The Ballad of Villon and Fat Madge', in which the copulatory antics of hero and heroine are described 'Inside this brothel where we drive our trade', remained unpublished until Wise's private edition of 1910. Even the less Rabelaisean and more charming eroticism of the Villon poem 'The Complaint of the Fair Armouress' led to the substitution of asterisks for six of its lines when it appeared in *Poems and Ballads: Second Series* in 1878. In the seventh stanza, describing the girl's youthful beauty, only the first five of the eight lines were considered safe for publication by Andrew Chatto.

> The shapely slender shoulders small,
>   Long arms, hands wrought in glorious wise,
> Round little breasts, the hips withal
>   High, full of flesh, not scant of size,
>   Fit for all amorous masteries;
> The large loins, and the flower that was
>   Planted above my firm round thighs
> In a small garden of soft grass....[4]

If Chatto was cautious, this was primarily because Swinburne, a dozen years after *Poems and Ballads*, was still an object of suspicion to those who were able to make trouble for him in the press – and even in the courts. As late as 1883 an announcement involving him was issued by the newly formed Society for the Suppression of Blasphemous Literature.

> We propose to get up cases, as our funds will allow, against Professor Huxley, Dr Tyndall, Herbert Spencer, Swinburne, the author of 'Supernatural Religion', the publishers of Mill's works, the publishers of Strauss's works, Leslie Stephen, John Morley, the editor of the *Jewish World*, Dr Martineau and others, who by their writings have sown widespread unbelief, and in some cases rank Atheism, in cultivated families.[5]

'The Higher Pantheism in a Nutshell' might be a joke to Swinburne and his kind: to his opponents it was intolerable trifling with piety. Elsewhere, though it was difficult to separate some of the blasphemy from some of the indecency, there were even stronger grounds for action by such groups. Indeed, Swinburne had involved himself in a battle with the Society for the Suppression of Vice. The most famous of all self-appointed guardians of public morality, and known to its chagrin as 'The Vice Society' for short, it had been founded in 1802 with the backing of William Wilberforce, Zachary Macaulay and other men of influence. For more than half a century it pursued a campaign of systematic prosecutions of publishers of obscene or blasphemous literature. Between 1834 and the Obscene Publications Act of 1857, the Vice Society had brought 154 obscenity prosecutions and had gained convictions in every one. During one of its purges it managed to force the closure of thirty-seven of the fifty-seven shops in London whose books it pronounced indecent. When the Metropolitan Police raided pornographic bookshops in Holywell Street, the Vice Society's porters were there to assist them in carrying off the seized property through a largely hostile crowd.[6] The surprising thing is not that Swinburne and the Vice Society should have engaged in public battle in 1875 but, rather, that they had avoided it for so long.

The occasion of the encounter was the society's denunciation of a new edition of Rabelais, the Secretary, C. H. Collette, having written to the *Athenaeum* on 15 May 1875 to forward the 'bitter complaints' made to him by 'all classes of persons' against the book with its 'details of a low, degrading, filthy and disgusting character, without the merit *even* of wit'. Collette, who was the society's solicitor as well as its secretary, fulminated against what he called 'the book entitled Rabelais' and hinted that 'proceedings should be taken to stop the scandal' of its sale

Though Swinburne chose ridicule as his weapon against the Vice Society, such organizations were in earnest. Bell's, the publishers of the Bohn Library, were obliged to withdraw their own edition of Rabelais. The Vice Society's successor, the National Vigilance Association, successfully prosecuted Jules Garnier's illustrations of Rabelais. The Association also persuaded the courts to condemn the works of Maupassant and Zola as obscene and to send their English publisher to prison.[7] Both organizations were virulently anti-Catholic as well, John Kensit leading both the National Vigilance Association and the Protestant Truth Association.

In the *Athenaeum* of 29 May 1875 Swinburne, armed with the lance of ridicule, joined battle with the natural enemy. As though urging blinkered Collette on to greater triumphs after dealing with 'the book entitled Rabelais', he indicated the true corrupters of England's morals.

Of the book entitled Dryden, the book entitled Pope, and the book entitled Swift, I need scarcely speak, and should indeed, in the presence of the Society for the Suppression of Vice, prefer to pass them by with a shudder and a blush. I believe that the book entitled Fielding is still permitted to circulate – by leave, no doubt of the Society. I have not heard that the book entitled Byron has yet been withdrawn from circulation. Of the book entitled Shelley, a few copies are still, I believe, procurable – even though one chapter of it, at least, was in time past withdrawn at the bidding of this very Society.

However, there was one other book, in Swinburne's view, which merited urgent action by the Society, its early chapters containing stories of incest and unnatural vice, as well as numerous verbal indecencies.

A larger Society is now at work, devoted to the dissemination of a book which, on the principle of the present Society, does most emphatically demand and require universal and rigid suppression or castration. Let the Society for the Suppression of Vice come forward as an Anti-Bible Society, and though we may still laugh at its folly, we shall no longer loathe the pretension and the hypocrisy which will have ceased to distinguish 'The Society for the Suppression of the Bible'.

Fortunately for Swinburne, Collette's two distinguishing characteristics were total sincerity and innate stupidity. He solemnly and publicly assured the world that the Vice Society had no present policy for suppressing the Bible – or even Shakespeare. Collette, as Swinburne assured Edwin Harrison, had 'walked open-eyed into the trap I had set for him'.[8]

*   *   *

The brush with the Vice Society was one of many quarrels, some of them extremely public, in which Swinburne involved himself as his health deteriorated still more alarmingly during the 1870s. His letters continued to denounce Byron's detractor as Mrs Bitcher Spewe, while adding a new figure of ridicule, 'Fuxton Boreman'. This name was bestowed on the critic and editor H. Buxton Forman, editor of Shelley and now suspected as the prime mover in the matter of the forged first editions previously attributed to T. J. Wise.[9] There were less good-humoured dismissals of other authors, including George Eliot, whose moral intensity was almost the precise opposite of Swinburne's aestheticism. By contrast with the Brontës, whom he admired, George Eliot was 'an Amazon thrown sprawling over the crupper of her spavined and spur-galled Pegasus'.[10] Gosse found him obsessed by the notion that 'George Eliot was hounding on her myrmidons to his destruction'.[11]

He seemed to revel in belligerence during this period, as Gosse thought. 'His firmness has become arrogance, his zeal violence.... Swinburne at the age of forty had adopted mannerisms of style and temper which could not but injure his future writings in prose.'[12] The truth was that Swinburne had been engaged in such battles with

gusto for several years already, even embroiling himself in trans-
atlantic hostilities in 1874.

The unlikely occasion of this was an interview with Ralph Waldo
Emerson reported in *Frank Leslie's Illustrated Newspaper* on 3
January. Emerson, in his seventieth year, was revered as more than
a mere writer, having become the first great sage and mystic of the
new democratic culture. It was not to be expected that this earnest
and homely philosopher would have much in common with
Swinburne. In the newspaper interview, however, Emerson
described Swinburne as 'a perfect leper and a mere sodomite',
adding a description of the poet attributed to Carlyle as 'a man
standing up to his neck in a cesspool, and adding to its contents'.

Whether Swinburne was guilty of errors of taste on such occasions
by replying in kind, as Gosse feared, is questionable. On hearing of
Emerson's remarks, however, he composed a letter combining lofty
scorn with pungent scurrility. It appeared in the *New York Daily
Tribune* on 25 February 1874, dealing a skilful retaliatory blow to
the 'impudent and foul-mouthed Yankee philosophaster', as
Swinburne later dubbed the great man.

> A foul mouth is so ill matched with a white beard that I would gladly
> believe the newspaper scribes alone responsible for the bestial utterances
> which they declare to have dropped from a teacher whom such disciples as
> these exhibit to our disgust and compassion as performing on their obscene
> platform the last tricks of tongue now possible to a gap-toothed and hoary-
> headed ape, carried at first into notice on the shoulder of Carlyle, and who
> now in his dotage spits and chatters from a dirtier perch of his own finding
> and fouling; coryphaeus or choragus of his Bulgarian tribe of auto-
> coprophagous baboons who make the filth they feed on.

Perhaps the only objection to this, in Swinburne's case, was that it
was likely to revive interest in the attack which had been made upon
him in the first place. For all that, the violence of revenge could be
enjoyed in the sure knowledge that Emerson's original indiscretion
would make it extremely unlikely that he could appeal to a court of
law for protection against such public travesties of his character as
this.

It was not always to be so and in the greatest public row of the
decade, involving a figure much less venerable than Emerson,
Swinburne was to succeed in getting his publishers sued for libel.
The apparent origin of this was an article in the *Contemporary
Review* for October 1871 by Thomas Maitland, entitled 'The

Fleshly School of Poetry'. This was principally an attack on the poetry of Dante Gabriel Rossetti, which the reviewer described as being without a gleam of nature or a sign of humanity. Rossetti was indecent for the most part and often blasphemous. There was also room to mention Swinburne as the inheritor of all that was foulest in Baudelaire: 'unnatural passion ... blasphemy ... wretched animalism'. In Swinburne's poetry 'the Bacchanal screams, the sterile Dolores sweats, serpents dance, men and women wench, wriggle and foam in an endless alliteration of heated and meaning-less words, the veriest garbage of Baudelaire'.

The appearance of this article was followed by hasty consultation between the Rossetti brothers, and between William Michael Rossetti and Swinburne, to discover who Thomas Maitland might be. His name was quite unknown among reviewers of the day and the suspicion grew that it must be a pseudonym. First from Frederick Locker and then from other sources came the editorial admission that the article was the work of Robert Buchanan, who had attacked *Poems and Ballads* with such relish in the *Athenaeum* five years earlier as 'prurient trash'. On 17 October, Dante Gabriel Rossetti wrote to his brother: 'What do you think? Ellis writes me that Maitland is – Buchanan! Do you know Buchanan's prose, and can you judge if it be so?'[13]

It was soon admitted that Buchanan had not only written this but that he now revealed himself as author of the satirical poem 'The Session of the Poets', published five years before in the *Spectator*, in which he had actually ridiculed himself along with the others to avoid suspicion of authorship. Now, as Swinburne bluntly put it, Buchanan had once more made a trumpet of his anus in order to announce his views to the world.

The first reactions of Buchanan's victims mingled annoyance with amusement at the absurdity of a man putting forward his critical views under a pseudonym. Dante Gabriel Rossetti addressed his publisher in verse on the matter.

> As a critic, the Poet Buchanan
> Thinks Pseudo much safer than Anon
>   Into Maitland he's shrunk
>   Yet the smell of the skunk
> Guides the shuddering nose to Buchanan.[14]

Swinburne who, since the *Athenaeum* review, had habitually referred to Buchanan by such epithets as 'polecat', 'bitch-born' and 'dung-dropping', seemed in two minds as to what to do. On 13 November he felt inclined to keep his foot from filth, as he called it, 'even though a scraper be at hand'.[15] In the first place, however, some reply must be made. Rossetti wrote to the editor of the *Contemporary*, informing him that Buchanan's identity as author of 'The Fleshly School of Poetry' was known to them. Buchanan's new *Drama of Kings* was being published and there was a suggestion among them that they should all review it separately, all using the pseudonym 'Thomas Maitland', in order to force him from cover. Rossetti abandoned a libellous open letter to Buchanan and instead made his reply in 'The Stealthy School of Modern Criticism', published in the *Athenaeum* on 16 December. In the same issue there appeared two letters. The first was from Buchanan's publishers, acquitting their author of writing the original essay. The second was from Buchanan himself, admitting that he *had* written it. His publishers had used the pseudonym.

At this point, Buchanan had made a sufficient ass of himself for the subjects of his essay to let the matter drop. But Swinburne was at work on an answering pamphlet, *Under the Microscope*, whose title was explained by the fact that microbes of Buchanan's species were visible only under such magnification. In the original essay, Buchanan had referred to Swinburne's poetic voice as 'falsetto', adding insinuatingly that 'a training in Grecian literature must tend to emasculate the student so trained'. Swinburne dealt with this in a passage of nicely balanced irony in which his friends might catch allusions to Buchanan's anal trumpetings. If a knowledge of the great authors of the past meant spiritual castration for modern poets:

> Well may we congratulate ourselves that no such process as robbed of all strength and manhood the intelligence of Milton, has had power to impair the virility of Mr Buchanan's virile and masculine genius. To that strong and severe figure we turn from the sexless and nerveless company of shrill-voiced singers who share with Milton the curse of enforced effeminacy; from the pitiful soprano notes of such dubious creatures as Marlowe, Jonson, Chapman, Gray, Coleridge, Shelley, Landor, 'cum semiviro comitatu', we avert our ears to catch the higher and manlier harmonies of a poet with all his natural parts and powers complete. For truly if love or knowledge of ancient art and wisdom be the sure mark of 'emasculation', and the absence of any taint of such love and any tincture of such knowledge (as then in consistency it must be) the supreme sign of perfect manhood, Mr Robert Buchanan should be amply competent to renew the thirteenth labour of Hercules.[16]

Hostilities between Swinburne and Buchanan continued for another three years, until Buchanan's friend Lord Southesk wrote *Jonas Fisher* in 1875. This was a reiteration in verse of the attacks already made in prose. Swinburne's first response was 'Epitaph on a Slanderer', which appeared in the *Examiner* on 20 November 1875.

> He whose heart and soul and tongue
> Once above ground stunk and stung,
> Now less noisome than before,
> Stinks here still but stings no more.

There was little that Buchanan could do, since he was not named as the object of the epitaph. Then, on 27 November, the *Examiner* announced that *Jonas Fisher* must be the work of either Buchanan or the devil. Swinburne seized on the phrase and wrote a letter, 'The Devil's Due', which appeared in the *Examiner* on 11 December. Swinburne signed himself with 'the honoured name' of Thomas Maitland and turned the entire letter into ironic praise of Buchanan as the author of *Jonas Fisher*. So far, he was probably safe from the law. Then he added a postscript, an allusion to Buchanan's protest that he had been on a cruise in the Hebrides when his publisher used the pseudonym of Thomas Maitland for 'The Fleshly School of Poetry'.

The writer of the above being at present away from London, on a cruise among the Philippine Islands, in his steam yacht (the *Skulk,* Captain Shuffleton master), is as can be proved on the oath or the solemn word of honour of the editor, publisher, and proprietor, responsible neither for an article which might with equal foundation be attributed to Cardinal Manning, or to Mr Gladstone, or any other writer in the *Contemporary Review,* as to its actual author; nor for the adoption of a signature under which his friends in general, acting not only without his knowledge but against his expressed wishes on the subject, have thought it best and wisest to shelter his personal responsibility from any chance of attack. This frank, manly and consistent explanation will, I cannot possibly doubt, make everything straight and safe on all hands.

To their dismay, Peter Taylor and William Minto, owner and editor of the *Examiner,* now discovered that *Jonas Fisher* was the work of the Earl of Southesk. By his remarks in the letter, particularly in the derisive postscript, Swinburne had delivered himself and them into the hands of Buchanan. They found themselves the recipients of a writ for libel.

The first reaction to this was a spirited outbreak of squabbling among the potential defendants. Taylor and Minto at once revealed Swinburne's identity as author of the letter in the hope that Buchanan's lawyers would sue the author rather than them. This seemed quite likely until Buchanan's junior counsel, C. R. McClymont, intervened. Not only was he a Balliol man and a former pupil of Jowett, he had also been a member of one of the Tummel Bridge reading parties with Swinburne. Additionally, McClymont was a friend of Swinburne's Old Mortality contemporary John Nichol. While McClymont persuaded Buchanan to sue Taylor and Minto rather than Swinburne, Robert Williams for the defence was trying to undermine this by assuring McClymont that Swinburne was denouncing him behind his back. In the end, however, it was the camaraderie of Jowett's men which prevailed, leaving Taylor and Minto to face their accusers.

The case came on in June 1876, while Swinburne waited nervously at Holmwood, hoping not to be involved. In the event, he received a subpoena on 19 June, requiring his presence at the trial which was held on 29 and 30 June. It was a case in which the judge, Mr Justice Archibald, had no great sympathy for either side. Though he commended *Poems and Ballads* to destruction, it was difficult to see Buchanan as innocence defamed in the light of the attacks he had made eagerly upon other men. At the same time, Taylor's counsel was less concerned to defend his client than to deflect the plaintiff's wrath upon Swinburne. He insisted 'that the question was about the conduct of Taylor, not that of Rossetti or Swinburne; that Taylor had no animosity against Buchanan; that Buchanan had been told who was the author of the article and offered the manuscript, but that he had refused to take action against Swinburne'.[17] This was true and no doubt the intervention of McClymont as Swinburne's friend might have had some part in the matter. Yet there was also the practical consideration that Buchanan could come forward against Taylor and claim that Taylor had injured him without the least provocation to do so. That would have been a far more difficult case to establish against Swinburne.

The jury heard Mr Justice Archibald's summing up and retired. They came back with a verdict for Buchanan but, though he had asked for damages of £5000, they awarded him only £150. When the case was over, it was suggested to Swinburne that he might show his decency in the matter by contributing towards the defence costs. He refused. At the time his refusal appeared ungracious but, in the light of later revelations as to the way in which Taylor and Minto had struggled to escape by making him the sacrifice to Buchanan's wrath, he had some justification for washing his hands of them.

*   *   *

Though the world might not have noticed it, Swinburne at forty sounded and acted privately like a cantankerous old man. Friendships and associations of youth, a mere ten years before, were the casualties of this deterioration. The break with Lord Houghton was almost complete when Swinburne, in May 1874, informed John Morley that he now shrank from the rancid unction of his old friend's adulation. He was separated, too, from Dante Gabriel Rossetti, after Rossetti's attempt at suicide in 1872. No reason was given him, merely a request transmitted by William Michael Rossetti that he should not attempt to see Dante Gabriel again. Swinburne at first played the part of the loyal and long-suffering friend in the face of this slight. By the beginning of 1877, however, he was writing privately to a new friend, Theodore Watts-Dunton, denouncing 'Houghtons and Rossettis (D. G.)' in apposition to the true friendships of Jowett, Nichol and, inevitably, Watts-Dunton himself.[18] At the time of Dante Gabriel's death, Swinburne turned even more bitterly against his former idol for his neglect of their beloved Lizzie.

Despite this break, Swinburne's friendships with the rest of the Rossetti family survived. William Michael, the younger brother, was in many ways the least characteristic of the Tudor House group, combining art criticism and literary editing with a post in the Inland Revenue Department at Somerset House. He was one of Swinburne's most constant friends and advisers, acting as go-between in the unpleasantness with John Camden Hotten and remaining the poet's friend for life. Serious-minded and yet solicitous for Swinburne's welfare, he endured both the estrangement between his brother and his friend, and Swinburne's gleeful Sadean fantasies, for which William Michael had little taste.

Dante Gabriel and Houghton lived on until 1882 and 1885 respectively, increasingly exiled from Swinburne's thoughts. Yet there were more distressing developments than these, partings made under circumstances far more painful. In 1879 Gosse heard from Swinburne of the final insults contrived by the 'blackguard' Charles Augustus Howell. In his own decline, Howell was allegedly reading out Swinburne's flagellation fantasies and other spirited indecencies to groups of men and women who, presumably, rewarded him in some fashion for this entertainment. There was nothing whatever that could be done, and Swinburne braved the matter out by denouncing Howell as a scoundrel who was below his notice. Only when the manuscripts came on to the market could they be bought and suppressed.

For all that, the story of Swinburne's middle years was not merely one of failing friendships and increasing isolation. The 1870s were, for instance, the decade of his ripening and enduring acquaintance with Edmund Gosse, who became something of a Boswellian figure from then on. Gosse was one of the young admirers of Swinburne in the 1860s, the son of the eminent naturalist and Plymouth Brother Philip Gosse, whose paternal care and spiritual anguish are described by Edmund in *Father and Son*. Edmund Gosse first corresponded with Swinburne at the age of eighteen in 1867. They met at a party in 1870, after which the hostess confided to Gosse, 'Algernon took to you at once, as is seldom the case with him.'[19] A strong mutual interest in seventeenth-century literature held them in literary sympathy, and led to projected collaboration on a dictionary of English drama. At a different level, Gosse's marriage and the advent of two children brought out Swinburne's peculiar interest in the very young which was to characterize much of his emotional life during the years which remained to him. He himself showed no more enthusiasm for a wife or for parenthood than he had ever done, dismissing marriage in 1876 as no more than 'a salutary check on the vulgar propensities of our natural inferiors'.[20]

In respect of his poetry, the changing friendships and declining health of the 1870s hardly affected the quantity of Swinburne's output. *Bothwell* and *Erectheus* had been published, *Tristram of Lyonesse* was in progress when, in 1878, he issued *Poems and Ballads: Second Series*. It was dedicated to one friend from whom he was separated by distance but not affection, Sir Richard Burton. They had not met for some time, Swinburne hearing that the Burtons were in India. Yet, as he insisted, this could never detract from the feeling between them.

The book contained some of his most accomplished poems, though it seemed to reflect the new tenor of his life, a sense of the past evoked by the worship of his own youth and its presiding gods. Hugo and Gautier were the subjects of six poems. There was the elegiac tribute to his dead father, as well as meditations on the landscapes of his earlier life. Perhaps those who believed that his creative talent had ossified after *Atalanta* and the first volume of *Poems and Ballads* might have felt themselves vindicated by the way in which the new book relied on translations of Villon, on poems in French and even in Latin to complete the bulk of its predecessors. Latin verses by an English poet had been an entirely appropriate offering to the reading public of Milton's day, but in the mass middle-class literacy of the later nineteenth century they suggested a clever schoolboy showing off his exercises.

The title as well as the tone of such poems as 'Relics' revealed the new Swinburne, the poet of middle age looking back with a degree of emotional self-indulgence which seemed dangerously close to that of the sentimental ballad, given his metrical precision.

> This flower that smells of honey and the sea,
> White laurustine, seems in my hand to be
>   A white star made of memory long ago
> Lit in the heaven of dear times dead to me.

The poetry had an easy appeal, a clarity and simplicity in recalling Swinburne's past through a series of cameos, as in his memory of Italy and of San Gimignano.

> Thou hast a word of that one land of ours,
> And of the fair town called of the Fair Towers,
>   A word for me of my San Gimignan,
> A word of April's greenest-girdled hours.
>
> Of the old breached walls whereon the wallflowers ran
> Called of Saint Fina, breachless now of man,
>   Though time with soft feet break them stone by stone,
> Who breaks down hour by hour his own reign's span.

Buchanan himself could hardly have complained over the morality of this second book of *Poems and Ballads*. True, there was a passing and discreetly phrased tribute to *Mademoiselle de Maupin*, but the 'biting lips, lithe limbs, supple flanks, hair that stings or burns, and kisses', which had made Sir William Hardman call the 1866 volume a rival to 'the most erotic work ever before produced', might be looked for in vain.[21] The book was, accordingly, received with more respect. The anonymous reviewer in the *Athenaeum* on 6 July 1878, where Buchanan had opened his attack in 1866, was none other than Swinburne's new friend, Theodore Watts-Dunton. Since the review opened with the questionable assumption that

Songs Before Sunrise was a 'a vast advance' upon the original *Poems and Ballads,* it is hardly surprising that the new collection should be presented as 'the most striking book' to appear in England for many years.

In the light of the bizarre and lengthy conclusion to Swinburne's life, Watts-Dunton's remarks in the *Athenaeum* were far more important than a mere reviewer's opinions. The world, it seemed, had misunderstood Algernon, and Watts-Dunton set about recovering his lost moral reputation for him. Even the original *Poems and Ballads* had been a victim of misrepresentation. Whatever its author had claimed, it was not immoral or amoral but a great achievement in 'ethical preaching'. Taking two poems which had caused most outrage in 1866, Watts-Dunton dismissed the lesbian passion of 'Anactoria' as merely incidental to its main purposes. It might appear to the careless reader to be a lurid display of physical passion between two women, but its true theme was the portrayal of man, faced by 'the inscrutable ways of God'. Again, the unperceptive reader might have been misled into thinking that 'Dolores', with the girl's voluptuous white limbs and red, cruel mouth, the bitings, stingings, the blushes of amorous blows on her nude body, was a gleeful celebration of sexual violence. Not at all. It was quite the reverse, Watts-Dunton insisted, a stern moral warning against indecent excesses of this kind, 'a wail from the bed of vice ... a Jeremiad on the misery of pleasure'. Even in the published portion of Swinburne's incomplete *Tristram of Lyonesse* the same was true. Tristram might appear to be discoursing of love and passion, but what he was really preoccupied by was 'pantheism and evolution'.

Whether as a reaction to this or not, Swinburne disappeared from his rooms and vanished into his metropolitan haunts on a drinking bout of quite alarming proportions. He was found in a sad state by Lord Houghton. Lady Jane Swinburne, complaining that since his father's death she had no authority over him and could no longer persuade him to return to Holmwood, talked helplessly of medical supervision as the only expedient.[22] With emotional energy undepleted, at least in his capacity for rage, he threw himself again into his current battle, where the antagonist was F. J. Furnivall.

Furnivall was nothing if not a scholar, the editor of Shakespeare and of Old English texts, founder of the New Shakspere [*sic*] Society. Their first encounter, in 1868, illuminates the lengths to which Swinburne and his contemporaries were prepared to go in search of material to gratify their particular sexual obsession.

Furnivall, sharing at least one such compulsion with Swinburne, had produced a saga of school occurrences, a book eagerly received by Swinburne. This was no furtive piece of pornography, not even one of Hotten's curious books, but *The Babees Book*, a medieval text edited by Furnivall himself, containing 'The Birched School-boy', and issued in 1868 under the unimpeachable imprint of the Early English Text Society. It was in 1875 and 1876 that Swinburne contributed his essays on Shakespeare to the *Fortnightly Review*, later collecting them in his *Study of Shakespeare* published in 1880. Furnivall first took him to task privately in 1875 over such questions as the dating of the plays and the authorship of *Henry VIII*. They exchanged coolly hostile arguments in the pages of the *Academy* early in January 1876. On 17 January Swinburne wrote to Furnivall in his most casually arrogant manner, consenting to be attacked as much as Furnivall pleased but declining further discussion or argument. There were only three men living with whom he felt he could debate such matters on equal terms. Furnivall was not one of them.

By 1877, the quarrel had broken out publicly again. Swinburne, in the *Athenaeum* of 14 April, denounced Furnivall's 'gross and infantile incompetence to hold or to utter an opinion worth uttering or holding on the text of Shakespeare'. The New Shakspere Society he described as 'a dynasty of dunces mainly, or chiefly rather of churls'. Privately, Swinburne described his *Athenaeum* piece to Gosse as the flagellation of a 'howling churl'. The appearance of *A Study of Shakespeare* drove Furnivall almost beyond the confines of reason. He raged at 'Mr Swinburne's shallow ignorance and self-conceit', invited him to 'teach his grandmother to suck eggs', and described his ear for verse as 'a poetaster's, hairy, thick, and dull'. The two men snapped and snarled at one another like ill tempered schoolboys in the matter of Shakespearean scholarship. Furnivall now referred to Swinburne as 'Pigsbrook', while Swinburne dubbed him 'Brothelsdyke' in exchange. Unable to gain an advantage in this, Furnivall sent libellous postcards about Swinburne to the poet's friends. Members of the New Shakspere Society who protested at this were expelled. Furnivall was unmoved: 'I am glad to be rid of you', was his printed card to the Duke of Devonshire.[23]

The New Shakspere Society acquired as president the ageing figure of Robert Browning. Swinburne wrote to him, denouncing Furnivall and ending such friendship as remained between Browning and himself. To Gosse, he complained of 'Browning's having disgraced himself for life by his acceptance of the presidency of a blackguard's gang of blockheads'.[24] There was, as Gosse remarked, a good deal of mud-slinging in the years which followed, until newspaper editors wearied of the fun and refused to insert any more letters from either champion. 'Furnivall kept up for some time, by halfpenny post, a running fire of scurrilities, and then the grotesque warfare came to a sullen end.'[25]

* * *

This pantomime of scholarly ill temper was a mere public diversion, a distraction from the sickness and desolation of his private life. In the autumn of 1877 he complained that he was too ill to hold a pen. He spent much of January 1878 in Glasgow with John Nichol. He evidently regaled Nichol with the choicer passages of *Lesbia Brandon*, which Chatto was requested to send to Glasgow on this occasion, and he met the young poet John Davidson. Nichol was reputed to have 'taught' Swinburne to drink at Oxford and their reunion was marked by alcoholic excesses on Swinburne's part which perturbed even his host.

Late in February Swinburne returned to London, making preparations for Nichol to visit him there. By the end of the month, Lady Jane Swinburne was thoroughly alarmed. Algernon was nowhere to be found and was not answering her letters. She wrote to the housekeeper at Great James Street, Jane Magill, inquiring after her son. He reappeared at his lodgings soon afterwards, too ill to leave them for some time, as he informed Chatto. Victor Hugo invited him to Paris in May for the centenary celebrations of Voltaire. It was out of the question for a bedridden invalid, as he now called himself, to consider such a journey. The doctor was in attendance at Great James Street and very little, apart from pretty children like Edmund Gosse's young daughter, seemed to rouse Swinburne's enthusiasm.

It was in July that he went missing again and was, on this occasion, retrieved by Lord Houghton. Lady Jane's despair was lightened briefly when her son was persuaded to go to Malvern with Jowett. Whatever good this did him was short-lived. During the winter which followed, Gosse described him as looking worn and feeble, tottering like an old man, and glad of a hand to help him up or down stairs. In appearance he was the ghost of the shrill, vivacious poet of the 1860s, an apparition 'in a close-fitting long Melton coat of dark blue, and the neatest of little shoes, his top hat balanced on his great mop of hair'.[26]

In the autumn of 1878, having moved to new rooms at Guildford Street, Russell Square, he wrote to Theodore Watts-Dunton, who had reviewed *Poems and Ballads: Second Series* so portentously in the *Athenaeum*, begging for a visit. Like almost all friends and acquaintances of this period, Watts-Dunton adopted the adjective 'sad' in his report of Swinburne's state and prospects. The star of romantic revolution and literary rebellion had fallen lower than seemed possible. Unable to face a return to the more decorous regime of Holmwood, Swinburne had avoided seeing his mother for well over a year. The famous readings, at which devotees had fallen on their knees before the marvels of 'Dolores' and other poems, had dwindled to domestic farce. Gosse recalled arriving at Great James Street for a reading of the essay on Charlotte Brontë. Swinburne stood alone in the middle of the room, one hand in the breast of his coat, the other jerking at his side. 'He had an arrangement of chairs, with plates and glasses set on the table, as if for a party. He looked like a conjurer who was waiting for his audience.' After a while, he brushed aside some of the glasses and sat down to read Gosse a poem. By the end of it, no one else had arrived and the room was darkening in the summer twilight. Presently, Swinburne said, 'I hope I didn't forget to ask them!' He disappeared into the bedroom and returned almost at once. 'Ah! I find I didn't ask any of those men, so we'll begin at once.' But the essay on Charlotte Brontë proved too much for him and he chose, instead, those passages of *Lesbia Brandon* 'of which he never wearies'. He read with 'amazing violence', Gosse recorded, and then seemed 'quite exhausted, and sank in a kind of dream into the corner of his broad sofa, his tiny feet pressed tight together, and I stole away'.[27]

Until the summer of 1879, Swinburne continued to appear occasionally at other men's social gatherings, including a party of Lord Houghton's where he met 'a harmless young nobody', whose name proved to be Oscar Wilde.[28] By the beginning of June 1879, his health was at its worst, and he evidently succumbed to alcoholic dysentery. Yet his very weakness was to prove his salvation. While the intractable Algernon was in no state to resist the plans made for him, Lady Swinburne and Watts-Dunton exchanged telegrams. There was no time to lose, since Holmwood was to be sold and plans for the poet's future must be made at once. This was evidently the occasion on which Watts-Dunton arrived at Swinburne's rooms in a four-wheeler and carried the patient off, not to his own rooms, but to the house of his married sister, Mrs Mason, at Ivy Lodge, Putney.

From this temporary haven he was brought by Watts-Dunton to Holmwood and safely installed there by 13 June.

Walter Theodore Watts-Dunton was five years older than Swinburne, the son of a Huntingdon solicitor, and a solicitor himself by profession. He was a bachelor who had combined his legal career with an enthusiasm for literature, and had finally settled in London in 1872. Among his friends were George Borrow and the Rossettis, from the former of whom he derived a strong interest in gipsy girls, or rather in gipsy girls as romanticized by the middle-class literary imagination. For many years after 1879, Watts-Dunton was an easy target of ridicule. His photographs, taken in middle life, show the shaggy, drooping moustache, the bright avaricious eyes, the tall, balding head, which might have done credit to a figure in stage farce. Added to this was the absurdity of such a man acting as domestic and moral nursemaid to the incorrigible Algernon, deciding who was to be admitted to the presence of his charge and who excluded. There was also the prospect of Watts-Dunton, the tamer of a revolutionary poet, the representative of temperance who outwitted his patient's penchant for drink, the prude who cut off Algernon's recital to the luncheon guests of the doings of the old man of Peru. That all this should have happened, not at Holmwood, nor at East Dene, but at No. 2 The Pines, Putney, seemed excruciatingly comic.

How long Swinburne could have survived without the intervention of Watts-Dunton is a matter of speculation. With or without such intervention, however, his work as a poet was virtually complete. There were to be poems written during the years at The Pines, but few of them ranked with *Atalanta* or the 1866 volume of *Poems and Ballads*.

By 1876 Watts-Dunton had begun his career as a literary critic for the *Examiner*, but his association with Swinburne went back to October 1872 and the rift between the poet and John Camden Hotten. On 1 October that year, their mutual friend, the painter Ford Madox Brown, had invited Watts-Dunton to dinner to meet Swinburne and give legal advice on a subject of some importance. 'The poet Swinburne is here at this moment, and was speaking to me about his publisher, Hotten. I told him I should much wish that I might have your advice in a rather puzzling matter with him.'[29]

However absurd he might seem as a mentor and exclusive companion for the young poet, Watts-Dunton at least had his legal wits about him and dealt decisively with Hotten, in a manner which

Howell had neither inclination nor ability to emulate. Nor was that all. Watts-Dunton's London lodgings were at 15 Great James Street, a few minutes away from Swinburne's. The neighbours became acquaintances and then friends. They began to dine together at the London Restaurant, on the corner of Chancery Lane and Fleet Street. Since his removal from the Arts Club, the arrangement suited Swinburne well. It was true that Watts-Dunton shared none of the Sadean enthusiasms or revolutionary excesses which still preoccupied Swinburne, but he was at least a tolerant companion. Despite the experience of being chased from 3 Great James Street by a naked poet, Watts-Dunton persevered. He became invaluable in the business affairs of both Swinburne and Dante Gabriel Rossetti. In return he was invited to hear Swinburne read his poetry, and became a dutiful and receptive listener. By 1874 and the publication of *Bothwell* he had combined the role of literary agent with that of legal and financial adviser.

More to the point, Watts-Dunton had literary ambitions of his own, beyond mere critical writing for the *Examiner*. If there had to be a man of business deeply involved in Swinburne's affairs, he was by no means the worst. He had already begun work on *Aylwin*, a novel of gipsies, girl-children and Celtic mystery, though it was not to be published for many years, and he was an intelligent and agreeable companion in Swinburne's solitary life. He left Great James Street before Swinburne but the association between them continued. When the crisis of 1878–9 came, it was not remarkable that Lady Swinburne and even her son should have turned to Watts-Dunton as the one dependable man of sense among all their acquaintances. The alternative was ominous. The sale of Holmwood would make it difficult for Lady Swinburne to provide a home for Algernon, even if he accepted such an arrangement. She had little control over him and the prospect must therefore be, at the best, 'medical supervision', as she called it. At the worst, it might be the confinement of a man who could no longer regulate his own life.

Swinburne returned to London briefly in the second half of June 1879, evidently under Watts-Dunton's supervision, to arrange the disposal of his rooms in Guildford Street. In July he was back at Holmwood for the last time, working on *A Study of Shakespeare*. His 'illness', Lady Jane Swinburne announced, was a thing of the past. By September, Holmwood had been sold and Lady Jane was about to make her new home in Wiltshire, at Leigh House, Bradford-on-Avon. While Swinburne himself was preoccupied with his book on Shakespeare, the proceeds of the Holmwood sale were divided up and invested by others to provide for his future. Lady Swinburne joined in this, promising Watts-Dunton that nothing would be said to Algernon about such matters until they had been arranged. The poet's younger brother, Edward Swinburne, making one of his rare appearances in Algernon's life, pointed out to Watts-Dunton ways and means of investing the capital so that it would be difficult for the prodigal to spend it, in the event of some future 'paroxysm of extravagance'.[30] Lady Swinburne arranged payment to Watts-Dunton of £200 a year for sheltering Algernon under his roof and, with that, the arrangements were completed. Swinburne himself seemed indifferent to the disposal of his person and possessions.

Watts-Dunton had suggested to Swinburne a 'run down' to Putney for the sake of his health, and had carried him off to his sister's house, Ivy Lodge, Werter Road, off the High Street. On his first arrival there, Swinburne was so weak that Watts-Dunton had to assist him down from the carriage. There followed the invigorating morning drives to the windmill on Wimbledon Common, until the poet's strength had returned sufficiently for him to accomplish the journey on foot. At the same time, Watts-Dunton, with the eye of a born businessman, had noticed a number of handsome new villas, large and semi-detached, being built in the neighbourhood. He took a twenty-one-year lease on a spacious new house of this type at the foot of Putney Hill – No. 2 The Pines. Swinburne was to be his sub-tenant.

The reformation of the poet had already shown promising signs. Undesirable acquaintances from the past were either not admitted to the Putney house by Watts-Dunton or, more surprisingly, frozen off by Swinburne himself. One such encounter involved a drinking crony who made his way unsteadily down to the suburbs, rang the bell, and gripping the hall table for support, said hopefully, 'Hullo, Algernon, ole buck!' To his surprise he was confronted by a hardly recognizable version of the poet, 'speechless with rage, the new-born fire of ascetic disapprobation in his blue eyes'. Swinburne refused the outstretched hand and, a few minutes later, his former acquaintance was outside again with the door closed.[31]

Mrs Mason, Watts-Dunton's sister, had accommodated the two men until October 1879. Then a firm of carters brought 'one van of furniture, as per estimate and contract' from the Guildford Street lodgings to The Pines. Swinburne was to have two rooms there, one on the first floor looking out across the garden at the back – his library – and a bedroom on the floor above. The contents of the Holmwood library had been sold, when he told his mother that he would rather have the money than the books. By the end of September, the two men had moved into one half of The Pines, 'gipsying here with furniture enough for sleep, meals and a sitting-room', until their own rooms were ready. 'Exactly like the outlying (and prettiest) parts of Oxford,' Swinburne described the area to his mother, 'within less than an hour of Piccadilly – and no underground travelling!'[32] In these improbable surroundings, and in equally improbable company, he was to spend as long a period of his life as that which separated the first 'run down' to Putney with Watts-Dunton from his first sight of Eton as a boy of twelve.

Chapter 10

The Pines

AS soon as news of Swinburne's removal to The Pines became
public knowledge, it was accompanied by rumours that he had
been abducted by Watts-Dunton, who now had the poet under
restraint in a private suburban sanitorium. Lord Ronald Gower had
seen Watts-Dunton's four-wheeler at Hyde Park Corner on the
initial journey from Guildford Street to Putney. 'Hullo, Watts,
you've got Swinburne there,' he said. 'Where are you taking him
to?' Watts-Dunton fended off Gower's attempt to board the carriage and said firmly, 'I'm taking him with me to Putney.' From this
small beginning, the abduction rumour began.[1]

Its falsity was soon proved to the poet's friends. Lord Houghton
was one of the first to be given a detailed account of his new home by
Swinburne himself.

> I keep no chambers in town henceforth, or (probably) for ever – finding
> after but too many years' trial that in the atmosphere of London I can never
> expect more than a fortnight at best of my usual health and strength. Here I
> am, like Mr Tennyson at Farringford, 'close to the edge of a noble down',
> and I might add 'Far out of sight, sound, smell, of the town', and yet within
> an easy hour's run of Hyde Park Corner and a pleasant drive of Chelsea,
> where I have some friends lingering.[2]

Edmund Gosse was one of many among Swinburne's friends who
took a less sanguine view of the arrangement. He referred to the
poet's 'captivity at The Pines', to the supervising by Watts-Dunton
as being 'bullied by the old horror of Putney', and to the 'rattlesnake
fascination' which his mentor seemed to exercise upon Swinburne.[3]
Yet if Watts-Dunton heard of such accusations, he was more than
recompensed by the gratitude of Lady Jane Swinburne, who visited
The Pines in October 1880 and wrote to him later of her relief at
seeing Algernon 'well and happy', in contrast to what he had been.
She even hoped for the return of his religious faith, 'when that fatal
tendency from which he has suffered so much is got the better of'.[4]
Algernon, too, showed a ready gratitude to his new saviour, which
twelve years as an inmate of The Pines served only to confirm. On

the death of his brother Edward, he wrote to Watts-Dunton on 31 July 1891, 'I cannot but keep thinking . . . how long since, how many years ago, I should have died as my poor brother has just died, if instead of the worst of wives I had not found the best of friends.'[5]

How was it that Watts-Dunton, not on the face of it the most inspiring or stimulating companion among Swinburne's acquaintances, should have gained this moral ascendency over the self-willed and cantankerous subject of so many moral reproaches? His technique was essentially that of his *Athenaeum* review the year before, in which he chose to reinterpret the morally objectionable 'Dolores' or 'Anactoria', rather than to deplore them. So, at Putney, he appeared to adopt Swinburne's style rather than to alter it. Swinburne's weakness, perhaps greater than his alcoholic or sado-masochistic compulsions, was vanity. He needed the reassurance that he was, as he lamented from behind Nichol's locked door, a poet of European reputation. In Watts-Dunton, he found a steady supply of a stimulant more potent than brandy or Sade – praise and adulation.

The initial letter to Houghton showed that Swinburne had already been persuaded to think of himself not as a hopeless drunkard doomed to suburban confinement for his own safety, but as another Tennyson living in sylvan seclusion at an address as imposing as Farringford. Even the problem of drink was not so daunting, once Swinburne's addiction to the esteem of his companion and himself had been confirmed. According to Watts-Dunton's future wife, and to other friends of The Pines, Swinburne's alcoholism was overcome by his own imitative vanity and the shrewdness of his friend.

Watts-Dunton, deciding that it would be unwise and probably impossible to bring Swinburne off his diet of brandy suddenly, first suggested that brandy and water was merely 'a drug, a medicine, to be taken only when prescribed by doctors'. The sight of it recalled sick-rooms and retching travellers on Channel steamers. The real poet's drink was vintage port, of the kind drunk by Tennyson at the rate of a bottle a day, a wine to keep poetic fire ablaze even in a man's declining years. Swinburne, who was still convalescing in bed at this stage, sat up eagerly when Watts-Dunton announced that he had a bottle of the very same wine which Tennyson drank and suggested that they should 'crack' it 'to drink old Tennyson's health and our very good selves'. For some weeks, Swinburne drank port eagerly, as the proposed means of literary inspiration. Then, on the grounds that 'gentlemen' drank it, the two friends turned to claret, by way of burgundy. Finally, according to the legend of The Pines, Watts-Dunton decreed that the only drink worth drinking was 'the wine of the country'. In Scotland it might be whisky, in France or Italy the wine of the region, in England it must be 'our own glorious and incomparable British beer!' From then on, Swinburne drank his morning glass at the Rose and Crown and his bottle of Bass at lunch. By 1882, when Swinburne missed the train from Trowbridge on his way back to Watts-Dunton after a visit to his mother, the alarm was short-lived. It was agreed, as Lady Jane Swinburne remarked, that the reformed drunkard could now be trusted not to have a relapse.[6]

For all that, his absences from The Pines were carefully monitored. He was a guest of his mother and sisters at Leigh House, Bradford-on-Avon, without Watts-Dunton. On other occasions, even when going to lunch with Jowett at Balliol, he was accompanied by his shadow. There were, of course, the annual seaside holidays, spent decorously with his friend at Eastbourne or Lancing, and there was one memorable visit to Paris in November 1882 to see Hugo and be present at the fiftieth anniversary performance of his play *Le Roi s'amuse*. Swinburne not only tolerated the presence of Watts-Dunton but, as Gosse heard, refused to go anywhere unless his friend were invited too. Both the performance of the play and the dinner to which Hugo invited them proved to be disappointing. Swinburne was getting increasingly deaf. Hugo clasped his hand and said that Swinburne was like a son to him, and he proposed Swinburne's health after dinner. Yet as the poet complained to his mother, even though he was sitting immediately opposite Hugo, 'my accursed deafness prevented my hearing a single word'.[7]

So much in Swinburne's first years at The Pines is indicative of old age and decrepitude that one may easily forget that he was only forty-two when he arrived there, though he remained for the last thirty years of his life. The faun-like figure was growing stout and, of course, the deafness grew steadily worse. It was this latter disability which disconcerted Max Beerbohm during lunch when Watts-Dunton suddenly roared at his friend: 'Well, Algernon, how was it on the heath to-day?' and when Beerbohm found himself later involved in a bellowed conversation with Swinburne on first editions of Jacobean plays.[8]

The change in mind was in many ways more remarkable than any outward alteration. There had, of course, always been the dualism in Swinburne's mind between democratic or revolutionary freedom and the Sadean delights of oppression and exploitation. As the walls of The Pines enclosed him he continued to write to Houghton about the Marquis and all his works, as well as the phenomena of 'Nigger Slavery' and the practice of whipping children in prison. Swinburne delightedly supported the last of these and wished Houghton success in his campaign on behalf of it.[9]

What seemed more surprising was the speed with which the former disciple of Mazzini and apostle of revolution turned against those men and causes whom he might have been expected to support. Even his attitude to Victoria herself underwent a transformation. In 1884 he described to Georgie Burne-Jones a plan for a new drama based upon the relationship between Victoria and her servant John Brown. It was to be written in French, entitled *Sir Brown* and set at 'Osborne's House, Ile de Wigth'. The two lovers, having disposed of Prince Albert, are to consign the royal children, including the Princes de Galles to the Tour de Londres, in order to indulge in their mutual sexual frenzy. It seems that the play was not written. Indeed, by the Golden Jubilee of 1887, Swinburne was viewing the monarchy with an indulgent eye. In June the Jubilee issue of the *Nineteenth Century* carried his poem 'The Jubilee', which was later reprinted as 'The Commonweal'. The reference to Victoria was light and gracious.

> And now that fifty years are flown
>   Since in a maiden's hand the sign
>   Of empire that no seas confine
> First as a star to seaward shone,
>   We see their record shine.
>
> A troubled record, foul and fair,
>   A simple record and serene,
>   Inscribes for praise a blameless queen
> For praise and blame an age of care
>   And change and ends unseen.

It was perhaps no coincidence that the rhythm of the new Swinburne was modelled so closely on Tennyson the civic bard in such poems as the 'Ode on the Death of the Duke of Wellington'. Like the Laureate himself, he now became the object of pilgrimage who venerated his 'blameless queen' and all that she represented, in his turn. He turned not only against the methods of revolution but also against the unimperial liberalism of Gladstone, whom he accused of leaving General Gordon to his fate in Khartoum. His new Toryism was

evinced, for example, by the lines written in an autograph album
during the critical Midlothian election campaign of 1879–80.

> Choose, England: here the paths before thee part.
> Wouldst thou have honour? Be as now thou art;
> Wouldst thou have shame? Take Gladstone to thy heart.[10]

In more specific terms, the poet who had denounced the execution of Fenians in 1867 turned violently against the cause of Irish
Nationalism and, indeed, the home rule which Gladstone
favoured. One Fenian representative, innocent of this, visited The
Pines to ask the former rebel to write an 'Ode on the Proclamation
of an Irish Republic'. To the man's dismay and to Watts-Dunton's
amusement, Swinburne flew into a rage and threatened to kick the
Fenian downstairs unless he left the house at once.[11] The heresy of
the Fenians and of Irish Nationalism, in Swinburne's view, was the
destruction of the ideal republic by division. As he wrote to his
mother, 'the first principle of a Republican is and must be Unity. . . .
Republicans ought in common consistency and honesty to be the
first to protest against a party of anarchists and intriguers whose
policy is to break up the state'.[12] It was one thing to advocate
tyrannicide to other members of Old Mortality, but the assassination of Lord Cavendish, Chief Secretary to the Lord Lieutenant of
Ireland, and his assistant in Phoenix Park, Dublin, was a different
matter. Swinburne denounced the assassins in *The Times* as 'infamous cowards', not the true revolutionaries of whom Mazzini
approved – 'he would have been as likely to approve or to condone
the crimes of the Mafiosi'.[13] The only men more contemptible than
the assassins were those like Gladstone and the Liberals 'who accept
money and support from those who approve the crime of the
Phoenix Park'.[14]

By the time that England's policy in South Africa led to declaration
of war on the Boers in 1899, Max Beerbohm imagined Watts-
Dunton taking Swinburne on one side and giving a word of advice.
'"Now Algernon, we're at war, you know – at war with the Boers. I
don't want to bother you at all, but I do think, my dear old friend,
you oughtn't to let slip this opportunity of", etc., etc.'[15] No one was
unduly astonished when Swinburne's first poetic attempt on the
subject ended with the jingoistic imperative, 'Strike, England, and
strike home', nor when he celebrated England alone against world
opinion, summoning the shades of Milton and Wordsworth on the
occasion.

Alone, as Milton and as Wordsworth found
And hailed their England, when from all around
    Howled all the recreant hate of envious knaves,
Sublime she stands.[16]

To judge Swinburne in the light of later twentieth-century hypersensitivity to being thought 'imperialist' or 'colonialist' is, of course, absurd. Yet even in terms of European politics his attitude had changed markedly. He rejoiced in the assassination of Czar Nicholas in 1881, partly from a natural dislike of extreme autocracy but also because he had supported Turkey and the rapine of Sadick Bey against Russian expansionism. Again, for personal reasons, he lamented the defeat of the Italian colonial expedition at Adowa, Abyssinia, in 1896. 'Italy has always been next – and very near – to England in my love and loyalty', he told his mother on hearing of the disaster.[17]

Perhaps the most telling *volte-face* in terms of his political allegiances was the one which came later in the same year. His youth had been characterized by hysterical hatred of Napoleon III even more strongly than by positive adulation of Mazzini. At the time of the Franco-Prussian War, he had been torn between natural allegiance to France and the knowledge that French victory would mean the triumph of the hated emperor. Much of his attachment to Hugo was explicable as admiration of the great republican exile. With the coming of the Third Republic in 1870, France was at length free and one of Swinburne's great political dreams appeared to have been realized. After a quarter of a century, most of it spent in the seclusion of The Pines, he thought otherwise. The mere absence of Napoleon III had not made for wisdom or probity on the part of the new rulers. Nicholas II, successor to the assassinated Czar, was invited as a guest of the French government, fostering the old alliance of the two countries. Swinburne at last burst out into a rhetorical denunciation of the 'prostitute hospitality' of the 'strumpet Republic'. He abominated Czarist tyranny, but the great Republic proved, after all, to be no more than the tyrant's whore.[18]

It is tempting to dismiss much of this as the influence of close confinement, year after year, with such a mind as that of Watts-Dunton. Yet there is evidence of a new moral censoriousness in Swinburne even before the departure for Putney. In 1877, for instance, he had published a letter in the *Athenaeum* on 16 June attacking the novels of Zola in terms which might almost have done credit to the Vice Society. *L'Assommoir*, he described as:

comparable only for physical and for moral abomination to such works as, by all men's admission, it is impossible to call into such a court as the present . . . for the simple and sufficient reason, that the mention of their very names in print is generally, and not unnaturally, considered to be of itself an obscene outrage on all literary law and prescription of propriety.

Acting the part of the outraged reader, Swinburne denounced the worst passages of Zola as physically impossible for him to cite and morally impossible for the editor to print.

Under the one head I rank such passages as deal with physical matters which might almost have turned the stomach of Dean Swift. The other class consists of those which contain such details of brutality and atrocity practised on a little girl, as would necessitate the interpolation of such a line as follows in the police report of any and every newspaper in London:- 'The further details given in support of the charge of cruelty were too revolting for publication in our columns.'

Clearly there had been a profound change in the moral outlook of Swinburne since, sixteen years earlier, he had screamed with laughter at Sade's description of Rodin, gleefully cutting open his daughter's belly while, at the same time, raping his own sister. Yet the case of Zola was more instructive than a mere protest in the *Athenaeum* might suggest. After his arrival at The Pines, Swinburne acquired an additional publisher, Henry Vizetelly. Vizetelly published a wide range of European fiction, including Maupassant, Gautier, Flaubert, Dostoevsky and Tolstoy. He published the Mermaid series of Elizabethan and Jacobean dramatists, to which Swinburne contributed an introduction to the Thomas Middleton volume, under the general editorship of Havelock Ellis. He also published the English translations of Zola.

Vizetelly stood far removed from the dingy pornographers of Holywell Street. As a publisher of fine editions and modern fiction, his reputation stood high. Then, in 1888, the newly formed National Vigilance Association, urged on by the *Methodist Times*, brought a prosecution in respect of such French fiction as Zola's *La Terre* and Gautier's *Mademoiselle de Maupin*. As a precaution, Vizetelly issued *Extracts Principally from English Classics*, including *Poems and Ballads*, inviting the National Vigilance Association to prosecute it as being far more obscene than anything in Zola. It was to no avail. At his trial, the jurors asked that the passages cited from French fiction should not be read out, being too indecent for a court of law. Vizetelly, who was seventy years old and weary of the whole business, changed his plea to guilty and was fined £100. *The Times* remarked smugly that publishers of Zola, in future, would not get off so lightly.[19]

The National Vigilance Association scanned his lists once more and seized on other novels by Maupassant and Zola to bring further charges. This time, despite his age and a deterioration in his health, he was sent to prison for three months. The sentence was imposed in respect of such classics of French literature as Maupassant's *Bel-Ami*. There were protests against his imprisonment and, indeed, against the National Vigilance Association, which had inherited an unctuous puritanism and an evangelical demagogy from its predecessors in the Vice Society. Yet Swinburne, for all his taunting of moral censorship in his youth, maintained an authoritarian aloofness as his publisher went to gaol and out of business. Zola's name, he remarked, should be represented by a dash, like an unprintable obscenity.

If Swinburne was guilty of moral duplicity it was, of course, nothing by comparison with the flawless hypocrisy of the nation's political leaders. Four years after Vizetelly's imprisonment, Zola visited England. The old publisher was writing the last pages of his autobiography at the time and he observed the festivities with wry detachment.

> I cannot help remarking that the irony of fate has so willed it, that, after having been prosecuted for issuing M. Zola's novels by the solicitor-general of one administration, I read in the newspapers at the very moment I am penning these concluding lines, of the enthusiastic reception of M. Zola at the Institute of Journalists, with Sir Charles Russell, the attorney-general of another administration, giving the signal for the rounds of ringing cheers with which the representatives of British journalism welcomed the great French novelist.[20]

Indeed, it was the same Charles Russell who in 1876, when paid as counsel to do so, had eagerly denounced *Poems and Ballads* as evidence of 'the indecent garbage of the French Baudelaire'.

*   *   *

Swinburne's changing attitudes and opinions affected many of his personal attachments in later life. Charles Augustus Howell and Simeon Solomon were both cast off when he found that they were selling his letters to them. William Bell Scott was denounced for his intimate portrait of Swinburne in the posthumously published

Autobiographical Notes. Watts-Dunton did his best to deter old friends like Burton or Burne-Jones from visiting the poet, as well as younger ones like Gosse. There was also the painter Whistler, author of the 'Dear Theodore, What's Dunton?' quip. Swinburne had long admired his work and had written 'Before the Mirror', collected in *Poems and Ballads*, to accompany Whistler's 'The White Girl'. Yet in the *Fortnightly Review* for June 1888, he broke publicly with Whistler, endorsing Watts-Dunton's view of him as 'a bit of a charlatan'. To T. J. Wise, Watts-Dunton confessed proudly: 'I persuaded Swinburne to write the really brilliant article.'[21]

Time alone solved many problems of admission to The Pines. Dante Gabriel Rossetti died in 1882, Houghton in 1885 and Burton in 1890. In the following decade, Jowett died in 1893, Nichol in 1894 and Burne-Jones in 1898. On hearing of Jowett's death, Swinburne filled a page with instant reminiscences, recalling his friend's 'hardihood and energy', his literary enthusiasms, and describing him with political pride as 'the last of the old Whigs'.[22] Among his lost friends he missed Jowett perhaps more than any other. They had not been separated by Watts-Dunton, who approved of Jowett and had been admitted to the exclusive company of the Malvern reading parties. In return he rewarded Jowett by incorporating him in a summer reminiscence of Oxford.

> We walk through flowery ways
> From Boar's Hill down to Oxford, fain to know
> What nugget-gold, in drift of Time's long flow,
> The Bodleian mine hath stored for richer days;
> He, fresh as on that morn, with sparkling gaze,
> Hair bright as sunshine, white as moonlit snow,
> Still talks of Plato, while the scene below
> Breaks gleaming through the veil of sunlit haze.[23]

There were, of course, friends who outlived Swinburne and, meanwhile, braved the displeasure of Watts-Dunton when necessary to visit The Pines. Among the survivors were Gosse, and also William Michael Rossetti, who outlived both the so-called 'housemates' of Putney, dying in 1919. There were also new acquaintances like Thomas J. Wise, the bibliophile, who had an eager eye upon Swinburne's manuscripts and their posthumous value. Such selected visitors still came to readings by 'The Bard', as Watts-Dunton began to call his companion. These were not, of course, the 'corybantic' performances of the kind witnessed in Great James

Street but sedate recitals before selected guests. Those who attended were treated to a display which perfectly matched other aspects of the new, reformed Swinburne who disowned the verses 'Dolorida', once written for Adah Isaacs Menken, and who found himself revolted by homosexuality to the extent of cancelling his praise of Walt Whitman and dismissing his former admirer John Addington Symonds as 'Soddington Symonds'.

That Watts-Dunton, or an alternative mentor, was necessary to Swinburne's salvation is as evident as that an appalling secular sanctimoniousness soon took over the Putney *ménage*. Yet Swinburne did not die and, indeed, began to work at a prodigious rate. After two years at Putney, the last part of his great dramatic trilogy was published as *Mary Stuart*. It had, said Edmund Gosse tactfully, 'the negative merit of brevity'. The reception of it was cool but Swinburne, at forty-four, was still alive and writing, which was more than might have been expected five years earlier. The editor of the *Encyclopaedia Britannica* invited him to write the article on Mary Queen of Scots for the forthcoming edition.[24]

In the following year, 1882, there appeared the completed *Tristram of Lyonesse*. The poem had, of course, been begun long before and its subject had even been treated in Swinburne's contribution to *Undergraduate Papers*. Now it was dedicated to Watts-Dunton, 'my best friend', with a prefatory poem assuring the world:

> There is a friend that as the wise man saith
> Cleaves closer than a brother.

The friend read *Tristram* and confessed to Swinburne some misgivings over its publication. The love of Tristram and Iseult was the problem, since the public might object to 'a poem so amatory in tone'. Not only would there be a scandal of the 1866 kind, but 'the second and fourth cantos might be challenged by the public Prosecutor'.[25] The sections likely to cause trouble were represented by such scenes as the lovemaking of Tristram and Iseult in the second canto, 'The Queen's Pleasance'.

> So they lay
> Tranced once, nor watched along the fiery bay
> The shine of summer darkness palpitate and play.
> She had nor sight nor voice; her swooning eyes
> Knew not if night or light were in the skies;
> Across her beauty sheer the moondawn shed

Its light as on a thing as white and dead;
Only with stress of soft fierce hands she prest
Between the throbbing blossoms of her breast
His ardent face, and through his hair her breath
Went quivering as when life is hard on death;
And with strong trembling fingers she strained fast
His head into her bosom; till at last,
Satiate with sweetness of that burning bed,
Her eyes afire with tears, he raised his head
And laughed into her lips; and all his heart
Filled hers; then face from face fell, and apart
Each hung on each with panting lips, and felt
Sense into sense and spirit in spirit melt.

Such, in Watts-Dunton's view, was the material which would bring Dan Chatto, and perhaps even Swinburne himself, before the Central Criminal Court. It seems absurd until one realizes that Vizetelly was sent to prison on the strength of such passages cited in his indictment as that from Maupassant's *Une Vie*. In this the embarrassment of Jeanne is described when she realizes that the hotel staff guess that her husband is taking her to bed during the afternoon, on their honeymoon.[26]

In Swinburne's case, the problem was resolved by padding out one hundred and seventy pages of *Tristram* with two hundred pages of other poems which were unobjectionable, except in aesthetic terms. Twenty-one sonnets on the English Dramatic Poets were accompanied by such infantile pieces as 'Seven years Old', 'Eight Years Old', 'A Child's Laughter', 'A Child's Thanks' and similar aberrations which would have made Swinburne's youthful ghost wince in dismay. The book escaped prosecution, and even censure. 'The amatory complexion of *Tristram* was not objected to by anybody,' wrote Gosse sadly. 'What was objected to in the poem, alas! was its lack of vital interest.'[27]

* * *

Unfortunately, the poems which accompanied *Tristram* were not merely makeweight in Swinburne's estimation. In his middle forties he had discovered a new source of joy and pleasure which cast a radiance upon The Pines and upon the humdrum routine of his walks across the common. Children, and more particularly babies, seemed guaranteed to enchant him. The first and most natural reaction to this enthusiasm on the part of a man of his age and taste was to assume that he found little girls – or little boys – sexually agreeable. Or perhaps he merely wished to impress upon their infant minds the more exotic ideas of the Marquis de Sade. His mother wrote in some alarm, reminding him of the biblical injunction against corrupting the young. She need not have worried; it was not Sadean glee but emotional senility which had led to her son's simple delight in infancy. The new centre of Swinburne's life was Bertie, the son of Watts-Dunton's sister, Miranda, who lived at Ivy Lodge. Bertie was five when his uncle and Swinburne set up house at The Pines. Swinburne bought him preserved fruits from Fortnum and Mason and indulged him like a benevolent supernumerary uncle. The books which he now ordered from Chatto were of a very different sort. The classics of European literature had been shouldered aside by *Aunt Judy's Magazine*, *Everyday Life in our Public Schools*, *Adventures of Herr Baby* and their kind. Later, Swinburne and Bertie progressed to *Dick's Holidays* and *The Union Jack*. By the time of Bertie's tenth birthday, their favourite reading included *For Name and Fame* by the boys' novelist of imperial adventure G. A. Henty, and such gems as *A Terrible Coward* and *Brownsmith's Boy* by Manville Fenn.[28]

Bertie grew up rather faster than Swinburne, who remained in a state of infantile fascination. Bertie was twenty-five when Max Beerbohm visited The Pines and witnessed the poet cooing amiably to Watts-Dunton about his morning walk, 'how he had seen in a perambulator on the heath to-day "the most BEAUT-iful babbie ever beheld by mortal eyes"'.[29] Robert Graves, an object of Swinburne's admiration, recalls how the ageing poet 'often used to stop my perambulator when he met it on Nurses' Walk, at the edge of Wimbledon Common, and pat me on the head and kiss me: he was an inveterate pram-stopper and patter and kisser'. In this account, Swinburne was on an allowance of twopence a day from Watts-Dunton to buy his beer at the Rose and Crown. 'I did not know that Swinburne was a poet,' Graves added, 'but I knew that he was a public menace.' It was some consolation to be patted on the head by a man who had been blessed by Walter Savage Landor, who in turn had been patted on the head by Samuel Johnson.[30] Regarded as an object of ridicule by the nursemaids themselves, though adored by the flattered mothers of the offspring, Swinburne poured out his tributes to infant beauty and coyness in such poems as 'A Child's Laughter'.

All the bells of heaven may ring,
All the birds of heaven may sing,
All the wells on earth may spring,
All the winds on earth may bring,
    All sweet sounds together....

In short, the state to which the disciple of Sade and revolution had been reduced would be hard to parallel in terms of irony, except perhaps in the earlier novels of Evelyn Waugh.

It was not only infancy but the newly refurbished memory of schooldays which exercised an influence over Swinburne as he passed from his forties into his fifties. At Eton's 450th anniversary in 1891, the school remembered its famous contemporary poet, the successor of Shelley, and invited him to participate. Swinburne responded with 'Eton: an Ode for the Four Hundred and Fiftieth Anniversary of the Foundation of the College'. He sent it to the Vice-Provost, Francis Warre Cornish, with a schoolboyish note: 'Here is my copy of verses – shown up in time as I understand – and I only hope I shall not be put in the bill for showing up too few.' He was invited to the anniversary celebrations on 23 June but, according to Gosse, Watts-Dunton declined to sanction this absence from The Pines and Swinburne 'submitted with a little sigh'.[31] The shadows of Putney, it seemed, closed like twilight upon him.

In the circumstances, it is almost a relief to discover that Swinburne was unreformed by the regime of The Pines, in one respect at least. Watts-Dunton, listening to the poet pacing the floor above him, imagined him at work upon some great and purer successor to *Tristram* but the truth was often otherwise. As if in a last act of defiance, Swinburne turned to the production of flagellation literature. Poetry of this kind, recognizably in Swinburne's manner, appeared in a surreptitiously marketed and very expensive magazine, *The Pearl*, which ran from July 1879 until December 1880. The issue for May 1880 contains 'Frank Fane – A Ballad', describing the ordeal of a hero whose name was to feature in longer poems by Swinburne on the subject. The scene is set in Whippingham School, which gave its name to *The Whippingham Papers*, published with equal caution in 1888. In this later book, the style of Swinburne is evident in such pieces as 'Reginald's Flogging'.

The only question which remains unresolved is whether Swinburne, the house-trained bard of Putney, was privately in touch with the more expensive pornographers of the late-Victorian period. It was Edward Avery, a bookseller of Greek Street, Soho, who issued Swinburne's work in *The Whippingham Papers*. Avery specialized in the production of what Chief-Inspector Edward Drew later described as 'elaborately bound books ... the grossest and most obscene pictures and photographs that one could well imagine, as well as a number of beautifully carved ivory models showing persons in the act of coition'. Avery enjoyed an undisturbed career from 1875 until 1900, when he was decoyed into selling one of his more explicit productions to a plain-clothes police officer. He went to prison for four months.[32]

It may be, of course, that the material which appeared in *The Pearl* and which Avery published was drawn from papers that had long since passed from Swinburne's possession. He may have been in touch with the publishers at the time. Certainly he exchanged letters with a far more influential pornographer than Avery. This was Charles Carrington, born Paul Ferdinando, who progressed from being an errand-boy and lavatory attendant in London to being the first and most ambitious publisher of English erotica in Paris. He survived the protests of the English police and the threats of their French colleagues, dying blind and syphilitic in 1922.

It was to Carrington that Swinburne confessed an ancient literary hoax. The story of the girl and her lover in his poem 'Laus Veneris' was taken from a French text of 1530 by Antoine Gaget, quoted in the original in *Poems and Ballads*. Pressed for details, Swinburne admitted that Gaget and the text were his own invention, as a justification of the poem which followed. Carrington was a natural admirer of Swinburne's work, his own publications showing an almost exclusive interest in sadism and sexual oddity. Ironically, Swinburne's own sexual eccentricity now seemed much less eccentric, at least to judge from the unremitting demand of English readers for products of Carrington's kind. *The Memoirs of Dolly Morton* (1899), *Woman and her Master* (1904), *The Beautiful Flagellants of New York* and *Sadopaedia* (1907) were a few of Carrington's gems. Many of his works were even semi-respectable, allowing purchasers to read with a sense of scholarly self-improvement the ordeals of such adolescent criminals as Sarah Barnes, Elaine Cox and Charlotte Burton, in *Les Châtiments de Jadis*. Indeed, Swinburne may have recognized in these Victorian prison scenes the counterpart of his own schoolroom contributions to *The Whippingham Papers*, including perhaps the prose story, 'A Boy's First Flogging at Birchminster'.

Among the secret poems of Putney, there was the still unpublished school epic *The Flogging Block*, whose resemblance is less to
erotic literature than to many of the school stories quite openly
published at the time in boys' magazines. The poem was evidently
written early in the 1880s and was followed in the 1890s by a poem
in a similar style, though not epic in length, 'Eton: another Ode'. In
this, Swinburne parodies his own 'Eton: an Ode', written for the
anniversary celebrations of the school in 1891. Oddest of all,
perhaps, Swinburne dedicated this latest piece to his cousin, Mary
Gordon, now Mary Disney Leith.

Mary's husband, being somewhat older than herself, had died in
1892 and she began writing to Swinburne again, as though to revive
an old affection. Flagellation was an enthusiastically introduced
topic in her letters, revealing her as an appreciative recipient and
dedicatee of these new pieces. The customs of The Pines, reflecting
those of the public-school system, led to Swinburne's referring to
Watts-Dunton as his 'Major' and to himself as Watts-Dunton's
'Minor'. Mary, now in her fifties, joined eagerly in the game by
correspondence, and occasionally as a visitor. In the school fantasies
which she and Swinburne shared she once again saw herself in the
role of a junior boy who was his 'Minor'. The letters which she wrote
also followed the odd custom of changing round the initial letters of
words so that, for example, 'My Dearest Cousin', was writtten by
her as 'Cy Merest Dozen'. As a code it was so simple and so easily
broken that there would have been little point to it. Perhaps it
reflects, rather, a certain feminine coyness on her part over the
feelings expressed and the matters discussed. This is so, for instance,
when Mary thanked Swinburne for his birching poem, 'Eton:
another Ode', but wished that he had dealt with a later period in
their lives than his own schooldays, 'I wish that it wealt with a pater
leriod'. As for the mode of punishment, however, she adds an
unambiguous 'Florebit'.[33]

Whatever the damage to modern susceptibilities from such
behaviour as Swinburne and Mary described, she at least was able to
take some refuge still in the moral probity of her enthusiasm.
Indeed, Swinburne had at hand an unlikely source of inspiration, as
the following passage shows.

> To be whacked occasionally is part and parcel of our very existence, and
> it's my belief that it's good for the human boy. But to be touched up *twice*, in
> the space of as many calendar minutes, is literally more than flesh and blood
> can bear. . . . Now the chance of stroke number two falling upon wale

number one is remote, and it may even be said that the chance of stroke number six exactly coinciding with any previous wale is also remote. But a second innings.... A second innings on a bad wicket![34]

This mixture of facetious erudition and furtive sado-masochism, echoing the correspondence of Swinburne and Mary, is not, of course, from any work of pornography but from *The Twins of Tendering: A Public School Story* by Captain Charles Gilson, already known as author of *The Lost Column*. It was published in the year of Swinburne's death, a genre of fiction which he had begun to acquire for the pleasure of reading to little Bertie. He had no need to buy Carrington's expensively produced copies of *The Memoires of Dolly Morton* or *The Beautiful Flagellants of New York*. If Victorian England reduced many of its inhabitants to a lame dependence on stimulus of this sort, it also provided for them on a scale which no mere pornographer could rival.

*   *   *

There was no dramatic change in the routine of The Pines, nothing which specifically differentiated one year from another until the nineteenth century and the Victorian period had ended. Swinburne, almost completely deaf, talking in a sweet, fluting voice, was the absurd target of young men like Beerbohm and an object of pilgrimage to others. He was, as Watts-Dunton called him, 'The Bard', and upon the death of Tennyson in 1892 there was a question of making him Poet Laureate. General opinion seemed to favour him and when Gladstone, as prime minister, consulted the queen, she was reported to have said, 'I am told that Mr Swinburne is the best poet in my dominions.' It was true that he had written questionable verses in the past, but there seemed little doubt as to his reformation. As lately as 1887 there had been the celebrated attack on Walt Whitman's morality, for instance, the denunciation of Whitman's Muse as 'a drunken apple-woman, indecently sprawling in the slush and garbage of the gutter amid the rotten refuse of her overturned fruit-stall'.[35] But Gladstone was unenthusiastic. He had no reason to like Swinburne, either personally or politically. When the appointment was at last made, it was Alfred Austin who was chosen, a poet unkindly remembered for such couplets as that attributed to him during the illness of the Prince of Wales from typhoid in 1871.

> Across the wires the electric message came,
> He is no better, he is much the same.[36]

In 1908, six months before his death, there was another flurry of expectation. It had been suggested that Swinburne should be offered the next Nobel Prize for Literature. Initially, he was not in favour of the idea because Rudyard Kipling had already received the prize for 1907 and to accept it subsequently would seem to be conceding Kipling's superiority. But Watts-Dunton urged acceptance and, as Swinburne told William Michael Rossetti, claimed that for Swinburne to be Nobel prizewinner would be a great triumph for free thought. Neither of them need have worried about its implication for, when the time came, Swinburne was not offered the prize.[37]

The routine of The Pines had continued with little alteration, including the familiar morning walk by Swinburne to Putney Heath, and the glass of beer at the Rose and Crown, whether or not on an allowance of twopence a day. Though he beamed indulgently into the prams of Nurses' Walk, admiring their occupants, he was discouraging to those who crossed his path for the purpose of introducing themselves. Eric Mackay, a minor poet of the day who wished to dedicate his next book of verse to Swinburne, was accorded a typical reception. He lay in wait by the path until Swinburne appeared, 'pelting along deep in thought'. Mackay stepped out suddenly, raising his hat and bowing.

'I believe I have the honour of addressing Mr Swinburne, the great poet.'

'My name is Swinburne. What do you want of me?'

'May I have the honour of a few words with you, sir? My name is Eric Mackay. I wrote to you....'

'Certainly not. I do not know you, sir. Good morning.'

And Swinburne stamped off indignantly across the heath. When Mackay wrote, angrily announcing that he would *not* dedicate his book to the poet, Swinburne replied to his letter succinctly.

Mr Swinburne has received a letter from a Mr Mackay – whom he does not know – in which Mr Mackay informs Mr Swinburne that he does *not* propose dedicating any book of his to Mr Swinburne, nor, indeed, of so much as mentioning his name in future, by which decision Mr Swinburne is honoured, and relieved.[38]

To his visitors at The Pines, he was the courteous but faded little poet, with an enthusiasm for books and pedantry which was more than anything reminiscent of an eccentric don. He, who had once seemed so revolutionary a force in English poetry, showed little enthusiasm for some of the new writers coming into fashion. Though he liked Thomas Hardy, he described Bernard Shaw as 'a scurrilous buffoon' for his reviling of Shakespeare, and he extended this dislike to include Ibsen. Though Ibsen and Zola, once more, were condemned in his 1902 essay on Dickens for their obscenity, the former was quite the opposite of all that Swinburne had admired in the past. There could be nothing less like *Poems and Ballads* or *l'art pour l'art* than Ibsen's moralizing, pervasive at the best and, at its worst, clumsily intrusive.

From the world beyond the book-lined room with its view across the back garden of The Pines, from beyond suburban Putney, came news of the changes which time and mortality brought about in the Swinburne family itself. In July 1891, he was with his mother when they heard first of Edward Swinburne's serious illness and then of his death, alone in St John's Wood, deserted by his wife. Edward had never had much involvement in his older brother's life, beyond suggesting to Watts-Dunton in 1879 that his money should be tied up in investments which would make it difficult for him to squander the capital. Ironically, Algernon's first reaction on hearing of his death was to congratulate himself on being the partner in a morally superior relationship with Watts-Dunton, by contrast with his brother's attachment to a faithless wife.

In the summer of 1896, Lady Jane Swinburne left Bradford-on-Avon to live at Barking Hall in Suffolk, which had been her birth-place. Swinburne visited her later, and her eighty-seventh birthday was celebrated there in the autumn. In October, Swinburne was preoccupied by the death of William Morris, and then, on 26 November, Lady Jane herself died at her new home. It was arguably the last great crisis of Swinburne's life, and prompted him to express feelings which were both characteristic and ambiguous, as in his letter to his sister Alice on 4 December:

> I know no such comfort in sorrow as the sight of little children. A look or a smile from them not only *re*-assures one that 'of such is the kingdom of heaven', but takes one thither and makes one a denizen of that kingdom – for a few minutes, anyhow.[39]

Precisely what 'the kingdom of heaven' meant to an atheist whose model of perfection had been the Marquis de Sade might seem open to question. It merely illustrates the recurrent truth in the Victorian period that though religious belief was often inconsistent and plagued by doubt, so was the 'unbelief' of atheists. In Swinburne's case, his views seemed to undergo an almost daily modification. For his surviving three sisters, however, his affection remained unaltered. On 11 June 1897 he wrote to Alice Swinburne, 'I often and often think of what you said to me on Dec. 1st just outside the Churchyard after the funeral – that we must be more and closer to each other now than ever.'[40] Two years later, in January 1899, Charlotte Swinburne died and Alice herself four years after that in September 1903. There remained only Isabel Swinburne, 'Abba', who was to survive her brother by six years. The loss of Alice was one which Swinburne felt particularly, describing her to Isabel as having a 'heroic and heavenly sweetness of nature' which he had found in no other human being but Mazzini.[41]

By the age of sixty-six, after he had lived for almost a quarter of a century at The Pines, the family for which Swinburne cared had been reduced to two members, Isabel Swinburne and Mary Leith. Yet after the bereavements inevitable at his age, the stage at Putney was rapidly reset for farce. There had, of course, been the amusement of Theodore Watts's becoming Theodore Watts-Dunton, but this was as nothing by comparison with Watts-Dunton's announcement, at the age of seventy-three, that he was to marry Clara Reich. She was twenty-one and had been visiting The Pines since her mother first brought her there as a schoolgirl of sixteen. *Aylwin*, with its penchant for the romantic gipsy-child, had been published in 1898, bringing fame to Watts-Dunton as an author. As he blossomed out of bachelor life, he addressed Clara eagerly as 'Darling Girl-Wife', and 'Darling Bright-Eyes'.[42] As Clara herself remarks, when the time came for her to change from the short skirts of a schoolgirl, ending at the knees, into a longer adult style, her septuagenarian fiancé was persuaded to 'intercede with my mother' in favour of retaining the 'juvenile short frocks'.[43]

Swinburne accepted the changes at The Pines with genial tolerance. 'You must not call me "Mr Swinburne" now, remember, but "Algernon",' he told the young bride after her marriage at St James's, Piccadilly. 'I hope you will look upon me as a brother-in-law.'[44] Meanwhile, Watts-Dunton's enthusiasm for his 'young rascal', as he called Clara, prompted Swinburne to take the precaution of descending the stairs very loudly and giving the sitting-room door handle a long, slow rattle before opening it.[45]

Despite the salubrious routine of The Pines, it was evident towards the end of his sixties that Swinburne's health had begun to deteriorate. Until 1903 he had been vigorous in action and regular in his daily exercise. 'Algernon is in great force,' announced Watts-Dunton, reporting to Clara on the condition of 'The Bard'. Then, in November, he contracted pneumonia. At the time of his celebrated faint in the British Museum and at the removal to Putney in 1879 Swinburne's health had been a matter of national interest. So it was now. Clara Watts-Dunton, as she was to be in two years more, saw the orange placards of the *Pall Mall Gazette* bearing in large black type the headline: 'Serious Illness of Mr Swinburne'.[46]

Pneumonia at the age of sixty-six was hazardous but not, in this instance, fatal. Nurses were installed at The Pines. Swinburne was petulant and abusive, resenting their intrusion, but he recovered all the same. Watts-Dunton became more cautious over his 'minor's' health. When 'The Bard' returned damp from the rain on Putney Heath, Watts-Dunton grew insistent over a change of clothes and dry socks. 'No excuses about not needing to change or keeping luncheon waiting were of the least use,' said Clara. 'Walter fidgeted until he had put on dry things, and refused to look happy until he saw the Bard appear, high and dry and jubilant, to take his place at the table.'[47] Visitors were apt to find Swinburne in the dining-room, keeping the table between him and them, as he surreptitiously dried his socks before the fire and danced furtively in bare feet to avoid the reproaches of Watts-Dunton.

In the spring of 1909 it was Watts-Dunton who caught cold. He was not well enough to come down to lunch and, evidently, he had influenza. Swinburne inquired after his friend and Clara described Watts-Dunton's indisposition as 'a bit of a cold'. When the patient had not appeared at lunch on the following day, Swinburne insisted on going to his room to see him after the meal. After the visit Swinburne withdrew to his own room for his customary afternoon siesta, returning later to read to Watts-Dunton the book which they were currently following, *Ivanhoe*. But the reading had to be postponed. On the following day, 1 April, Swinburne went for his morning walk in cold and blustery weather, without an overcoat. Watts-Dunton was irritated and ordered his secretary, Thomas Hake, to confront 'The Bard' on his return and see that he changed his clothes.

By the next day, Swinburne was confined to his bed and the doctor had been fetched. The patient was irritable and his condition was deteriorating. He was moved to another bed in his library and two nurses were stationed outside the open door, so that he should not be further annoyed by their presence in the room itself. That presence was soon necessary, however, as Clara arrived to find a nurse trying to insert an oxygen tube between Swinburne's lips while the patient beat at it with his hands and cried, 'Take it away, take it away!' Clara persuaded him that its effect was merely that of a beneficial sea-breeze, and Swinburne resisted no more.

Three days later, 5 April, was his seventy-second birthday, but by then he was in a fever, and the messages of congratulation lay unopened. His case was diagnosed as double pneumonia and he had lapsed into delirium. There had been some apprehension over this and over the words which might come unimpeded into the hearing of the nurses. The language of lesbian passion, the enthusiasm of the flagellation brothel, the obscenities with which he mocked and savaged his literary enemies were, however, not heard. His mind had wandered back beyond the years of The Pines and the book-lined room overlooking the suburban garden, beyond the alcoholic misery of the 1870s and the drawing-room passions of St John's Wood. Even Mazzini's Italy and the girls of Venice were forgotten, and Balliol and the Oxford of the young Pre-Raphaelites. He was back at last in the ideal Aegean of East Dene, the classical Arcadia of Eton, and the comfortable world of Pino, Mimmie and Mary Gordon. He talked and talked in words which the nurses could not understand but which were the Greek of his beloved Sappho and Aeschylus.

Clara went to him repeatedly as his breathing grew harsher, and reported that she heard strange chords of music in the room, coming from no evident source. The words of the delirium had ended and Swinburne was alone, silent in whatever vision presented itself behind his closed eyelids. On 9 April, Watts-Dunton managed to get up in the evening and went to Swinburne's room. There was no longer any need for medical diagnosis of the poet's condition. Watts-Dunton reappeared presently, in great distress, and said, 'Oh, Clara, Clara!' as he put his arms round his wife. Swinburne died at ten o'clock on the following morning.[48]

*　　*　　*

There was almost at once a lively dispute between secularism and religion over the disposal of Swinburne's remains. For a man of his eminence to escape some form of religious ceremony at his funeral was extraordinarily difficult. What, in any case, did he believe or disbelieve? The answer was made more complex by his confession to Lucy Brown Rossetti, for instance, that he felt inclined to a religious belief in immortality, despite the unwitting efforts of foolish clergymen to destroy intelligent belief. To his mother, he had described his wish – rather than his ability – to believe, in 1892. 'It is so beautiful and delightful to think of "being together when this life is over", as you say, and of seeing things no longer "in a glass darkly", but all who have ever tried to do a little bit of what they thought right being brought together.'⁴⁹ Those who contended for Swinburne's belief might easily demonstrate that he had neatly summarized the undogmatic piety of many Victorians. Anticlericalism had perhaps been a stronger motive in his case than philosophical atheism. Appropriately, his words to Lucy Brown Rossetti echoed those of his great friend Jowett to Margot Asquith: 'My dear child, you must believe in God in spite of what the clergy tell you.'⁵⁰

One thing which seemed generally agreed was that Swinburne should be buried with his parents and his dead sisters in the churchyard of East Dene. On 15 April the coffin was taken by train to Portsmouth and then laid under a tarpaulin in the bows of the ferry steamer for Ryde. Watts-Dunton and Isabel Swinburne were too ill to accompany the mourners but Clara stood on the upper deck and watched the foam of a sunlit wave burst over the bow of the steamer and the covered coffin.

At the churchyard there was another altercation over the disposal of Swinburne's remains. He had given no specific instructions in the matter and Watts-Dunton was left to exchange vague and ineffectual telegrams with the rector, John Floyd Andrewes. Watts-Dunton had however promised Swinburne that the burial service should not be read over him, and he insisted on this to the surviving sister, Isabel Swinburne. She took to her bed and did not attend the funeral. But did the promise mean that no phrases of any kind from the liturgy were to be uttered, or merely that there should be no formal religious service? On the evening before the funeral, Watts-Dunton sent another telegram from Putney to East Dene. The mourners were to gather round the grave in silence, throw flowers into it, and then disperse.

The rector had agreed that there would be no service and he tactfully avoided quoting anything from the New Testament. But when the cortège arrived at the churchyard gate, he greeted it with several phrases from the liturgy, perhaps from force of habit. At the graveside he spoke flatteringly of Swinburne and his poetry, but also used the words 'earth to earth, dust to dust', and '*requiescat in pace*'. There was a vociferous interruption from one of the mourners, and a good deal of subsequent recrimination. The Rector protested that he had not held a service and that, in any case, Swinburne was a baptized member of the Church who had sought burial in consecrated ground. The words to which members of secularist organizations were objecting were of the vaguest and most undogmatic kind. Had there been no attempt to give some form of address, the public would have concluded: 'They are going to bury him like a dog.'[51]

* * *

Of the survivors, Watts-Dunton died in 1914, William Michael Rossetti in 1919, and the young admirer Edmund Gosse in 1928. The poet's sister and only living member of his immediate family, Isabel, died in 1915, his cousin Mary following her in 1926. Clara Watts-Dunton lived on until 1938, cherishing the memory of her husband and his famous 'housemate'.

The problem of reconciling Swinburne's intimations of immortality with his opposition to all forms of religion was nothing compared with the difficulty of preserving the image of him which his remaining family and intimates chose to recall. The mass of surviving letters and manuscripts attracted the attention of two men, Thomas James Wise, as bibliographer and collector, and Edmund Gosse as the potential biographer. Watts-Dunton himself had already declined the latter role, under pressure from Clara, who professed to regard biography as 'mere stodge and Baedekerism'.[52]

As a likely biographer, Gosse soon found himself in difficulties. Swinburne's memory was fiercely defended by his sister and his cousin Mary. Mary insisted that Swinburne had never been drunk in his life, and that all his years had been spent in communion with the Church of England. Mary could hardly add that the poet had had no interest in flagellation, but when the name of Adah Isaacs Menken was mentioned, both women announced that 'Algernon was far too well-bred a gentleman ever to *speak* to a woman of that class!'[53]

Watts-Dunton, as Swinburne's heir, had become the possessor of manuscript letters and literary works which seemed to prove the truth beyond any question, and which were a source of embarrassment to their new owner. There were the unpublished fragments of *Lesbia Brandon*, which Gosse and Wise saw and jointly agreed 'ought never to be published'.[54] There were pieces like *The Flogging Block*, which never have been published and whose discovery must have caused Watts-Dunton to reflect that even the benevolent despotism of The Pines had not been foolproof. There were the notorious letters to Charles Augustus Howell, bought back to save public embarrassment. Watts-Dunton claimed that he burnt them in 1886, when they were retrieved. Unfortunately, eighteen of them at least survived and were bought by Wise for his Swinburne collection.

When Gosse published his *Life of Algernon Charles Swinburne*, it was out of the question for him to use manuscript material of this kind. As if to justify the incomplete portrait of the poet which he had drawn, Gosse sent a private memoir to eminent contemporaries in which he described, with examples, the alcoholic and sado-masochistic excesses of Swinburne's private life. The recipients were not, on the whole, surprised. Most of them had already guessed that there was some sexual oddity in Swinburne's life. A. C. Bradley, the Shakespearean scholar, had suggested at the time of the biography that if Swinburne was 'excessively given to fornication', Gosse ought to say so, in order to counter the post-humous rumours that the poet was homosexual. Sir Walter Raleigh, Merton Professor of English at Oxford, had merely supposed Swinburne to be impotent, while A. E. Housman replied philosophically that at least masochism must have been cheaper to indulge than sadism. As to the publication of such material, Max Beerbohm and John Bailey believed that the sexual aberrations must remain secret, though Beerbohm hoped Swinburne would be revealed as a colourful 'toper'. Raleigh alone advocated the full publication of the memoir: 'There is nothing very awful about it.'[55]

Gosse, on the other hand, seemed increasingly to feel the awful-ness of the letters which he passed on to Wise as the requirements of biography yielded to those of bibliography. 'They should be des-troyed at once,' he insisted, sending to Wise the letters of Simeon Solomon to Swinburne, replete with sadistic and homosexual refer-ences.[56] Wise kept them. Later on, Gosse despatched the letters of Swinburne's cousin Mary to 'Cy Merest Dozen', with their enthusiastic appreciation of school discipline. His message to Wise was succinct: 'For goodness' sake tear them up.'[57] Wise preserved these also.

The collection of Thomas J. Wise, the Ashley Library, passed at his death to the British Museum. In 1959, as the first volume of

Cecil Y. Lang's comprehensive edition of the *Swinburne Letters* appeared, the truth about the poet was at last documented. His obsessions were, of course, evident in general terms before this, at least since the eventual publication of *Lesbia Brandon* in 1952 and, in a sense, since *Poems and Ballads* in 1866. It was, perhaps, inevitable that the most scandalous details of Swinburne's personal life should remain suppressed until a period so accustomed to such indulgences that their revelation was greeted in the terms in which he received Sade's *Justine:* 'Is this all?'

* * *

As a poet, Swinburne falls into that group described by T. S. Eliot in *The Sacred Wood,* where the question is how much of his work to ignore as well as how much to read. It is easy to explain why he should have been led into the empty sonority of much of his later verse in an age which placed a high value on rhetoric. Yet Swinburne as the bright star of mid-Victorian poetry is the author of *Atalanta, Poems and Ballads*, and very little more. To explain that the mass of his later poetry casts an interesting light on contemporary culture hardly makes it much more enjoyable – or tolerable. At his best, in the 1860s, he shows a modernity and a strength which justifiably marked him out as the leader of the new generation.[58]

His decline from that point can be variously explained as mere failure of poetic inspiration, 'ossification' of his receptivity to new experience, the artistic suicide of becoming the poet of a political cause (however admirable), the misjudgement of wearing himself out with unwieldy poetic dramas rather than, perhaps, in writing the prose fiction for which he had shown such initial aptitude. Gosse dated the dulling of Swinburne's emotional responses from 1877, Harold Nicolson tentatively put the date 1857, when he was twenty.[59]

Whatever defiance he showed to his critics over *Poems and Ballads*, Swinburne thereafter grew more cautious in writing of such subjects and, indeed, arbitrarily attuned himself to political demands in *Songs Before Sunrise.* Yet it was in the style of *Poems and Ballads* that he excelled: passionate, sensual, and suggestive. It was in this vein that art and life flowed together. Gosse, in his confidential memoir, remarked that Swinburne's generative instinct was not strongly developed, that he was not sexually very active. Indeed, the evidence of both his life and his writing shows repeatedly that Swinburne's obsession, whether in poems like

'Anactoria' or in the capers of the Regent's Park brothel, is not with the sexual but with the erotic.

The distinction is important to an understanding of his compulsions. Mental excitement of suggestion and stimulus was more to him, in this respect, than the physical excitement of sexual fulfilment. Mary Gordon, playing the part of a boy in a birch-obsessed school, even at a distance and by correspondence, was more desirable than Mary Gordon as a wife or sexual partner. The splendid and violent Dolores, by turns an aggressive and submissive animal, held more excitement than all the tangible physical qualities of Adah Isaacs Menken could offer. Swinburne's eroticism might be bluntly described as a stimulation of the mind rather than the genitals. Hence, in old age, the enthusiasm for subjects such as *The Flogging Block*, whose appeal might puzzle a reader oriented towards sexual activity. Hence, in more overt sexual terms, the preoccupation with lesbianism, where the man is involved only as observer and not as actor. There is a sense in which the progress from the loves of Lesbia Brandon or Dolores to the arid emotions of *The Flogging Block* is a refinement of stimulus to the cerebral and the symbolic.

Swinburne's appreciation of feminine beauty is beyond question in his poetry and in the caressing prose which describes the women of Rossetti's paintings. Yet the caresses are reserved for women as created by the artist. Here, too, the concern of the erotic is with symbol, abstraction and fetish, rather than with the biological act of copulation. His acknowledged master is Gautier, in whose fiction eroticism attained its most refined and almost abstract form. The finale of *Mademoiselle de Maupin* requires no actors, merely the bed in which Rosette has slept bearing the imprint of two bodies upon it, the nature of their love determined by the discovery of another woman's pearls in the sheets.

As the charged eroticism of *Lesbia Brandon* faded in the secret schoolroom obsessions of The Pines, so Swinburne's political ideals accommodated themselves to an unenlightened Toryism. He appeared jingoistic and self-righteous. He had, of course, been self-righteous even as an undergraduate, in a different cause. During his years at Putney a good many contemporaries were moving in the same political direction. The queen, unpopular to varying degrees in her middle years, was the grand old lady of the golden and diamond jubilees, a totem of national self-satisfaction. The empire, which she had considered disbanding in 1865 as unmanageable and too extensive for military defence, was now held firmly and contributed greatly to the wealth of Britain.[60] To Swinburne, always receptive to political themes, the call of imperial achievement proved irresistible. Indeed, the circumstances of The Pines offered little alternative. Even as a revolutionary he had, of course, retained a proper awareness of his noble origins. Other men were quick to remind him of them. 'I knew nothing about his social position,' said one Dutch visitor to Putney, 'but he was manifestly a foreigner and an English aristocrat.'[61] In the end, it was always open to an aristocratic revolutionary to decide that he was an aristocrat first and a revolutionary second.

Perhaps his greatest achievement was to live on in the memory of the twentieth century as a curiosity of society and literature, a more vivid cameo of the Victorian writer in his world than that presented by men and women whose works were to be more highly valued. It was almost enough to see Swinburne, whether or not one read him. Beside his oddities, his presence as a 'flag', in Gosse's term, of mid-Victorian rebellion, George Eliot and Henry James seem humdrum, and even Tennyson appears insubstantial. Ironically, even in his later isolation at The Pines, he became a figure who was instantly recognized. At the height of his fame, Gosse recalled, his appearance was so well known that a firm of tailors used to publish photographic portraits of the immaculate aesthete as 'an illustration of our full dress suit'.[62]

Because his commitments were few and the calls upon his energy and time rarely urgent, he could afford to live his life as though regaling his contemporaries with a flawless theatrical performance. Though that performance was sometimes absurd, it was never dull; though it caused exasperation and even uproar, it was generally well attended. Arnold Bennett arrived in Putney on 9 April 1909, during the final scenes.

A few yards beyond where the autobuses turned was a certain house with lighted upper windows, and in that house the greatest lyric versifier that England ever had, and one of the great poets of the whole world and of all ages, was dying.... The next day all the shops were open and hundreds of fatigued assistants were pouring out their exhaustless patience on thousands of urgent and bright women; and flags waved on high, and the gutters were banked with yellow and white flowers, and the air was brisk and the roadways were clean. The very vital spirit of energy seemed to have scattered the breath of life generously, so that all were intoxicated by it in the gay sunshine. He was dead then. The waving posters said it....[63]

Notes

Abbreviations

Bonchurch – *The Complete Works of Algernon Charles Swinburne*, ed. Edmund Gosse and Thomas James Wise (1925–7).

Gosse, *Life* – Edmund Gosse, *The Life of Algernon Charles Swinburne* (1917).

Hake and Compton-Rickett – Thomas Hake and Arthur Compton-Rickett, *The Letters of A. C. Swinburne* (1918).

Lafourcade – Georges Lafourcade, *Swinburne: A Literary Biography* (1932).

La Jeunesse – Georges Lafourcade, *La Jeunesse de Swinburne* (1928).

Lang – *The Swinburne Letters*, ed. Cecil Y. Lang (1959–62).

Leith – Mrs Disney-Leith [Mary Gordon], *The Boyhood of Algernon Charles Swinburne* (1917).

Rossetti, *Letters* – *Letters of Dante Gabriel Rossetti*, ed. Oswald Doughty and John Robert Wahl (1965).

Manuscript sources are first noted with the name of the institution holding them, and subsequently with their serial numbers alone.

Chapter 1: Blue Blood

1 W. B. Scott, *Autobiographical Notes* (1892) II, 14.

2 Gosse, *Life*, p. 2.

3 Nikolaus Pevsner, *The Buildings of England: Northumberland* (1957), pp. 111–12.

4 Scott, *Autobiograhical Notes*, II, 19.

5 Gosse, *Life*, p. 3.

6 William Roberts, *The Memoirs of the Life and Correspondence of Mrs Hannah More* (1834), 4 vols. I, 282.

7 Gosse, *Life*, p. 3.

8 *Examiner*, 22 March 1812.

9 Gosse, *Life*, pp. 3–4.

10 *Revue Bleue*, LXXIV (1936), 154; Lang, II, 18.

11 Gosse, *Life*, p. 4.

12 Thomas Barnes, eleventh Earl of Dundonald, and H. B. Fox Bourne, *The Life of Thomas, Lord Cochrane, 10th Earl of Dundonald* (1869), II, 238.

13 Gosse, *Life*, p. 4.

14 Lang, II, 30.

15 Thomas Brettell, *A Topographical and Historical Guide to the Isle of Wight* (1840), p. 1.

16 *Letters of Queen Victoria*, ed.

A. C. Benson and Viscount Esher (1908), II, 36.

17 G. Brannon, *The Pleasure Visitor's Companion in Making the Tour of the Isle of Wight* (1850), p. 38.

18 Gosse, *Life*, p. 6.

19 Brannon, *Isle of Wight*, pp. 69–70.

20 Harold Nicolson, *Tennyson* (1960), p. 224.

21 British Museum MS. Ashley 5752 ff. 189–212.

22 Bonchurch XVIII, 485; Lang, VI, 195.

23 Lafourcade, p. 183.

24 Lang, I, 184–5.

25 Ashley 5752 f. 191.

26 'A Forsaken Garden', *Poems and Ballads: Second Series* (1878).

27 *The Times Literary Supplement*, 3 June 1909; Lang, III, 12.

28 'The Triumph of Time', *Poems and Ballads* (1866).

29 Leith, pp. 1, 6–7.

30 *ibid.*, p. 9.

31 Quoted in Humphrey Hare, *Swinburne, A Biographical Approach* (1949), p. 5.

32 Leith, p. 6.

33 *ibid.*, p. 5.

34 Ashley 5752 ff. 40–49.

35 Leith, p. 25.

36 *ibid.*, p. 23.

37 *La Jeunesse*, I, 27.

38 Leith, p. 7.

39 *ibid.*, p. 8.

40 *Poetical Works of William Cowper*, ed. H. S. Milford (1934), pp. 246–7.

41 Lord Suffield, *My Memories 1830–1913* (1913), p. 39.

42 C. A. Wilkinson, *Reminiscences of Eton* (1888), p. 41.

43 *ibid.*, p. 46.

44 Henry S. Salt, *Memories of Bygone Eton* (1928), p. 225.

45 *ibid.*, p. 226.

46 *ibid.*, pp. 69–76.

47 Wilkinson, *Eton*, p. 324.

48 *ibid.*, pp. 324, 326.

49 *ibid.*, p. 321.

50 William Hardman, *A Mid-Victorian Pepys,* ed. S. M. Ellis (1923), p. 71.

51 Geoffrey Faber, *Jowett* (1957), p. 65.

52 John Addington Symonds MS. Autobiography, f.79.

53 *ibid.*, ff. 79–80.

54 Salt, *Eton*, p. 112.

55 Symonds, Autobiography, ff. 102–6.

56 Oscar Browning, *Memories of Sixty Years* (1910), p. 16.

57 *ibid.*, p. 16.

58 Leith, p. 227; Lang, IV, 321.

59 Salt, *Eton*, p. 126.

60 Gosse, *Life*, p. 319.

61 *ibid.*, p. 322.

62 *ibid.*, p. 14.

63 Osbert Sitwell, *Noble Essences* (1950), p. 113.

64 Gosse, *Life*, p. 322.

65 Salt, *Eton*, p. 125.·

66 Gosse, *Life*, pp. 320–1.

67 *ibid.*, p. 321.

68 *ibid.*, p. 321.

69 *ibid.*, p. 14.

70 Ashley 5753 f.25; Lang, I, 78.

71 A. C. Benson, *Memories and Friends* (1924), pp. 85–90.

72 *ibid.*, pp. 87–91.

73 Michael Holroyd, 'The Fraternity to Come', in *The Times Literary Supplement*, 24 February 1978, p. 224.

74 Hare, *Swinburne*, p. 18.

75 Bonchurch, XVIII, 266; Lang, III, 229.

76 Leith, p. 9.

77 Wilkinson, *Eton*, p. 179.

78 Gosse, *Life*, p. 26.

79 *ibid.*, p. 323.

Chapter 2: Oxford

1 Gosse, *Life,* pp. 15, 24.
2 Timothy Gowing, *A Voice from the Ranks* (1954), pp. 4–5.
3 Leith, p. 13.
4 Charles Kingsley, *Letters and Memoirs* (1877), I, 434.
5 *ibid.,* I, 433.
6 Gosse, *Life,* p. 29.
7 *Mysteries of Flagellation* (1863), *passim.*
8 Harold Nicolson, *Swinburne* (1926), p. 37.
9 Leith, p. 14.
10 Gosse, *Life,* p. 30; Leith, pp. 14–16.
11 Leith, p. 17.
12 'Duns Scotus's Oxford'.
13 Matthew Arnold, *Essays in Criticism* (1889), pp. x-ix.
14 Mrs Humphrey Ward, *A Writer's Recollections* (1918), pp. 131–2.
15 Geoffrey Faber, *Oxford Apostles* (1954), pp. 416–17.
16 Frank, Earl Russell, *My Life and Adventures* (1923), p. 106.
17 Nicolson, *Swinburne,* p. 40.
18 Symonds, Autobiography, f. 333; Phyllis Grosskurth, *John Addington Symonds* (1964), p. 51.
19 E. F. Benson, *As We Were* (1930), pp. 146–7.
20 Margot Asquith, *Autobiography* (1920), p. 136.
21 Benson, *As We Were,* pp. 147–8.
22 *ibid.,* p. 147.
23 Horatio F. Brown, *John Addington Symonds, A Biography* (1903), p. 132.
24 Symonds, Autobiography, ff. 336–7.
25 Faber, *Jowett,* p. 359.
26 Bodleian Library MS. Top. Oxon. d. 242 f.4.
27 W. A. Knight, *Memoir of John Nichol* (1896), p. 127.
28 Top. Oxon. d. 242 f.26.
29 Bonchurch, XVIII, 4; Lang, I, 18.
30 Top. Oxon. d. 242 f.21.
31 Gosse, *Life,* p. 41; Nicolson, *Swinburne,* p. 43.
32 Gosse, *Life,* p. 41.
33 Evelyn Abbott and Lewis Campbell, *Life and Letters of Benjamin Jowett* (1897), II, 197.
34 'A Song in Time of Order', *Poems and Ballads.*
35 Gosse, *Life,* p. 40.
36 *ibid.,* p. 52.
37 Knight, *Memoir of John Nichol,* p. 134.
38 Gosse, *Life,* pp. 337–8.
39 *ibid.,* p. 338.
40 Not the present debating-chamber, of course, but what is now the Old Library.
41 Val Prinsep, 'A Chapter from a Painter's Reminiscences', in *Magazine of Art* (1904), pp. 167–8.
42 *Letters of George Birkbeck Hill,* ed. Lucy Crump (1904), p. 41.
43 Gosse, *Life,* p. 35.
44 *ibid.,* p. 43.
45 *La Jeunesse,* I, 151n.
46 J. E. Alden, *The Pre-Raphaelites and Oxford* (1948), p. 36.
47 G. H. Fleming, *That Ne'er Shall Meet Again* (1971), p. 103.
48 Prinsep, in *Magazine of Art,* p. 168.
49 Gosse, *Life,* p. 43.

50 Lang, VI, 11.
51 'Sonnet with a Copy of *Mademoiselle de Maupin'*, *Poems and Ballads: Second Series*.
52 *ibid.*
53 Gosse, *Life,* p. 36.
54 Bonchurch, I, 5–6.
55 *Undergraduate Papers* (1858), p. 41.
56. *ibid.*, pp. 97–102.
57 *Letters of George Birkbeck Hill,* p. 65.
58 *La Jeunesse,* II, 121.

59 Bonchurch, XVIII, 4; Lang, I, 17–18.
60 Top. Oxon. d. 242 f.50.
61 Pisanus Fraxi [H. S. Ashbee], *Catena Librorum Tacendorum* (1885), pp. 260–7.
62 Gosse, *Life,* p. 68.
63 *ibid.,* p. 69.
64 *ibid.,* pp. 62–3.
65 *ibid.,* p. 58.
66 Abbott and Campbell, *Jowett,* I, 328.
67 Gosse, *Life,* p. 64.
68 *ibid.,* p. 34.

Chapter 3: The Protégé

1 Scott, *Autobiographical Notes,* II, 19.
2 *ibid.,* pp. 19–20.
3 *United Service Gazette*, 8 October 1842.
4 Raleigh Trevelyan, *A Pre-Raphaelite Circle* (1978), p. 241.
5 Gosse, *Life*, p. 324.
6 Trevelyan, *A Pre-Raphaelite Circle,* p. 35.
7 Bonchurch, XVIII, 11; Lang, I, 40.
8 Lang, I, 29.
9 Gosse, *Life,* p. 54.
10 Lang, I, 76.
11 Scott, *Autobiographical Notes,* II, 19.
12 Gosse, *Life,* p. 325.
13 Scott, *Autobiographical Notes,* II, 18.
14 Bonchurch, XVIII, 10; Lang, I, 39–40.
15 Trevelyan, *A Pre-Raphaelite Circle,* p. 72.
16 'A Study from Memory', *Tristram of Lyonesse and other Poems* (1882).
17 Gosse, *Life,* p. 55.
18 Bonchurch, XVIII, 10; Lang, I, 40.

19 'For a Venetian Pastoral', *Poems by Dante Gabriel Rossetti* (1870).
20 Bonchurch, XVIII, 8; Lang, I, 38.
21 *ibid.*
22 *New Writings by Swinburne*, ed. Cecil Y. Lang (1964), pp. 119–74.
23 *La Jeunesse,* I, 184n.
24 Bonchurch, XVIII, 9; Lang, I, 39.
25 'A Song in Time of Revolution', *Poems and Ballads* (1866).
26 *ibid.*
27 *La Jeunesse,* I, 187; Lang, II, 376.
28 'Three Faces', *A Century of Roundels* (1883).
29 Gosse, *Life,* p. 78.
30 *La Jeunesse,* II, 251.
31 12 January 1861.
32 T. Wemyss Reid, *Life of Richard Monckton Milnes, First Lord Houghton* (1890), I, 295–6.
33 W. H. Mallock, *Memoirs of Life and Literature* (1920), pp. 44–5.
34 Benson, *As We Were,* pp. 203–4.

35 James Pope-Hennessy, *Monckton Milnes: The Years of Promise* (1949), p. 100.
36 *ibid.*, p. 100.
37 Reid, *Monckton Milnes*, II, 485, 489.
38 *ibid.*, II, 491.
39 Pope-Hennessy, *Monckton Milnes: The Years of Promise*, p. 165.
40 *ibid.*, p. 165.
41 Fawn M. Brodie, *The Devil Drives: A Life of Sir Richard Burton* (1967), p. 111.
42 'To Sir Richard F. Burton', *Poems and Ballads: Third Series* (1889).
43 Gosse, *Life*, p. 122.
44 Brodie, *The Devil Drives*, p. 192.
45 Gosse, *Life*, pp. 121–2.
46 *ibid.*, p. 122.
47 Lang, I, 124.
48 T. J. Wise, *A Swinburne Library* (1925), p. 119; Lang, II, 283.
49 James Pope-Hennessy, *Monckton Milnes: The Flight of Youth* (1951), p. 119.
50 Brodie, *The Devil Drives*, p. 196.

Chapter 4: Figures in a Landscape

1 Derek Hudson, *Munby: Man of Two Worlds* (1974), p. 92.
2 Bonchurch, XX, 10; Lang, III, 169.
3 Hudson, *Munby*, p. 117.
4 *ibid.*, p. 161.
5 Georgiana Burne-Jones, *Memorials of Edward Burne-Jones* (1904), I, 207–8.
6 *ibid.*, I, 216.
7 W. M. Rossetti, *Dante Gabriel Rossetti: His Family Letters* (1895), I, 210.
8 *ibid.*, I, 210.
9 Gosse, *Life*, p. 84.
10 Rossetti; *Dante Gabriel Rossetti: His Family Letters*, I, 199.
11 'Genius in Beauty', *Ballads and Sonnets* (1881).
12 Gosse, *Life*, p. 66.
13 *ibid.*, p. 75.
14 Burne-Jones, *Memorials of Edward Burne-Jones*, I, 215.
15 Benson, *As We Were*, pp. 273–4.
16 Thomas Shelton, *A Tutor to Tachygraphy*, ed. William Matthews (1970), p. viii.
17 Rossetti, *Letters*, II, 397.
18 Burne-Jones, *Memorials of Edward Burne-Jones*, I, 222.
19 Leith, p. 103; Lang, I, 48.
20 Rossetti, *Letters*, II, 431–2.
21 *Letters of George Meredith*, ed. C. L. Cline (1970), I, 106.
22 *ibid.*, I, 104.
23 *ibid.*, I, 108.
24 *ibid.*, I, 106.
25 *ibid.*, I, 149.
26 Rossetti, *Dante Gabriel Rossetti: His Family Letters*, I, 229.
27 Benson, *As We Were*, p. 272.
28 Rossetti, *Letters*, II, 492.
29 'Hermaphroditus', *Poems and Ballads*.
30 *La Jeunesse*, I, 203
31 Gosse, *Life*, p. 82.
32 Benson, *As We Were*, pp. 60–4.
33 'The Triumph of Time', *Poems and Ballads*.
34 Gosse, *Life*, p. 102.
35 'Itylus', *Poems and Ballads*.
36 Gosse, *Life*, pp. 103–4.
37 *La Jeunesse*, II, 455; *The Times*, 15 April 1909.
38 Rossetti, *Letters*, II, 456.
39 Bonchurch, XVIII, 37; Lang, I, 142.
40 Lang, III, 331.
41 Public Record Office MS. K.B. 28/484/34.

42 Donald Thomas, *A Long Time Burning* (1969), p. 257.
43 Rossetti, *Letters,* II, 743.
44 Bonchurch, XV, 122.
45 *ibid.*, XV, 123.
46 *ibid.*, XV, 126.
47 Ashley, 5752, f.189.
48 Matthew Arnold, *Discourses in America* (1885), p. 131.
49 Edmund Gosse, *Portraits and Sketches* (1912), p. 3.
50 W. H. Auden, 'One Evening', *Another Time* (1940).
51 6 May 1865.
52 Bonchurch, XVIII, 33; Lang, I, 132.
53 *Letters of John Ruskin to Charles Eliot Norton* (1904), I, 157.
54 Lafourcade, pp. 125–6.
55 V. A. G. R. Lytton, *Life of Edward Bulwer, First Lord Lytton* (1913), II, 433.
56 23 December 1865.
57 *ibid.*
58 2 December 1865.
59 *John Bailey, 1864–1931, Letters and Diaries*, ed. Sarah Bailey (1935), p. 175.
60 Rossetti, *Letters,* II, 510.

Chapter 5: Orpheus in the Underworld

1 Bonchurch, XVIII, 7; Lang, I, 46.
2 Hardman, *A Mid-Victorian Pepys,* pp. 78–9.
3 Pope-Hennessy, *Monckton Milnes: The Flight of Youth,* p. 148; Lang, I, 57.
4 Public Record Office MS. K.B. 28/515/13.
5 Henry James, *The Middle Years* (1917), pp. 99–100.
6 Pope-Hennessy, *Monckton Milnes: The Flight of Youth,* p. 148; Lang, I, 54.
7 Lang, I, 57.
8 *Letters of Matthew Arnold,* ed. G. W. E. Russell (1895), I, 196.
9 Henry Adams, *The Education of Henry Adams* (1918), p. 139.
10 Gosse, *Life,* pp. 95–6.
11 Lang, I, 70–1.
12 William Hardman, *The Hardman Papers,* ed. S. M. Ellis (1930), p. 91.
13 Hudson, *Munby,* p. 220.
14 Gosse, *Life,* p. 139.
15 *La Jeunesse,* I, 231.
16 Bonchurch, XVIII, 33.
17 Ashley, 5753, f.16.
18 *ibid.*, f.17.
19 Gosse, *Life,* pp. 98–9.
20 Ashley, 5753, f.19.
21 Bonchurch, XVIII, 137; Lang, II, 297.
22 Mrs. R. W. Disney Leith, *The Children of the Chapel* (1864), pp. 128–31.
23 James Joyce, *Ulysses* (1925), p. 502.
24 Leith, p. 21; Lang, I, 105.
25 Leith, p. 25; Lang, I, 109.
26 Leith, pp. 30–1; Lang, I, 109–11.
27 Leith, p. 26.
28 *Lesbia Brandon,* ed. Randolph Hughes (1952), pp. 38–9.
29 *ibid.,* p. 39.
30 Hake and Compton-Rickett, p. 149; Lang, 277.
31 *La Jeunesse,* II, 285.
32 *Love's Cross-Currents: A Year's Letters* (1905), pp. 93, 97.
33 *ibid.*, pp. 248–9.
34 *ibid.*, p. 253.
35 *ibid.*, p. 53.
36 *ibid.*, pp. 34–5.
37 *ibid.*, p. 18.
38 *ibid.*, pp. 210–11.
39 *Lesbia Brandon,* p. 89; Rossetti, *Dante Gabriel Rossetti: His Family Letters,* I, 199.

40 *Lesbia Brandon*, p. 105.
41 Lang, I, 83, 283.
42 Francis Kilvert, *Kilvert's Diary*, ed. William Plomer (1976), I, 123.
43 *ibid.*, III, 218–19
44 D.A.F. de Sade, *La Nouvelle Justine* (1797), chapter 18.
45 G. Meredith, *The Ordeal of Richard Feverel* (1859),

chapter 2.
46 *The Complete Ronald Firbank*, ed. Anthony Powell (1961), p. 73.
47 *The Captain: A Magazine for Boys and Old Boys*, VII (1902), 349.
48 *ibid.*, II (1899), 30 ['Some Pretty Sisters']; XVI (1906–7), 67.

Chapter 6: *Poems and Ballads*

1 Leon Edel, *Henry James: The Untried Years, 1843–1870* (1953), p. 295.
2 Gosse, *Life*, p. 133.
3 Arnold, *Letters*, II, 43.
4 Gosse, *Portraits and Sketches*, p. 4.
5 7 June 1862.
6 *Hardman Papers*, p. 288.
7 Gosse, *Life*, pp. 161–2.
8 Bonchurch, XV, 211–12.
9 *ibid.*, XV, 208.
10 *Temple Bar*, July 1869.
11 Hallam Tennyson, *Alfred Lord Tennyson: A Memoir* (1897), I, 496.
12 Lang, I, 84.
13 *ibid.*, I, 182.
14 Meredith, *Letters*, 329–30.
15 Rossetti, *Letters*, II, 529.
16 *ibid.*, II, 873.
17 *ibid.*, II, 873.
18 Samuel Butler, *The Way of All Flesh* (1903), chapter 6.
19 Helen Rossetti Angeli, *Pre-Raphaelite Twilight* (1954), p. 13.
20 Lang, I, 123.
21 Angeli, *Pre-Raphaelite Twilight*, p. 24.
22 Gosse, *Life*, p. 90.
23 Public Record Office MS. K.B. 28/555/10.
24 Lona Mosk Packer, *The Rossetti-Macmillan Letters* (1963), pp. 25–6.
25 *ibid.*, p. 31.

26 T. J. Wise, *A Swinburne Library*, p. 229; Lang, I, 139–40n.
27 Gosse, *Life*, p. 141.
28 *ibid.*, p. 147.
29 *ibid.*, p. 214.
30 4 August 1866.
31 Rossetti, *Letters*, II, 856.
32 *Hardman Papers*, p. 192.
33 *ibid.*, p. 166.
34 *La Jeunesse*, I, 243.
35 *ibid.*, I, 244.
36 *ibid.*, I, 244.
37 Gosse, *Life*, p. 152.
38 *ibid.*, p. 153.
39 Lytton, *Life of Lord Lytton*, II, 435.
40 *ibid.*, II, 437.
41 Gosse, *Life*, p. 154.
42 Dewey Ganzel, 'Samuel Clemens and John Camden Hotten', *The Library* (Fifth Series), XX (1965), 230–42.
43 Pisanus Fraxi [H. S. Ashbee], *Index Librorum Prohibitorum* (1877), pp. 5–8; 229–30; *Centuria Librorum Absconditorum* (1879), pp. 346–54.
44 Fraxi, *Index Librorum Prohibitorum*, pp. 301–11; 345–56.
45 Gosse, *Life*, p. 160.
46 *ibid.*, pp. 160–1.
47 *ibid.*, p. 161.
48 *La Jeunesse*, I, 245.
49 Bonchurch, XVI, 356.

50 Public Record Office MSS. K.B. 28/600/3; 602/1, 2, 3; 604/2.

51 *Family Classical Library: No. XIX, Juvenal and Persius* (1831), p. 12.

52 *Index Expurgatorius of Martial* (1868), p. vi.

53 *R.* v. Thomson (1900), 64 J. P. 456.

54 W. M. Rossetti, *Swinburne's Poems and Ballads: A Criticism* (1866), p. 21.

55 Rossetti, *Letters,* II, 608.

56 Gerald B. Kauver and Gerald C. Sorensen (eds.), *The Victorian Mind* (1969), pp. 365–6.

Chapter 7: A Scandal in Bohemia

1 Lang, I, 284, 293.

2 Hake and Compton-Rickett, p. 21; Lang, II, 59; Clara Watts-Dunton, *The Home Life of Swinburne* (1922), p. 19.

3 Gosse, *Portraits and Sketches,* pp. 11–12.

4 Ashley 5753 f.11.

5 *ibid.,* f.21.

6 *ibid.,* ff. 17–18.

7 Hudson, *Munby,* p. 233.

8 *ibid.,* p. 233.

9 *ibid.,* p. 234.

10 *ibid.,* p. 246.

11 *ibid.,* p. 270.

12 *ibid.,* pp. 289–90.

13 Gosse, *Portraits and Sketches,* p. 17.

14 *ibid.,* p. 18.

15 *Mazzini's Letters to an English Family,* ed. E. F. Richards (1922), III, 199; Lang, I, 298.

16 Pope-Hennesy, *Monckton Milnes: The Flight of Youth,* p. 137.

17 Gosse, *Portraits and Sketches,* p. 18.

18 Lafourcade, p. 204; Lang, II, 137.

19 Gosse, *Life,* p. 199.

20 Ashley 5753 ff.14–15.

21 Gosse, *Portraits and Sketches,* p. 25.

22 *Poèmes et Ballades de Swinburne,* tr. Gabriel Mourey (1891), pp. v–x.

23 [Julian Field], *Things I Shouldn't Tell, (*1924) p. 114.

24 *ibid.,* pp. 114–15.

25 *ibid.,* p. 115.

26 Leith, p. 182; Lang, II, 23.

27 *La Jeunesse,* I, 178n.; Lang, II, 19.

28 Charles Terrot, *The Maiden Tribute* (1962), p. 65.

29 British Museum Private Case 14 de 3.

30 Bernard Falk, *The Naked Lady* (1934), p. 90.

31 *ibid.,* p. 123.

32 [Field], *Things I Shouldn't Tell,* p. 102.

33 Ashley 5753 f.30.

34 Lafourcade, p. 193; Lang, I, 307.

35 George R. Sims, *My Life* (1917), p. 42.

36 *ibid.,* p. 42.

37 *ibid.,* p. 44.

38 Private Case 14 de 3.

39 *ibid.*

40 Ashley 5753 f.65.

41 Lang, I, 260.

42 Ashley 5753 ff.60, 74.

43 Lafourcade, p. 196; Lang, I, 307, 310–11.

44 Ashley 5753 f.32.

45 [Field], *Things I Shouldn't Tell,* p. 105.

46 *ibid.*

47 *ibid.,* p. 107.

48 Gosse, *Portraits and Sketches,* p. 47.

49 *ibid.,* p. 11.

50 Nicolson, *Swinburne,* p. 143.

51 Gosse, *Life,* pp. 329–30.

52 Benson, *As We Were,* p. 275.
53 Lang, II, 35.
54 *Letters of Queen Victoria: Second Series,* ed. G. E. Buckle (1926), II, 470.
55 Lang, III, 122.
56 Bonchurch, XVIII, 134; Lang,

II, 293.
57 Lang, II, 108.
58 *ibid.,* II, 141.
59 *ibid.,* II, 33, 49.
60 Rossetti, *Letters,* II, 810–11.
61 Lang, II, 227–9.

Chapter 8: 'What Could be Done *With* and *For* Algernon?'

1 Lafourcade, pp. 194–5.
2 *ibid.,* p. 142; Lang, I, 195.
3 Gosse, *Life,* p. 166.
4 *ibid.*
5 *ibid.*
6 *La Jeunesse,* I, 255.
7 Leith, p. 93; Lang, I, 237.
8 *ibid.*
9 Leith, p. 81; Lang, I, 239.
10 *ibid.*
11 Leith, p. 95; Lang, I, 242.
12 Lafourcade, p. 154.
13 *ibid.,* p. 154.
14 *ibid.,* p. 155.
15 Leith, p. 98; Lang, II, 174.
16 Hudson, *Munby,* pp. 305–6.
17 Abbott and Campbell, *Jowett,* II, 10.
18 Symonds, Autobiography, f. 86.
19 *Poems of Arthur Hugh Clough* (1903), p. 201.
20 Bonchurch, XVIII, 90; Lang II, 153.
21 Leith, p. 62; Lang, II, 181.
22 Mallock, *Memoirs of Life and Literature,* pp. 54–5.
23 *ibid.,* pp. 55–8.
24 Gosse, *Life,* p. 202.
25 Abbott and Campbell, *Jowett,* II, 18.
26 Gosse, *Life,* p. 213.
27 Benson, *As We Were,* p. 151.
28 Faber, *Jowett,* p. 176.

29 *ibid.,* p. 366.
30 Rossetti, *Letters,* II, 823.
31 Leith, p. 85; Lang, II, 295.
32 Leith, p. 85; Lang, II, 295.
33 Lang, I, xlviii; II, 3–4.
34 Leith, p. 97; Lang, I, 306–7.
35 Leith, p. 97; Lang, I, 307.
36 Frank Harris, *My Life and Loves* (1963), p. 696.
37 Rossetti, *Letters,* II, 820.
38 Harris, *My Life and Loves,* p. 124.
39 Lang, II, 130.
40 *César Franck and his Circle* (1970), pp. 252–71.
41 Gosse, *Life,* p. 216.
42 *ibid.,* p. 215.
43 *ibid.,* p. 217.
44 Bonchurch, XVIII, 144–5; Lang, II, 310–12.
45 Lang, IV, 257.
46 *Academy,* 8 January 1876.
47 Hake and Compton-Rickett, pp. 30–4.
48 Bonchurch, XVIII, 96; Lang, II, 198.
49 Lang, II, 216.
50 Gosse, *Life,* p. 220.
51 Leith, p. 86; Lang, II, 295.
52 Lang, II, 374–5.
53 Ashley 5753 ff. 18–19.
54 *Philological Quarterly,* XIII (1934), 297; Lang, 233.

Chapter 9: 'Dear Theodore, What's Dunton?'

1 Bonchurch, XVIII, 24–5; Lang, I, 128.
2 Wise, *A Swinburne Library,* p. 200; Lang, IV, 267.

3 *The Ashley Library, A Catalogue* (1922–31), IX, 138.
4 Ashley 5071.
5 Hypatia Bradlaugh Bonner,

Charles Bradlaugh: A Record of His Life and Work (1898), II, 332.
6 *The Times*, 4 September 1851.
7 Donald Thomas, *A Long Time Burning*, pp. 258–9; 267–9.
8 Hake and Compton-Rickett, p. 57.
9 John Carter and Graham Pollard, *An Enquiry into the Nature of Certain Nineteenth Century Pamphlets* (1934).
10 Gosse, *Life*, p. 236.
11 Gosse, *Portraits and Sketches*, p. 16.
12 Gosse, *Life*, p. 236.
13 Rossetti, *Letters*, III, 1017.
14 *ibid.*, III, 1020.
15 Lang, II, 169.
16 Bonchurch, XVI, 441–2.
17 Lafourcade, p. 248.
18 Bonchurch, XVIII, 274; Lang, III, 265.

19 Gosse, *Portraits and Sketches*, p. 7.
20 Hake and Compton-Rickett, p. 62; Lang, III, 140–1.
21 *Hardman Papers*, p. 164.
22 Pope-Hennessy, *Monckton Milnes: The Flight of Youth*, p. 136; Lang, IV, 56.
23 Gosse, *Life*, pp. 249–50.
24 *ibid.*, p. 251.
25 *ibid.*, p. 251.
26 *ibid.*, p. 244.
27 *ibid.*, pp. 237–8.
28 *ibid.*, p. 243.
29 Thomas Hake and Arthur Compton-Rickett, *The Life and Letters of Theodore Watts-Dunton* (1916), I, 105.
30 Lang, IV, 85.
31 Hake and Compton-Rickett, *Watts-Dunton*, II, 105.
32 *ibid.*, II, 103; Leith, p. 150; Lang, IV, 95.

Chapter 10: The Pines

1 Clara Watts-Dunton, *The Home Life of Swinburne*, p. 70.
2 Gosse, *Life*, p. 245.
3 Lafourcade, p. 264.
4 *ibid.*, p. 263; Lang, IV, 166.
5 Lafourcade, p. 264; Lang, VI, 14.
6 Coulson Kernahan, *Swinburne as I Knew Him* (1919), pp. 8–16; Lang, IV, 313.
7 Leith, p. 65; Lang, IV, 316.
8 Max Beerbohm, *And Even Now* (1920), p. 67.
9 Lang, IV, 168–9.
10 Gosse, *Life*, p. 292.
11 *ibid.*
12 Leith, p. 232; Lang, V, 192.
13 *The Times*, 6 May 1887.
14 *ibid.*
15 Beerbohm, *And Even Now*, pp. 60–1.
16 Gosse, *Life*, p. 293.

17 Leith, p. 89; Lang, VI, 97.
18 Lang, VI, 114.
19 *The Times*, 1 November 1888.
20 Henry Vizetelly, *Glances Back Through Seventy Years* (1893), II, 432.
21 Gosse, *Life*, p. 273.
22 Balliol College MS.
23 Hake and Compton-Rickett, *Watts-Dunton*, II, 129.
24 Gosse, *Life*, p. 257.
25 *ibid.*, p. 261.
26 Donald Thomas, *A Long Time Burning*, pp. 476–7.
27 Gosse, *Life*, p. 262.
28 Lang, IV, 243, 264, 321, 324; V, 129.
29 Beerbohm, *And Even Now*, p. 69.
30 Robert Graves, *Goodbye to All That* (1957), pp. 1–2.
31 Gosse, *Life*, p. 275.
32 *Report from the Joint Select*

Committee on Lotteries and Indecent Advertisements (1908), p. 40.

33 Ashley 5752 ff. 40–1.
34 *The Captain*, XXI (1909), 104.
35 Gosse, *Life*, p. 277.
36 Benson, *As We Were*, p. 196.
37 Lang, VI, 17.
38 Kernahan, *Swinburne as I Knew Him*, pp. 59–60.
39 Leith, p. 216; Lang, VI, 119.
40 Leith, p. 216; Lang, VI, 125.
41 Leith, p. 90; Lang, VI, 168.
42 Hake and Compton-Rickett, *Watts-Dunton*, II, 191–2.
43 *ibid.*, II, 190.
44 *ibid.*, II, 182.
45 *ibid.*, II, 182.
46 Clara Watts-Dunton, *The Home Life of Swinburne*, pp. 248–9.
47 *ibid.*, p. 250.
48 *ibid.*, pp. 251–62.
49 Leith, p. 212; Lang, VI, 35.

50 Margot Asquith, *Autobiography*, p. 136.
51 Clara Watts-Dunton, *the Home Life of Swinburne*, pp. 268–73; *The Times*, 16 and 19 April 1909.
52 Clara Watts-Dunton, *The Home Life of Swinburne*, p. 277.
53 Ashley 5753 f. 10.
54 Gosse, *Life*, p. 164n.
55 Ashley 5753 ff. 60–74.
56 Ashley 1755 f. 19.
57 Ashley 5752 f. 38.
58 T. S. Eliot, *The Sacred Wood* (1920), p. 131.
59 Gosse, *Life*, p. 236; Nicolson, *Swinburne*, p. 9.
60 *Lertters of Queen Victoria: Second Series*, I, 250.
61 Gosse, *Life*, p. 290.
62 *ibid.*, p. 289.
63 Arnold Bennett, *Books and Persons* (1920), p. 92.

Select Bibliography

The aim of the following bibliography is to list the major texts of Swinburne, a selection of the more important biographical and critical studies and material which relates him to the society in which he lived. Further material is listed in the relevant sections of the *New Cambridge Bibliography of English Literature* and in the annual volumes of *The Year's Work in English Studies*, published by the English Association.

1 Manuscript Sources

Balliol College MS., Swinburne's notes on Jowett.
Bodleian Library MS. Top. Oxon. d. 242, Minute Book of the Old Mortality Society.
British Museum MSS. Ashley 1755, Letters of Simeon Solomon, Edmund Gosse.
—— Ashley 5071, 'The Complaint of the Fair Armouress', (*Translations from the French of Villon*).
—— Ashley 5256, 'The Flogging Block'.
—— Ashley 5264, 'Lesbia Brandon'.
—— Ashley 5271, 'Eton: Another Ode', 'Cuckoo Weir: An Ode'.
—— Ashley 5752, Letters of Edmund Gosse to T. J. Wise, Lady Jane Swinburne to Swinburne, Mary Gordon to Swinburne, etc.
—— Ashley 5273, Edmund Gosse, 'Confidential Paper on Swinburne's Moral Irregularities', with letters from six recipients.

2 Swinburne Texts

The Complete Works of Algernon Charles Swinburne, ed. Edmund Gosse and Thomas James Wise, 20 vols. (1925–7) [Bonchurch edition].
The Poems of Algernon Charles Swinburne, 6 vols. (1904).
The Tragedies of Algernon Charles Swinburne, 5 vols. (1905–6).
A Choice of Swinburne's Verse, ed. Robert Nye (1973).
Lesbia Brandon, ed. Randolph Hughes (1952).
Love's Cross-Currents: A Year's Letters (1905).
New Writings by Swinburne, ed. Cecil Y. Lang (1964).
Swinburne as Critic, ed. Clyde K. Hyder (1972).

3 Swinburne Letters

The Complete Works of Algernon Charles Swinburne, ed. Edmund Gosse and Thomas James Wise (1925–7), XVIII and XX.
HAKE, THOMAS, and COMPTON-RICKETT, ARTHUR, *The Letters of A. C. Swinburne* (1918).

LANG, CECIL Y., *The Swinburne Letters*, 6 vols. (1959–62).

LEITH, MRS R. W. DISNEY, *The Boyhood of A. C. Swinburne* (1917).

WISE, THOMAS JAMES, *The Ashley Library: A Catalogue*, 11 vols. (1922–31).

——, *A Swinburne Library* (1925).

4 General Bibliography

ABBOTT, EVELYN, and CAMPBELL, LEWIS, *The Life and Letters of Benjamin Jowett*, 2 vols. (1897).

ADAMS, HENRY, *The Education of Henry Adams* (1918).

ALDEN, J. E., *The Pre-Raphaelites and Oxford* (1948).

ANGELI, HELEN ROSSETTI, *Pre-Raphaelite Twilight: The Story of Charles Augustus Howell* (1954).

ARNOLD, MATTHEW, *Discourses in America* (1885).

——, *Letters of Matthew Arnold, 1848–1888*, ed. G. W. E. Russell, 2 vols. (1895).

ASQUITH, MARGOT, *The Autobiography of Margot Asquith* (1920).

BAILEY, JOHN, *John Bailey, 1864–1931, Letters and Diaries*, ed. Sarah Bailey (1935).

BEERBOHM, MAX, 'No. 2. The Pines', in *And Even Now* (1920).

BELL, ALAN, 'Gladstone Looks for a Poet Laureate', in *The Times Literary Supplement*, 21 July 1972.

BENNETT, ARNOLD, *Books and Persons* (1920).

BENSON, A. C., *Memories and Friends* (1924).

BENSON, E. F., *As We Were* (1930).

BONNER, HYPATIA BRADLAUGH, *Charles Bradlaugh: A Record of his Life and Work*, 2 vols. (1898).

BRANNON, G., *The Pleasure Visitor's Companion in Making the Tour of the Isle of Wight* (1850).

BRETTELL, THOMAS, *A Topographical and Historical Guide to the Isle of Wight* (1840).

BRODIE, FAWN M., *The Devil Drives: A Life of Sir Richard Burton* (1967).

BROWN, HORATIO F., *John Addington Symonds, A Biography* (1903).

BURNE-JONES, GEORGIANA, *Memorials of Edward Burne-Jones*, 2 vols. (1904).

CARTER, JOHN, and POLLARD, GRAHAM, *An Enquiry into the Nature of Certain Nineteenth Century Pamphlets* (1934).

CHEW, SAMUEL C., *Swinburne* (1931).

COLLINS, L. C., *Life and Memoirs of John Churton Collins* (1912).

DAVIES, LAURENCE, *César Franck and his Circle* (1970).

DAVIS, H. W. C., *Balliol College* (1899).

DOUGHTY, OSWALD, *A Victorian Romantic: Dante Gabriel Rossetti* (1960).

ELIOT, T. S., *The Sacred Wood* (1920).

EMPSON, WILLIAM, *Seven Types of Ambiguity* (1930).

FABER, GEOFFREY, *Jowett: A Portrait with Background* (1957).

——, *Oxford Apostles: A Character Study of the Oxford Movement* (1933).

FALK, BERNARD, *Naked Lady: A Biography of Adah Isaacs Menken* (1934).

[FIELD, JULIAN], *Things I Shouldn't Tell* (1924).

FLEMING, G. H., *That Ne'er Shall Meet Again: Rossetti, Millais, Hunt* (1971).

FRAXI, PISANUS [H. S. ASHBEE], *Index Librorum Prohibitorum* (1877).

——, *Centuria Librorum Absconditorum* (1879).

——, *Catena Librorum Tacendorum* (1885).

FULLER, JEAN OVERTON, *Swinburne, A Critical Biography* (1968).

GANZEL, DEWEY, 'Samuel Clemens and John Camden Hotten', in *The Library* (Fifth Series), XX (1965).

GAUNT, WILLIAM, *The Pre-Raphaelite Tragedy* (1942).

——, *The Aesthetic Adventure* (1945).

——, *Victorian Olympus* (1952).

GOSSE, EDMUND, *The Life of Algernon Charles Swinburne* (1917).

——, *Portraits and Sketches* (1912).

GROSSKURTH, PHYLLIS, *John Addington Symonds, A Biography* (1964).

HAKE, THOMAS, and COMPTON-RICKETT, ARTHUR, *The Life and Letters of Theodore Watts-Dunton*, 2 vols. (1916).

HARDMAN, WILLIAM, *A Mid-Victorian Pepys*, ed. S. M. Ellis (1923).

——, *The Letters and Memoirs of Sir William Hardman: Second Series*, ed. S. M. Ellis (1925).

——, *The Hardman Papers: A Further Selection*, ed. S. M. Ellis (1930).

HARE, HUMPHREY, *Swinburne, A Biographical Approach* (1949).

HARRIS, FRANK, *My Life and Loves* (1963).

HENDERSON, PHILIP, *Swinburne: The Portrait of a Poet* (1974).

HILL, GEORGE BIRKBECK, *Letters of George Birkbeck Hill*, ed. Lucy Crump (1904).

HOLROYD, MICHAEL, 'The Fraternity to Come,' in *The Times Literary Supplement*, 24 February 1978.

HUDSON, DEREK, *Munby: Man of Two Worlds* (1972).

HYDE, H. MONTGOMERY, *A History of Pornography* (1964).

HYDER, CLYDE K. (ed.), *Swinburne: The Critical Heritage* (1970).

KAUVER, GERALD B., and SORENSEN, GERALD C., (eds.) *The Victorian Mind* (1969).

KERNAHAN, COULSON, *Swinburne as I Knew Him* (1919).

KILVERT, FRANCIS, *Kilvert's Diary*, ed. William Plomer, 3 vols. (1976).

KNIGHT, W. A., *Memoir of John Nicol* (1896).

LAFOURCADE, GEORGES, *La Jeunesse de Swinburne, 1837–1867*, 2 vols. (1928).

——, *Swinburne: A Literary Biography* (1932).

LEITH, MRS R. W. DISNEY, *The Children of the Chapel* (1910).

LYTTON, V. A. G. R., *The Life of Edward Bulwer, First Lord Lytton*, 2 vols. (1913).

MALLOCK, W. H., *Memoirs of Life and Literature* (1920).

MARCUS, STEVEN, *The Other Victorians* (1966).

MAZZINI, GIUSEPPE, *Mazzini's Letters to an English Family*, ed. E. F. Richards, 3 vols. (1922).

MEREDITH, GEORGE, *Letters of George Meredith*, ed. C. L. Cline, 3 vols. (1970).
NICOLSON, HAROLD, *Swinburne* (1926).
——, *Tennyson* (1960).
PACKER, LONA MOSK, *The Rossetti-Macmillan Letters* (1963).
POPE-HENNESSY, JAMES, *Monckton Milnes: The Years of Promise, 1809–1851* (1949).
——, *Monckton Milnes: The Flight of Youth, 1851–1885* (1951).
POUND, EZRA, *Literary Essays of Ezra Pound*, ed. T. S. Eliot (1954).
PRAZ, MARIO, *The Romantic Agony* (1933).
PRINSEP, VAL, 'A Chapter from a Painter's Reminiscences', in *Magazine of Art* (1904), pp. 167–72.
REID, T. WEMYSS, *The Life, Letters, and Friendships of Richard Monckton Milnes, First Lord Houghton*, 2 vols (1890).
RIDLEY, NANCY, *Northumbrian Heritage* (1968).
ROSSETTI, DANTE GABRIEL, *Collected Works of Dante Gabriel Rossetti*, ed. William Michael Rossetti, 2 vols. (1888).
——, *Letters of Dante Gabriel Rossetti*, ed. Oswald Doughty and John Robert Wahl, 4 vols. (1965).
ROSSETTI, WILLIAM MICHAEL, *Dante Gabriel Rossetti: His Family Letters with a Memoir*, 2 vols. (1895).
——, *Swinburne's Poems and Ballads: A Criticism* (1866).
RUSKIN, JOHN, *Letters of John Ruskin to Charles Eliot Norton*, 2 vols. (1904).
SALT, HENRY S., *Memories of Bygone Eton* (1928).
SASSOON, SIEGFRIED, *Meredith* (1948).
SCHULDT, EDWARD P., 'Three Unpublished Balliol Essays of A. C. Swinburne', *Review of English Studies*, New Series, XXVII (1976), 422–30.
SCOTT, WILLIAM BELL, *Autobiographical Notes*, 2 vols. (1892).
SIMS, GEORGE R., *My Life: Sixty Years' Recollections of Bohemian London* (1917).
SITWELL, OSBERT, *Noble Essences* (1950).
STUBBS, WILLIAM, *Letters of William Stubbs, Bishop of Oxford*, ed. W. H. Hutton (1904).
SUFFIELD, LORD, *My Memories 1830–1913*, ed. Alys Lowth (1913).
TENNYSON, ALFRED LORD, *Alfred Lord Tennyson: A Memoir*, ed. Hallam Tennyson, 2 vols. (1897).
THOMAS, DONALD, *A Long Time Burning: The History of Literary Censorship in England* (1969).
THOMAS, EDWARD, *Algernon Charles Swinburne: A Critical Study* (1912).
TREVELYAN, RALEIGH, *A Pre-Raphaelite Circle* (1978).
VICTORIA, QUEEN, *Letters of Queen Victoria*, ed. A. C. Benson, Viscount Esher and G. E. Buckle, 9 vols. (1908–32).
WARD, MRS HUMPHREY, *A Writer's Recollections* (1918).
WATSON, GODFREY, *Northumberland Villages* (1976).
WATTS-DUNTON, CLARA, *The Home Life of Swinburne* (1922).
WATTS-DUNTON, THEODORE, *Aylwin* (1898).

The Whippingham Papers: A Collection of Contributions in Prose and Verse, Chiefly by the Author of 'The Romance of Chastisement', pub. Edward Avery (1887).

WILKINSON, C. ALLIX, *Reminiscences of Eton* (1888).

WILSON, EDMUND, *The Bit Between My Teeth* (1966).

Index of Names

Note: For Swinburne's literary works, please see
'Swinburne, literary works'